Y0-BEB-143

The World's Body

JOHN CROWE RANSOM

The World's Body

LOUISIANA STATE UNIVERSITY PRESS · BATON ROUGE

Paperback edition manufactured by
Kingsport Press, Inc., Kingsport, Tennessee

To my friends and former colleagues on the staff of the College of the South West of England, at Exeter.

Preface

TO ADVERTISE scrupulously the nature of my book, I must say that these are not altogether papers in criticism; many of them will have to come under some other heading. For the author their relation to criticism, and their value, has been this: they are preparations for criticism, for the understanding and definition of the poetic effects. They are about poetic theory itself. That is one of the most fascinating fields of speculation; I suppose it can be one of the idlest.

It is my impression that the serious critic should serve a sort of apprenticeship with his general principles. But the studies can scarcely afford to be pursued in any way except in the constant company of the actual poems. About ten years ago, when I did not know this, I wrote out and sent to a publisher a general æsthetic of poetry, a kind of Prolegomena to Any Future Poetic, thinking that the public needed one, as perhaps it does. The intelligent publisher declined my project politely and returned my manuscript, which the other day I had the pleasure of consigning to the flames.

But for the animating idea which informed my little

effort of that time I have no repentance. I was concerned with urging that it is not a pre-scientific poetry but a post-scientific one to which we must now give our consent. I suppose I was rationalizing my own history, for I came late into an interest in poetry, after I had been stuffed with the law if not the letter of our modern sciences, and quickly I had the difficulty of finding a poetry which would not deny what we in our strange generation actually are: men who have aged in these pure intellectual disciplines, and cannot play innocent without feeling very foolish. The expense of poetry is greater than we will pay if it is something to engage in without our faculties. I could not discover that this mortification was required.

Among these papers the general ones offer various versions of what approaches, I hope, to a fairly single and coherent poetic doctrine. And I will supplement them here with still another version, a last one as I now believe, shorter and more dogmatic, for the benefit of some unusually close and generous reader who is disposed to make the most of my essays, and by way of a preface.

The kind of poetry which interests us is not the act of a child, or of that eternal youth which is in some women, but the act of an adult mind; and I will add, the act of a fallen mind, since ours too are fallen. It has been forgotten by most of the formal æstheticians that poetry is an event in time. Under the present circumstances it is an inevitable and perhaps spectacular event, which interrupts the history of men officially committed under civilization to their effective actions and abstract studies. It is revulsive, or revolutionary, by intention.

But I would like to suggest a distinction. First we should see what poetry properly is not, though it is what poetry has often been declared to be. There is a kind of poetry which proceeds out of failure. To its author the natural world has dispensed too liberally of its blows, privations, humiliations, and silences in answer to his prayers for sympathy. He therefore invents a private world where such injustice cannot be, and enjoys it as men enjoy their dream. The impulse is known very well, and has had many celebrations, as this one:

Ah, Love, could thou and I with Fate conspire
To grasp this sorry scheme of things entire,
Would we not shatter it to bits, and then
Remould it nearer to the heart's desire?

The poetry I am disparaging is a heart's-desire poetry. If another identification is needed, it is the poetry written by romantics, in a common sense of that term. It denies the real world by idealizing it: the act of a sick mind. A modern psychologist puts a blunt finger in a rather nasty manner upon this sort of behavior. It indicates in the subject a poor adaptation to reality; a sub-normal equipment in animal courage; flight and escapism; furtive libido. It is only reasonable if such acts, even if they are performed in the name of poetry, should be treated under the pathological categories. But it is unfortunate that some theorists, who would not know better because of their comparative unacquaintance with poetry, have concluded that it is all of this order.

There is a tragedy of success which is more teasing, and not much less bleak, than the tragedy of failure. See CXXIX among Shakespeare's sonnets, and Ecclesiastes, *passim*. For even though we have our heart's desire, as happens frequently enough, it tastes like ashes; there is little to it. The presumption is that we desired it too exclusively, and that the maximum efficiency with which we toiled for it was too much efficiency. In the labor we sacrificed nearly everything, and naturally the reward is as tenuous as the labor. Where is the body and solid substance of the world? It seems to have retired into the fulness of memory, but out of this we construct the fulness of poetry, which is counterpart to the world's fulness.

The true poetry has no great interest in improving or idealizing the world, which does well enough. It only wants to realize the world, to see it better. Poetry is the kind of knowledge by which we must know what we have arranged that we shall not know otherwise. We have elected to know the world through our science, and we know a great deal, but science is only the cognitive department of our animal life, and by it we know the world only as a scheme of abstract conveniences. What we cannot know constitutionally as scientists is the world which is made of whole and indefeasible objects, and this is the world which poetry recovers for us. Men become poets, or at least they read poets, in order to atone for having been hard practical men and hard theoretical scientists.

For such moderns as we are the poetry must be modern: It is not as in a state of innocence, to receive the fragrance of the roses on the world's first morning, that our moderns the scarred veterans may enact their poetry, but in the violence of return and regeneration. They re-enter the world, but it is the world which they have marked with their raids, and there is no other world they can enter. It is by its thickness, stubbornness, and power that it must impress them. First must come respect, and then, if then, love.

It is a paradox that poetry has to be a technical act, of extreme difficulty, when it wants only to know the untechnical homely fulness of the world. The race in its unconscious strategy pushes its sciences always harder, and they grow more and more exclusive as they prosper. But at the same time it devises the arts, and even sets them up in a sort of honor as an equal and opposite activity, and keeps them always changing their forms in order to have their full effect. They are probably the best devices there could be for the purpose, and the way they work is the proper object of critical studies.

John Crowe Ransom

The editors of this edition have kindly suggested that I may wish to enter a few further observations in this Preface, and I do; it is morally obligatory. The fifteen essays which follow must stand here just as they were in the original edition of 1938. That was the year of my fiftieth birthday. But this is 1968, and suddenly I am an octogenarian. I do not mind, as it seems to have brought a fresh accession of generosity. Probably it is a commonplace that the opinions of a literary critic improve as he ages. Insofar as this book goes, I spotted some time ago its two most odious errors, committed in two harsh essays against two of the most important poets in our language. Now I can do justice to the reputations of these gentlemen, and replace the slights which I put upon them with the greenest laurels I can find. Yet that seems hardly the sort of job for a Preface, and so I refer the reader to the Postscript which follows the book.

JOHN CROWE RANSOM
Gambier, Ohio
April 5, 1968

Contents

Acknowledgments

THESE essays, minus perhaps some joints and sticking-plaster with which I have now put them together, have all had periodical publication. The present arrangement of them does not quite conform to the order of original publication. In reprinting them I wish to thank *The American Review, The Southern Review, The Virginia Quarterly Review,* and *The Yale Review.*

I owe much to the friends who have played the game of dialectic with me. It is my impression that some of these are persons (and for that matter that this is an age) of more than usual critical distinction. I am most under obligations to Mr. Allen Tate, with whom I have generally been in close communication, and whose views of poetry I share, so far as I know them, with fewest and slightest reservations. Between us, when the talk was at a certain temperature, I have seen observations come to the surface in a manner to illustrate the theory of anonymous or communal authorship. I hope that he looks upon this phenomenon as indulgently as I do, for in the following pages he will see that I take my profit from it without much further acknowledgment.

The World's Body

A Poem Nearly Anonymous

IT was published in 1638, in the darkness preceding our incomparable modernity. Its origins were about as unlikely as they could be, for it was only one of the exhibits in a memorial garland, a common academic sort of volume. It appeared there without a title and signed only by a pair of initials, though now we know it both by a name and by an author. Often we choose to think of it as the work of a famous poet, which it was not; done by an apprentice of nearly thirty, who was still purifying his taste upon an astonishingly arduous diet of literary exercises; the fame which was to shine backwards upon this poem, and to be not very different from the fame which he steadily intended, being as distant as it was great. Unfortunately it is one of the poems which we think we know best. Upon it is imposed the weight of many perfect glosses, respecting its occasion, literary sources, classical and contemporary allusions, exhausting us certainly and exhausting, for a good many persons, the poem. But I am bound to consider that any triteness which comes to mind with mention of the poem is a property of our own registration, and does not affect its freshness, which is perennial. The poem is young, brilliant, insubordinate. In it is an artist who wrestles with an almost insuperable problem, and is kinsman to some tortured modern artists. It has something in common with, for example, *The Waste Land.* In short, the poem is *Lycidas.*

A symbol is a great convenience in discussion, and therefore I will find one in the half-way anonymity of the poem; symbolic of the poet's admirable understanding of his art, and symbolic of the tradition that governed the art on the whole in one of its flourishing periods. Anonymity, of some real if not literal sort, is a condition of poetry. A good poem, even if it is signed with a full and well-known name, intends as a work of art to lose the identity of the author; that is, it means to represent him not actualized, like an eye-witness testifying in court and held strictly by zealous counsel to the point at issue, but freed from his juridical or prose self and taking an ideal or fictitious personality; otherwise his evidence amounts the less to poetry. Poets may go to universities and, if they take to education, increase greatly the stock of ideal selves into which they may pass for the purpose of being poetical. If on the other hand they insist too narrowly on their own identity and their own story, inspired by a simple but mistaken theory of art, they find their little poetic fountains drying up within them. Milton set out to write a poem mourning a friend and poet who had died; in order to do it he became a Greek shepherd, mourning another one. It was not that authority attached particularly to the discourse of a Greek shepherd; the Greek shepherd in his own person would have been hopeless; but Milton as a Greek shepherd was delivered from being Milton the scrivener's son, the Master of Arts from Cambridge, the handsome and finicky young man, and that was the point. In proceeding to his Master's degree he had made studies which gave him dramatic insight into many parts foreign to his own personal experience; which was precisely the technical resource he had required the moment he determined to be a poet. Such a training was almost the regular and unremarked procedure with the poets of his time. Today young men and women, as noble as Milton, those in university circles as much as those out of them, try to become poets on another plan, and with rather less success. They write their autobiographies, following perhaps the example of Wordsworth, which on the whole may have been unfortunate for the prosperity of the art; or they write some of their intenser experiences, their loves, pities, griefs, and religious ecstasies; but too literally, faithfully, piously, ingenuously. They seem to want to do without wit and playfulness, dramatic sense, detachment, and it cuts them off from the practice of an art.

Briefly, it was Milton's intention to be always anonymous as a poet, rarely as a writer of prose. The poet must suppress the man, or the man would suppress the poet. What he wanted to say for himself, or for his principles, became eligible for poetry only when it became what the poet, the *dramatis persona* so to speak, might want to say for himself. The poet could not be directed to express faithfully and pointedly the man; nor was it for the sake of "expression" that the man abdicated in favor of the poet.

Strictly speaking, this may be a half-truth. But if we regard with a reformer's eye the decay, in our time, of poetry, it becomes almost the whole truth we are called to utter. I do not mind putting it flatly; nor drawing the conclusion that poetry appeared to the apprentice Milton, before it could appear anything else, and before it could come into proper existence at all, as a sort of exercise, very difficult, and at first sight rather beside the point. It was of course an exercise in pure linguistic technique, or metrics; it was also an exercise in the technique of what our critics of fiction refer to as "point of view." And probably we shall never find a better locus than *Lycidas* for exhibiting at once the poet and the man, the technique and the personal interest, bound up tightly and contending all but equally; the strain of contraries, the not quite resolvable dualism, that is art.

For we must begin with a remark quite unsuitable for those moderns to whom "expression" seems the essential quality of poetry. *Lycidas* is a literary exercise; and so is almost any other poem earlier than the eighteenth century; the craftsmanship, the formal quality which is written on it, is meant to have high visibility. Take elegy, for example. According to the gentle and extremely masculine tradition which once governed these matters, performance is not rated by the rending of garments, heartbreak, verisimilitude of desolation. After all, an artist is standing before the public, and bears the character of a qualified spokesman, and a male. Let him somewhat loudly sweep the strings, even the tender human ones, but not without being almost military and superficial in his restraint; like the pomp at the funeral of the king, whom everybody mourns publicly and nobody privately. Milton made a great point of observing the proprieties of verse. He had told Diodati, as plainly as Latin elegiacs allowed, that "expression" was not one of the satisfactions which they permitted to the poet: "You want to know in verse how much I love and cherish you; believe me that you will scarcely discover this in verse, for love like ours is not contained within cold measures, it does not come to hobbled feet." As for memorial verse, he had already written, in English or Latin, for the University beadle, the University carrier, the Vice-Chancellor, his niece the Fair Infant Dying of a Cough, the Marchioness of Winchester, the Bishop of Winchester, the Bishop of Ely; he was yet to write for his Diodati, and for Mrs. Katharine Thomason. All these poems are exercises, and some are very playful indeed. There is no great raw grief apparent ever, and sometimes, very likely, no great grief. For Lycidas he mourns with a very technical piety.

Let us go directly to the poem's metre—though

this feature may seem a bristling technicality, and the sort of thing the tender reader may think he ought to be spared. I do not wish to be brutal, but I am afraid that metre is fundamental in the problem posed to the artist as poet. During the long apprenticeship Milton was the experimentalist, trying nearly everything. He does not ordinarily, in the Minor Poems, repeat himself metrically; another poem means another metre, and the new metre will scarcely satisfy him any better than the last one did. Evidently Milton never found the metre in which as a highly individual poet he could feel easy, and to which he was prepared to entrust his serious work, until he had taken the ragged blank verse of contemporary drama and had done something to it; tightening it up into a medium which was hard enough to exhibit form, and plastic enough to give him freedom. In other words, it defined the poet as somebody with a clipped, sonorous, figurative manner of speaking; but it also gave a possible if indirect utterance to the natural man. Here let us ask the question always in order against a Milton poem: What was the historic metrical pattern already before him, and what are the liberties he takes with it? For he does not cut patterns out of the whole cloth, but always takes an existing pattern; stretches it dangerously close to the limits that the pattern will permit without ceasing to be a pattern; and never brings himself to the point of defying that restraint which patterns inflict upon him, and composing something altogether unpatterned. That is to say, he tends habitually towards the formlessness which is modern, without quite caring to arrive at that destination. It is the principle we are interested in, not the literal answer to the question, which I will try to get over briefly.

The answer given by the Milton scholars, those who know their Italian, might well be that in this poem he made a very free adaptation of the canzone. This was a stanza of indeterminate length, running it might be to twenty lines or so, marked by some intricate rhyming scheme, and by a small number of six-syllable lines inserted among the ten-syllable lines which constituted the staple. The poet was free to make up his own stanza but, once that was given, had to keep it uniform throughout the poem. Milton employs it with almost destructive freedom, as we shall see. Yet, on the other hand, the correct stanza materials are there, and we can at least say that any one of the stanzas or paragraphs might make a passable canzone. And lest his irregularities be imputed to incompetence, we must observe the loving exactitude of his line-structure, that fundamental unit of any prosody, within the stanzas. He counts his syllables, he takes no liberties there: consisting with our rather fixed impression that he scarcely knew how in all his poetry to admit an imperfect line.

The Milton scholars know their Italian, and have me at a disadvantage. Milton knew his Italian. But he also knew his Spenser, and knowing that, it seems unnecessary to inquire whether he knew his Italian too; for he had only to adapt a famous Spenserian stanza, and his acquaintance with the canzone becomes really immaterial. I imagine this point has a slight importance. It would have something to do with the problem of the English poet who wants to employ an English technique in addressing himself to an English public which can be expected to know its English formal tradition. Spenser anticipated Milton by employing the canzone effectively in at least two considerable poems; they were not elegies, but at least they were marriage hymns. In 1596 he published his *Prothalamion,* upon the occasion of a noble alliance; the stanzas are exactly uniform, and they compose an admirable exercise in Italian canzoni. But he had published in 1595 his *Epithalamion,* upon the occasion of his own wedding, which is much more to Milton's purpose, and ours. Here are ten eighteen-line stanzas, but here are also twelve nineteen-line stanzas, and one of seventeen lines; and one of the eighteen-line stanzas does not agree in pattern with the others. If these details escape the modern reader, it is not at all certain that they were missed by Spenser's public. I should like to think that the poetical consciousness of the aristocratic literati of that age was a state of mind having metrical form in its foreground, and Spenser intended frankly to make use of the situation. Perhaps he calculated that if they would go to the trouble to analyze a poem composed of intricate but regular canzoni, they might go to still greater pains to analyze a poem whose canzoni were subtly irregular. I suppose this was something of a miscalculation, like other of his plans. But if it were a just calculation: then the advantage to be reaped by their going to such pains—it was their advantage as much as his—was the sort of addition to total effect which a labor of love can furnish. A public like Spenser's, if we are to construe it at its best, participates in the poem as does the author, and it is unfortunate if there lives today some modern Spenser who does not hope for such a reward to his efforts. But probably the sad truth is that a subtle art is unlikely in the first place, whose artist does not reckon upon the background of a severe technical tradition, and the prospect of a substantial public body of appreciation.

The enterprising Spenser prepared the way for the daring Milton, who remarks the liberties which his celebrated exemplar has taken and carries his own liberties further, to a point just this side of anarchy. The eleven stanzas of *Lycidas* occupy 193 lines, but are grossly unequal and unlike. Such stanzas are not in strictness stanzas at all; Milton has all but scrapped the stanza in its proper sense as a formal and binding element. But there is perhaps an even more startling lapse. Within the poem are ten lines which do not rhyme at all, and which technically do not belong therefore in any stanza, nor in the poem.

Now we may well imagine that the unrhymed lines did not escape Milton's notice, and also that he did not mean nor hope that they should escape ours.

The opening line of the poem is unrhymed, which is fair warning. The ten unrhymed lines should be conspicuous among the 183 rhymed ones, like so many bachelors at a picnic of fast-mated families. Let us ask what readers of *Lycidas* have detected them, and we shall see what readers are equipped with the right sensibility for an effect in form. And if the effect in this case is an effect of prose formlessness, and if nevertheless it is deliberate, we had better ask ourselves what Milton wanted with it.

It is tempting to the imperious individualism of the modern reader, especially if he has heard somewhere about the enormous egoism of John Milton, to say that the "expression" in these lines must have seemed to their author "inevitable," and superior to any obligation to the law of the form. Just as we find them, they had leapt out of the tense creative fury of the poet, notable, possibly prophetic; and what higher considerations were there anywhere requiring him in cold blood to alter them? But that does not make sense as an account of the poetic processes of a Milton. The ten lines, as it happens, look at them hard as we like, do not seem more important than ten others, and are not the lines by which he could have set special store. As a matter of fact, he might have altered them easily, tinkering with them as long as necessary in order to bring them within the metre, and they would scarcely have been, by whatever standard, any the worse. So great is the suggestibility of the poet's mind, the associability of ideas, the margin in the meaning of words. It is the inexperienced artist who attributes sanctity to some detail of his inspiration. You may ask him to write a poem which will make sense and make metre at the same time, but in the performance he will sacrifice one or the other; the consequence will be good sense and lame metre, or good metre and nonsense; if he is a man of interests and convictions, the former. But the competent artist is as sure of his second thoughts as of his first ones. In fact, surer, if anything; second thoughts tend to be the richer, for in order to get them he has to break up the obvious trains of association and explore more widely. Milton was not enamored of the ten lines, and they stand out from their context by no peculiar quality of their own but only because they do not belong to it metrically. Therefore I would say that they constitute the gesture of his rebellion against the formalism of his art, but not the rebellion itself. They are defiances, showing the man unwilling to give way to the poet; they are not based upon a special issue but upon surliness, and general principles. It is a fateful moment. At this critical stage in the poet's career, when he has come to the end of the period of Minor Poems, and is turning over in his head the grand subjects out of which he will produce great poems, he is uneasy, sceptical, about the whole foundation of poetry as an art. He has a lordly contempt for its tedious formalities, and is determined to show what he can do with only half trying to attend to them.

Or he thinks they are definitely bad, and proposes to see if it is not better to shove them aside.

In this uncertainty he is a modern poet. In the irregular stanzas and the rhymeless lines is registered the ravage of his modernity; it has bit into him as it never did into Spenser. And we imagine him thinking to himself, precisely like some modern poets we know, that he could no longer endure the look of perfect regimentation which sat upon the poor ideas objectified before him upon the page of poetry, as if that carried with it a reflection upon their sincerity. I will go further. It is not merely easy for a technician to write in smooth metres; it is perhaps easier than to write in rough ones, after he has once started; but when he was written smoothly, and contemplates his work, he is capable actually, if he is a modern poet, of going over it laboriously and roughening it. I venture to think that just such a practice, speaking very broadly, obtained in the composition of *Lycidas;* that it was written smooth and rewritten rough; which was treason.

I will make a summary statement which is true to the best of my knowledge. There did not at the time anywhere exist in English, among the poems done by competent technical poets, another poem so wilful and illegal in form as this one.

An art never possesses the "sincerity" that consists in speaking one's mind, that is, in expressing one's first impression before it has time to grow cold. This sincerity is spontaneity, the most characteristic quality in modern poetry. Art is long, and time is fleeting, and we have grown too impatient to relish more than the first motions towards poetic effect. The English and American Imagists exploited and consolidated this temper, which was no longer hospitable to a finished art. In their defence it may be said with justice that the writing of formal poetry, which they interrupted, was becoming a tedious parlor performance in which the poet made much ado about saying nothing of importance, while the man behind him quite escaped acquaintance through sheer lack of force. The verslibrists were determined to be bright, and fresh, and innocent of deep and ulterior designs; but their prose art was an anomaly. It wore out, and strict artistic economy has had a certain recovery; nothing like a complete one, for they left their mark upon our poetry, and I shall certainly not be so dogmatic as to say it has been entirely unfortunate.

It depends ultimately on taste whether we prefer prose to poetry, or prefer even a mixture of prose and poetry. Let us suppose two gentlemen talking a little wildly over their cups, until Mr. A insults Mr. B. Now if B is a modern man, he immediately strikes A down, with his knife if it happens to be in his hand, or his stick, or his fist. He has acted spontaneously, with a right and quick instinct, and he is admired for it. (I do not mean to raise any moral issues with my analogy.) But if the time is about a century or two earlier, B steps back and says drily: "My seconds will wait upon you, Sir." The next dawn A and B repair to the grove, attended by their respective partisans, draw their rapiers, and with great ceremony set in to kill each other. Or apparently they do; but if they are not really prepared to be hurt, nor to hurt each other, but are only passing the time until they are informed that their honors are satisfied, it is a bogus and ineffective action and the serious spectators feel cheated; that represents the sort of art against which the free versifiers revolted. If they fight till A puts his steel through the vitals of B, or *vice versa*, the spectators are well rewarded, and the ceremonial has justified itself, though it took time; that stands for the true art. But if they lose their tempers on the field and begin to curse, and kick, and throw stones and clods at each other, they are behaving too spontaneously for a formal occasion. Why were they not spontaneous yesterday if that was their intention? They will have to be recalled to the occasion and come to a conclusion under the terms nominated; and here we have the mixed affair of poetry and prose, a problem in taste; here, I am afraid, we have *Lycidas*.

At any rate Milton thought something of the kind. For he never repeated his bold experiment; and he felt at the time that it was not an altogether successful experiment. The last stanzas become much more patterned, and in the postscript Milton refers to the whole monody as the song of an "uncouth Swain," who has been "with eager thought warbling his *Dorick* lay." That is descriptive and deprecatory.

There is another possibility. Milton had much of the modern poet's awareness of his public; in this case the awareness of a public not quite capable of his own sustained artistic detachment. What sort of poem would it like? Too perfect an art might look cold and dead; and though an elegy had to be about the dead, it did not want itself to look dead, but to display incessant energy. So he read the formal poem he had written, and deformed it; or he had read other formal poems, like the *Epithalamion*, and remarked that the public, an increasingly mixed lot, thought them a little dull, and he now, as he composed his own poem, remembered to write into it plenty of formlessness. "The formalism," he was thinking, "if unrelieved, will dull the perceptions of my reader, and unprepare him for my surprises, and my tireless fertility. Therefore let him sense an exciting combat between the artist and the man, and let the man interrupt with his prose (comparative prose) the pretty passages of the artist." In that case the artist was only pretending to give way to the man, calculating with the cunning of a psychologist, perhaps of a dramatist, and violating the law of his art entirely for its public effect; a Jesuit of an artist. But the Jesuit, according to the Protestant tradition which reaches me, and which I will trust to the extent of this argument, has an excessive respect for the depravity of the humanity he ministers to, and he needs beyond other priests to be firmly grounded in his principles, lest from fighting the devil with fire he change his own element insensibly, become himself a fallen angel, and bear the reputation of one. The best thing to say for Milton is that his principles were strong, and he did not again so flagrantly betray them.

But if the poem is a literary exercise, it does not consist only in a game of metrical hide-and-seek, played between the long lines and short lines, the rhymed and unrhymed. It is also a poem in a certain literary "type," with conventions of subject-matter and style. Milton set out to make it a pastoral elegy, and felt honor-bound to use the conventions which had developed in the pastoral elegies of the Greeks, of Virgil, of the Italians, of Spenser; possibly of the French. The course of the poem in outline therefore is not highly "creative," but rather commonplace and in order, when the dead shepherd is remembered and his virtues published; when nature is made to lament him, and the streams to dry up in sympathy; when the guardian nymphs are asked why they have not saved him; when the untimeliness of his doom is moralized; when the corrupt church is reproached; when the flowers are gathered for the hearse; and finally when it appears to the mourners that they must cease, since he is not dead, but translated into a higher region, where he lives in bliss of a not definitive sort. In the pastoral elegy at large one of my friends distinguishes eleven different topics of discourse, and points out that Milton, for doubtless the first time in this literature, manages to "drag them all into one poem"; a distinction for him, though perhaps a doubtful one. But in doing so he simply fills up the poem; there are no other topics in it. And where is Milton the individualist, whose metrical departures would seem to have advertised a performance which in some to-be-unfolded manner will be revolutionary?

When we attempt to define the poetic "quality" of this poet's performances, we are forced to confess that it consists largely in pure eclecticism; here is a poet who can simply lay more of his predecessors under tribute than another. This is not to deny that he does a good job of it. He assimilates what he receives, and adapts it infallibly to the business in hand, where scraps fuse into integer, and the awkward articulations cannot be detected. His second-hand effects are not as good as new but better; the features of pastoral elegy are not as pretty in *Lycidas* as they were in Moschus, or Virgil, or Spenser, but prettier; though generically, and even in considerable detail, the same features. We remember after all that Milton intended his effects; and among others, this one of indebtedness to models. He expected that the reader should observe his eclecticism, he was scarcely alarmed lest it be mistaken for plagiarism. It is because of something mean in our modernism, or at least in that of our critics, that we, if we had composed the poem, would have found such an expectancy tainted with such an alarm. Like all the artists of the Renaissance, Milton hankered honestly after "Fame"; but he was not infected with our gross modern concept of "originality." The æsthetic of this point is perfectly rational. If a whole series of artists in turn develop the same subject, it is to the last one's advantage that he may absorb the others, in addition to being in whatever pointed or subtle manner his own specific self. His work becomes the climax of a tradition, and is better than the work of an earlier artist in the series. Unfortunately, there will come perhaps the day when there is no artist prepared to carry on the tradition; or, more simply, when the tradition has gone far enough and is not worth carrying further; that is, when it is worn out as a "heuristic" principle, and confines more than it frees the spirit. (Very few pastoral elegies can have been written since *Lycidas* in our language; very rew critics can have deplored this.) On that day the art will need its revolutionist, to start another tradition. It is a bold step for the artist to take, and Milton did not think it needful to take it here. The revolutionist who does not succeed must descend to the rating, for history, of rebel; the fool of a wrong political intuition.

But revolutions, for all that, little and private ones if not big and general ones, come frequently into a healthy literary history, in which variety is a matter of course. The poet may do better with a make-believe of his own than with a time-honored one. There is no theoretical limit upon the variety of literary types, and each good type permits of many explorers, but tends at last to be exhausted. The point of view of Greek shepherds, as romantic innocents and rustics, is excellent, and offers a wide range of poetic discourse concerning friendship, love, nature, and even, a startling innovation of the Italian pastoralists, the "ruin of the clergy." The point of view of the amorous cavalier presenting his compliments and reproaches to his lady is also a good one; it ran through many hundreds of lyrics in the sixteenth and seventeenth centuries, and is still better than no point of view at all, which we find in some very young poet speaking in his own person to his own love. The studied "conceit" of the seventeenth century offered another field of discourse in which poetic exercises took place; logical and academic, but having rich possibilities, and eligible even for religious experiences. The sonnet is primarily a metrical form, but behind it there is an ideal and rather formidable speaker, far from actual, who must get what he has to say into a very small space and, according to the rules, into a very concise style of utterance. The ballad offers a point of view quite alien to the ordinary cultivated poet, because speaking in that form he must divest himself of the impedimenta of learning and go primitive. All these forms lend themselves to individual variations and innovations; call for them, in fact, in the course of time, when the poet can find no fresh experience within the usual thing. It is entirely according to the æsthetic of this art if a poet wants to enter the book of literature with a series of

Choctaw incantations, provided he is steeped in Choctaw experience and able to make a substantial exhibit; or with a set of poems from the character of a mere Shropshire lad; or from that of a dry New England countryman. It is important mostly that the poet know his part and speak it fluently.

Of Milton's "style," in the sense of beauty of sound, imagery, syntax and dystax, idiom, I am quite unprepared to be very analytic. It is a grand style; which is to say, I suppose, that it is *the* grand style, or as much a grand style as English poets have known: the style produced out of the poet's remembrance of his classical models, chiefly Virgil. Milton has not been the only English poet to learn from Virgil, but he is doubtless the one who learned the most. Until the nineteenth century Virgil was perhaps the greatest external influence upon English literature. Dryden venerated but could not translate him:

> . . . must confess to my shame, that I have not been able to Translate any part of him so well, as to make him appear wholly like himself. For where the Original is close, no Version can reach it in the same compass. Hannibal Caro's, in the Italian, is the nearest, the most Poetical, and the most Sonorous of any Translation of the Æneid's; yet, though he takes the advantage of blank Verse, he commonly allows two lines for one of Virgil, and does not always hit his sence. . . . Virgil, therefore, being so very sparing of his words, and leaving so much to be imagined by the Reader, can never be translated as he ought, in any modern Tongue. To make him Copious,

is to alter his Character; and to translate him Line for Line is impossible; because the Latin is naturally a more succinct Language than either the Italian, Spanish, French, or even than the English (which, by reason of its Monosyllables, is far the most compendious of them). Virgil is much the closest of any Roman Poet, and the Latin Hexameter has more Feet than the English Heroick.

But in spite of the unfitness of an uninflected language like English, poets have occasionally managed a Virgilian style in it. We think at once of Marlowe. Naturally, it was not entirely beyond Shakespeare's powers; but Shakespeare at his highest pitch likes to rely on fury and hyperbole rather than the "smoothness" and "majesty" which Dryden commends in Virgil. Shakespeare writes:

> Rumble thy bellyful! Spit, fire! Spout, rain!

and

> You sulphurous and thought-executing fires,
> Vaunt-couriers of oak-cleaving thunderbolts,
> Singe my white head!

which is in a sublime style but not, if we care to be precise, the grand style. But Milton very nearly commanded this style. And with reason; for he had written Minor Poems in Latin as well as Minor Poems in English, and they were perhaps the more important item in his apprenticeship. This is one of the consequences:

> But now my Oate proceeds,
> And listens to the Herald of the Sea,
> That came in *Neptune's* plea,
> He ask'd the Waves, and ask'd the Fellon winds,

What hard mishap hath doom'd this gentle swain?
And question'd every gust of rugged wings
That blows from off each beaked Promontory,
They knew not of his story,
And sage *Hippotades* their answer brings,
That not a blast was from his dungeon stray'd,
The Ayr was calm, and on the level brine,
Sleek *Panope* with all her sisters play'd.
It was that fatall and perfidious Bark
Built in th'eclipse, and rigg'd with curses dark,
That sunk so low that sacred head of thine.

It is probable that no other English poet has this mastery of the Virgilian effect; it is much more Virgilian, too, than the later effect which Milton has in the lines of the *Paradise Lost*, where the great departure from the epical substance of the Virgil makes it needful to depart from the poetic tone. But Milton proves here that he had fairly mastered it. He had simply learned to know it in the Latin—learning by the long way of performance as well as by the short one of observation—and then transferred it to his native English; where it becomes a heightened effect, because this language is not accustomed at once to ease and condensation like this, and there is little competition. The great repute of the Miltonic style—or styles, variants of a style—in our literature is a consequence of the scarcity of Miltons; that is, of poets who have mastered the technique of Latin poetry before they have turned to their own.

But the author of *Lycidas*, attended into his project by so much of the baggage of tradition, cannot, by a universal way of thinking, have felt, exactly, free. I shall risk saying that he was not free. Little chance there for him to express the interests, the causes, which he personally and powerfully was developing; the poem too occasional and too formal for that. Of course the occasion was a fundamental one, it was no less than Death; and there is nobody so aggressive and self-assured but he must come to terms with that occasion. But a philosophy of death seems mostly to nullify, with its irony, the philosophy of life. Milton was yet very much alive, and in fact he regarded himself as having scarcely begun to live. The poem is almost wasted if we are seeking to determine to what extent it permitted Milton to unburden his heart.

But not quite. The passage on mortality is tense; Professor Tillyard finds the man in it. It goes into a passage on the immortality of the just man's Fame, which gives Milton's Platonic version of the ends of Puritanism. More important perhaps is the kind of expressiveness which appears in the speech of Peter. The freedom with which Milton abuses the false shepherds surpasses anything which his predecessors in this vein had indulged. He drops his Latinity for plain speech, where he can express a Milton who is angry, violent, and perhaps a little bit vulgar. It is the first time in his career that we have seen in him a taste for writing at this level. With modern readers it may be greatly to his credit as a natural man that he can feel strongly and hit hard. Later, in the period of his controversial prose, we get more of it, until we have had quite enough of this natural man. In the *Paradise Lost* we will get some "strong" passages again, but they are not Milton's response to his own immediate situation, they are dramatically appropriate, and the persons and scenes of the drama are probably remote enough to bring the passages under the precise head of artistic effect. This may be thought to hold for *Lycidas,* since it is Peter speaking in a pastoral part, and Peter still represents his villains as shepherds; but I feel that Peter sounds like another Puritan zealot, and less than apostolic.

Before I offer some generalizations about the poet and his art, I wish to refer, finally, to a feature of *Lycidas* which critics have rarely mentioned, and which most readers of my acquaintance, I believe, have never noticed, but which is technically astonishing all the same, and ought to initiate an important speculation upon the intentions of this poet. Pastoral elegies are dramatic monologues, giving the words of a single shepherd upon a single occasion; or they are dialogues giving, like so much printed drama, the speeches of several shepherds in a single scene. They may have prologues, perhaps so denominated in the text, and printed in italics, or in a body separate from the elegy proper; and likewise epilogues; the prologues and epilogues being the author's envelope of narrative within which is inserted the elegy. The composition is straightforward and explicitly logical.

Milton's elegy is otherwise. It begins without preamble as a monologue, and continues so through the former and bitterer half of the passage on Fame:

> But the fair Guerdon when we hope to find,
> And think to burst out into sudden blaze,
> Comes the blind *Fury* with th'abhorred shears,
> And slits the thin spun life. . . .

At this point comes an incredible interpolation:

> . . . But not the praise,
> *Phœbus* repli'd, and touch'd my trembling ears . . .

And Phœbus concludes the stanza; after which the shepherd apologizes to his pastoral Muses for the interruption and proceeds with his monologue. But dramatic monologue has turned for a moment into narrative. The narrative breaks the monologue several times more, presenting action sometimes in the present tense, sometimes in the past. And the final stanza gives a pure narrative conclusion in the past, without the typographical separateness of an epilogue; it is the one which contains Milton's apology for the "Dorick" quality of his performance, and promises that the author will yet appear in a serious and mature light as he has scarcely done on this occasion.

Such a breach in the logic of composition would denote, in another work, an amateurism below the level of publication. I do not know whether our failure to notice it is because we have been intoxicated by the wine of the poetry, or dulled by the drum-fire of the scholars' glosses, or intimidated by the sense that the poem is Milton's. Certainly it is Milton's; therefore it was intended; and what could have been in his mind? I have a suggestion. A feature that obeys the canon of logic is only the mere instance of a universal convention, while the one that violates the canon is an indestructibly private thing. The poor "instance" would like so much to attain to the dignity of a particular. If Milton had respected the rule of composition, he must have appeared as any other author of pastoral elegy, whereas in his disrespect of it he can be the person, the John Milton who is different, and dangerous, and very likely to become famous. (It is ironical that the lapse in question celebrates Fame.) The logical difficulties in the work of an artist capable of perfect logic may be the insignia of an individuality which would otherwise have to be left to the goodness of the imagination; and that is a calculation which lies, I think, under much modern art. There are living poets, and writers of fiction, and critics at the service of both, who have a perfect understanding of the principle. The incoherence or "difficulty" in the work is not necessarily to be attributed to the unresourcefulness of the artist, as if he could not have straightened everything out if he had desired, but sometimes to his choice. Under this head comes that licentious typography in which we may find one of the really magnificent manifestations of our modernity. The author is like some gentleman in the world of fashion who is thoroughly initiated, yet takes great pains to break the rule somewhere in order that nobody will make the mistake of not remarking his personality. If there is any force in this way of reasoning, we may believe that Milton's bold play with the forms of discourse constitutes simply one more item in his general insubordinacy. He does not propose to be buried beneath his own elegy. Now he had done a thing somewhat on the order of the present breach in his *L'Allegro* and *Il Penseroso*. There is a comparative simplicity to these pieces amounting almost to obviousness, but they are saved in several ways. For one thing, they are twin poems, and the parallelism or contrast is very intricate. More to our point, there is a certain lack of definition in the substantive detail; long sentences with difficult grammatical references, and uncertainty as to whether the invocation has passed into the action, and as to just where we are in the action. That trick was like the present one, indicating that the man is getting ahead of the poet, who is not being allowed to assimilate the matter into his formal style.

More accurately, of course, *they would like to indicate it;* the poet being really a party to the illusion. Therefore he lays himself open to the charge of being too cunning, and of overreaching himself; the effect is not heroic but mock-heroic. The excited Milton, breathless, and breaking through the logic of composition, is charming at first; but as soon as we are forced to reflect that he counterfeited the excitement, we are pained and let down. The whole poem is properly an illusion, but a deliberate and honest one, to which we consent, and through which we follow the poet because it enables him to do things not possible if he were presenting actuality. At some moments we may grow excited and tempted to forget that it is illusion, as the untrained spectator may forget and hiss the villain at the theatre. But we are quickly reminded of our proper attitude. If the author tends to forget, all the more if he pretends to forget, we would recall him to the situation too. Such license we do not accord to poets and dramatists, but only to novelists, whose art is young. And even these, or the best of these, seem now determined, for the sake of their artistic integrity, to surrender it.

So *Lycidas*, for the most part a work of great art, is sometimes artful and tricky. We are disturbingly conscious of a man behind the artist. But the critic will always find too many and too perfect beauties in it ever to deal with it very harshly.

Forms and Citizens

A FIRST-RATE poet performs in *Lycidas*, it is plain. And this is plain too: he performs because the decencies of an occasion require it of him, but the occasion catches him at a moment when his faith in the tradition of his art is not too strong, and in the performance rebellion is mixed up with loyalty. The study of the poem leads into a very broad field of discussion, and the topic is the general relation of the poet to his formal tradition.

By formal we are not to mean the metre only; but also, and it is probably even more important, the literary type, with its fictitious point of view from which the poet approaches his object, and its prescription of style and tone. And by tradition we should mean simply the source from which the form most easily comes. Tradition is the handing down of a thing by society, and the thing handed down is just a formula, a form.

Society hands down many forms which the individual is well advised to appropriate, but we are concerned here with those which may be called the æsthetic ones. They contrast themselves with the other and more common forms in the remarkable fact that they do not serve the principle of utility. This point has not been sufficiently remarked, so far as my reading indicates. There are economic forms;

there are also æsthetic forms, which are not the same thing. Or, there are work-forms and there are play-forms.

First, the economic forms. We inherit the traditional forms of such objects as plough, table, book, biscuit, machine, and of such processes as shepherding the flock, building, baking, making war. These forms are of intense practicality, and it is a good thing that they exist for the instruction of the successive generations, whose makeshifts, if they had to tutor themselves, would be blundering and ineffectual. Such forms write their own valuations, and very clearly. They are the recipes of maximum efficiency, short routes to "success," to welfare, to the attainments of natural satisfactions and comforts. They are the stock services which society confers upon its members, and the celebrated ones; doubtless in themselves alone a sufficient justification for constituted societies; sometimes, and especially where it is the modern temper which passes on it, the one usefulness which we can imagine attaching to societies, and the whole purpose of the social contract. But that is almost demonstrably an error, proceeding from a blind spot on the organ of insight which we are scarcely in a position to detect. Men absorbed in business and affairs may be excused for making that error, but it would be an egregious one for those who spend of their time and love upon æsthetic effects. It is in the æsthetic effects, if secured in those experiences that record themselves publicly as "art," or for that matter as manners and religion, that the given forms are both more and less than they seem, and not, on the whole, of any conceivable economic advantage.

Chiefly the error is an eidolon of period, a matter of the age and generation. Societies of the old order seemed better aware of the extent of their responsibilities. Along with the work-forms went the play-forms, which were elaborate in detail, and great in number, fastening upon so many of the common and otherwise practical occasions of life and making them occasions of joy and reflection, even festivals and celebrations; yet at the same time by no means a help but if anything a hindrance to direct action. The æsthetic forms are a technique of restraint, not of efficiency. They do not butter our bread, and they delay the eating of it. They stand between the individual and his natural object and impose a check upon his action; the reason must have been known well to the governors of old societies, for they honored the forms with unanimity; it must even yet be recoverable, for the argument shapes itself readily. To the concept of direct action the old society—the directed and hierarchical one—opposed the concept of æsthetic experience, as a true opposite, and checked the one in order to induce the other. Perhaps, since a social psychology is subtle, they fancied that the indissolubility of societies might depend as much on the definition they gave to play as on the definition they gave to labor. If so, our modern societies, with their horror of "empty" forms and ceremonies, and their invitation to men to be themselves, and to handle their objects as quickly and rudely as they please, are not only destroying old arts and customs, which they might not mind doing, but exposing incidentally their own solidarity to the anarchy of too much greed. But that is an incident. The formal tradition in art has a validity more than political, and the latter I am content to waive. What I have in mind is an argument from æsthetics which will justify any formal art, even a formal literature.

2

When a consensus of taste lays down the ordinance that the artist shall express himself formally, the purpose is evidently to deter him from expressing himself immediately. Or, the formal tradition intends to preserve the artist from the direct approach to his object. Behind the tradition is probably the sense that the direct approach is perilous to the artist, and may be fatal. It is feared that the artist who disregards the instruction may discover at length that he has only been artless; or, what is worse, that he will not make this important discovery, which will have to be made for him by the horrid way of autopsy. I suggest, therefore, that an art is usually, and probably of necessity, a kind of obliquity; that its fixed form proposes to guarantee the round-about of the artistic process, and the "æsthetic distance."

A code of manners also is capable of being taken in this fashion; it confers the same benefit, or the same handicap if we prefer, upon its adherent. Let us represent graphically, as in the figure I have entered below, the conduct of a man toward the woman he desires.

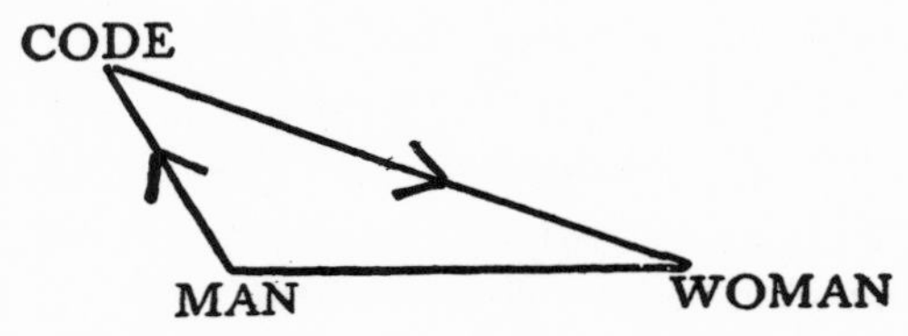

The event consists in his approach to the object. He may approach directly, and then his behavior is to seize her as quickly as possible. No inhibitions are supposed to have kept the cave-man or pirate, or any other of the admired figures of a great age when life was "in the raw," from taking this severely logical course. If our hero, however, does not propose for himself the character of the savage, or of animal, but the quaint one of "gentleman," then he has the fixed code of his *gens* to remember, and then he is estopped from seizing her, he must approach her with ceremony, and pay her a fastidious courtship. We conclude not that the desire is abandoned, but that it will take a circuitous road and become a romance. The form actually denies him the privilege of going the straight line between two points, even though this line has an axiomatic logic in its favor and is the shortest possible line. But the woman, contemplated in this manner under restraint, becomes a person and an æsthetic object; therefore a richer object.

In fact the woman becomes nothing less than an individual object; for we stumble here upon a fruitful paradox. The natural man, who today sometimes seems to be becoming always a greater man in our midst, asserting his rights so insistently, causing us to hear so much about "individualism," is a predatory creature to whom every object is an object of prey and the real or individual object cannot occur; while the social man, who submits to the restraint of convention, comes to respect the object and to see it unfold at last its individuality; which, if we must define it, is its capacity to furnish us with an infinite variety of innocent experience; that is, it is a source, from which so many charming experiences have already flowed, and a promise, a possibility of future experiences beyond all prediction. There must then, really, be two kinds of individualism: one is greedy and bogus, amounting only to egoism; the other is contemplative, genuine, and philosophical. The function of a code of manners is to make us capable of something better than the stupidity of an appetitive or economic life. High comedy, for example, is technically art, but substantially it is manners, and it has the agreeable function of displaying our familiar life relieved of its fundamental animality, filled, and dignified, through a technique which has in it nothing more esoteric than ceremonious intercourse.

To return to the figure, and to change the denotation slightly. Let us have a parallel now from the field of religion. The man is bereaved, and this time the object of his attention is the dead body of his friend. Instead of having a code of manners for this case, let him owe allegiance to a religious society, one which is possessed preferably of an ancient standing, and at all events of a ritual. The new terms for our graph become: Man and Corpse at the base, and Rite at the top and back. The religious society exists in order to serve the man in this crisis. Freed from his desolation by its virtue, he is not obliged now to run and throw himself upon the body in an ecstasy of grief, nor to go apart and brood upon the riddle of mortality, which may be the way of madness. His action is through the form of a pageant of grief, which is lovingly staged and attended by the religious community. His own grief expands, is lightened, no longer has to be explosive or obsessive. A sort of by-product of this formal occasion, we need not deny, is his grateful sense that his community supports him in a dreadful hour. But what interests us rather is the fact that his preoccupation with the deadness of the body is broken by his participation in the pageantry, and his bleak situation elaborated with such rich detail that it becomes massive, substantial, and sufficient.

We may of course eliminate the pageantry of death from our public life, but only if we expect the widow and orphan not really to feel their loss; and to this end we may inform them that they will not find it an economic loss, since they shall be maintained in their usual standards of living by the State. It is unfortunate for the economic calculus that they are likely to feel it anyway, since probably their relation to the one dead was not more economic than it was sentimental. Sentiments, those irrational psychic formations, do not consist very well with the indifference, machine-like, with which some modern social workers would have men fitting into the perfect economic organization. It is not as good animals that we are complicated with sentimental weakness. The fierce drives of the animals, whether human or otherwise, are only towards a *kind* of thing, the indifferent instance of a universal, and not some private and irreplaceable thing. All the nouns at this stage are common nouns. But we, for our curse or our pride, have sentiments; they are directed towards persons and things; and a sentiment is the totality of love and knowledge which we have of an object that is private and unique. This object might have been a simple economic object, yet we have elected to graft upon the economic relation a vast increment of diffuse and irrelevant sensibilia, and to keep it there forever, obstructing science and action. Sometimes we attach the major weight of our being, unreasonably, and to the point of absurdity, to a precious object. The adventitious interest, the sensibility that complicates and sometimes submerges the economic interest, does not seem to ask any odds of it, nor to think it necessary to theorize on behalf of its own existence. We may resent it, but eventually we have to accept it, as, simply, an "æsthetic" requirement, a piece of foolishness, which human nature will not forego. Wise societies legalize it and make much of it; for its sake they define the forms of manners, religions, arts; conferring a public right upon the sensibilia, especially when they organize themselves, or pile up notably, as they do, into the great fixed sentiments.

In Russia[1] we gather that there is a society bent seriously on "perfecting" the human constitution, that is, rationalizing or economizing it completely. The code of manners and the religious ritual are suspended, while the arts lead a half-privileged, censored, and furtive existence. Already a recent observer notes one result of the disappearance of the sex taboos: there is less sex-consciousness in Russia than anywhere in the Western world. That is to say, I suppose, that the loyal Russians approach the perfect state of animals, with sex reduced to its pure biological business. The above observer wonders painfully whether "love," of the sort that has been celebrated by so much history and so much literature, will vanish from Russia. It will vanish, if this society succeeds in assessing it by the standard of economic efficiency. The Russian leaders are repeating, at this late stage of history, with a people whose spirit is scored by all the traditional complications of human nature, the experiment of the Garden of

[1]I am not sure at this time of second publication just how true of Russia this representation may be.

Eden; when the original experiment should be conclusive, and was recorded, we may imagine, with that purpose in view. The original human family was instructed not to take the life of the beast-couples as its model; and did not, exactly, mean to do so; occupied itself with a certain pretty project having to do with a Tree of Rationalization; and made the mortal discovery that it came to the very same thing. The question is whether the ideal of efficient animality is good enough for human beings; and whether the economic law, by taking precedence at every point over the imperative of manners, of religion, and of the arts, will not lead to perfect misery.

3

And now, specifically, as to art, and its form. The analogy of the above occasions to the occasion called art is strict. Our terms now are Artist, Object, and Form. Confronting his object, the artist is tempted to react at once by registering just that aspect of the object in which he is practically "interested." For he is originally, and at any moment may revert to, a natural man, having a predatory and acquisitive interest in the object, or at best looking at it with a "scientific" curiosity to see if he cannot discover one somewhere in it. Art has a canon to restrain this natural man. It puts the object out of his reach; or more accurately, removes him to where he cannot hurt the object, nor disrespect it by taking his practical attitude towards it, exchanging his actual station, where he is too determined by proximity to the object, and contemporaneity with it, for the more ideal station furnished by the literary form. For example: there is the position, seemingly the silly and ineffectual one, of the man who is required by some quixotic rule of art to think of his object in pentameter couplets, therefore with a good deal of lost motion; and there is the far-fetched "point of view," which will require him to adapt all his thought to the rule of drama. The motion is well lost, if that is what it costs to frustrate the natural man and induce the æsthetic one. Society may not after all be too mistaken in asking the artist to deal with his object somewhat artificially. There will be plenty of others glad to deal with it immediately. It is perfectly true that art, *a priori,* looks dubious; a project in which the artist has a splendid chance for being a fool. The bad artists in the world are cruelly judged, they are the good journeymen gone wrong; and the good artists may be humorously regarded, as persons strangely possessed. But the intention of art is one that is peculiarly hard to pursue steadily, because it goes against the grain of our dominant and carefully instructed instincts; it wants us to enjoy life, to taste and reflect as we drink; when we are always tending as abstract appetites to gulp it down; or as abstract intelligences to proceed, by a milder analogue, to the cold fury of "disinterested" science. A technique of art must, then, be unprepossessing, and look vain and affected, and in fact look just like the technique of fine manners, or of ritual. Heroic intentions call for heroic measures.

We should not be taken in for a moment when we hear critics talking as if the form were in no sense a discipline but a direct help to the "expressiveness" —meaning the forthrightness—of the poem. This view reflects upon the holders credit for a reach of piety which is prepared to claim everything for the true works of art, and also a suspicion of ingenuousness for their peculiar understanding of the art-process. Given an object, and a poet burning to utter himself upon it, he must take into account a third item, the form into which he must cast his utterance. (If we like, we may call it the *body* which he must give to his passion.) It delays and hinders him. In the process of "composition" the burning passion is submitted to cool and scarcely relevant considerations. When it appears finally it may be said to have been treated with an application of sensibility. The thing expressed there is not the hundred-per cent passion at all.

If the passion burns too hot in the poet to endure the damping of the form, he might be advised that poetry can exercise no undue compulsion upon his spirit since, after all, there is prose. Milton may not always have let the form have its full effect upon the passion; some modern poets whom I admire do not; neither of which facts, however, disposes one to conclude that poetry is worse for the formal tradition. The formal tradition, as I have said, lays upon the poet evidently a double requirement. One is metrical or mechanical; but the measured speech is part of the logical identity of the poem; it goes into that "character" which it possesses as an ideal creation, out of the order of the actual. The other requirement is the basic one of the make-believe, the drama, the specific anonymity or pseudonymity, which defines the poem as poem; when that goes we may also say that the poem goes; so that there would seem to be taking place in the act of poetry a rather unprofitable labor if this anonymity is not clearly conceived when a poet is starting upon his poem, and a labor lost if the poet, who has once conceived it and established it, forgets to maintain it.

4

We accept or refuse the arts, with their complex intention, according as we like or dislike the fruits, or it may be the flowers, they bring to us; but these arts, and their techniques, may be always reinforced by the example of manners, and the example of religion; the three institutions do not rest on three foundations but on one foundation. A natural affiliation binds together the gentleman, the religious man, and the artist—punctilious characters, all of them, in their formalism. We have seen one distinguished figure in our times pronouncing on behalf of all three in one breath. In politics, royalism; in religion, Anglo-Catholic; in literature, classical. I am astonished upon discovering how comprehensively this formula covers the kingdom of the æsthetic life as it is organized by the social tradition. I am so grateful that it is with hesitation I pick a little quarrel with the terms. I would covet a program going something like this: In manners, aristocratic; in religion, ritualistic; in art, traditional. But I imagine the intent of Mr. Eliot's formula is about what I am representing; and on the other hand might be only the more effective to fight with for being so concrete. (Unfortunately its terms are not suited to Americans; but possibly this is so of mine too.) The word for our generation in these matters is "formal," and it might even bear the pointed qualification, "and reactionary." The phrase would carry the sense of our need to make a return to amenities which the European communities labored to evolve, and defined as their "civilization." For the intention of none of those societies can have been simply to confirm the natural man as a natural man, or to improve him in cunning and effectiveness by furnishing him with its tried economic forms. It wanted to humanize him; which means, so far as his natural economy permitted, to complicate his natural functions with sensibility, and make them æsthetic. The object of a proper society is to instruct its members how to transform instinctive experience into æsthetic experience.

Manners, rites, and arts are so close to each other that often their occasions must be confused, and it does not matter much if they are. The rule of manners is directed to those occasions when natural appetites and urges are concerned; when we hunger, or lust, or go into a rage, or encounter strange or possibly dangerous persons. The rites take place upon religious occasions; but I suppose this is tautology. It is my idea that religion is an institution existing for the sake of its ritual, rather than, as I have heard, for the sake of its doctrines, to which there attaches no cogency of magic, and for that matter a very precarious cogency of logic. The issues upon which the doctrines pronounce are really insoluble for human logic, and the higher religionists are aware of it. The only solution that is possible, since the economic solution is not possible, is the æsthetic one. When these issues press upon us, there is little that one man, with whatever benefit of doctrines, can do toward the understanding of the event which another man cannot do; and he had better not try too hard to understand the precise event, but enlarge its terms, and assimilate it into the form of an ornate public ritual through which the whole mind can discharge itself. This is a subtle technique, it has been a successful technique; in insisting upon it as the one thing I do not mean to subtract dignity from the world's great religions—which I revere. And what are the specific occasions for ritual? Those which are startling in our biological and economic history, and provoke reflection, and also, for fear we may forget to be startled when we are living for a long interval upon a dead level of routine, some arbitrary occasions, frequent and intercalated; therefore birth, marriage, death; war, peace, the undertaking of great enterprises, famine, storm; the seasons of the year, the Sabbath, the holidays. But as for the artistic process, what are its occasions? What prompts the artist? For we remark at once that many works of art embody ritual, and art is often apparently content to be the handmaiden to religion, as Hegel desired, and as she conceivably is in a painting by Michelangelo, or a poem on the order of *Lycidas*. We know also that works of art have been dedicated to the ceremonious life of society, commemorating chivalry, or some much easier code; art serving manners.

The occasions of art are innumerable; very probably its "future is immense." Its field is wider than that of manners, or than that of religion; the field of literary art alone is that. In fact it is about as wide as the field of science itself; and there I think lies the hint for a definition. What is the occasion which will do for the artist and the scientist indifferently? It is the occasion when we propose to "study" our object; that is, when we are more than usually undesirous and free, and find the time to become curious about the object as, actually, something "objective" and independent. Out of the surplus of our energy—thanks to the efficiency of our modern economic forms we have that increasingly—we contemplate object as object, and are not forced by an instinctive necessity to take it and devour it immediately. This contemplation may take one of two routes; and first, that of science. I study the object to see how I may wring out of it my physical satisfaction the next time; or even how I may discover for the sake of a next time the physical satisfaction which it contains, but not too transparently; analyzing and classifying, "experimenting," bringing it under the system of control which I intend as a scientist to have over the world of objects. It is superfluous to observe that I, the modern scientist, am in this case spiritually just as poor as was my ancestor the cave-man. My intention is simply to have bigger and quicker satisfactions than he had, my head still runs on satisfactions. But I may contemplate also, under another form entirely, the form of art. And that is when I am impelled neither to lay hands on the object immediately, nor to ticket it for tomorrow's outrage, but am in such a marvellous state of innocence that I would know it for its own sake, and conceive it as having its own existence; this is the knowledge, or it ought to be, which Schopenhauer praised as "knowledge without desire." The features which the object discloses then are not those which have their meaning for a science, for a set of practical values. They are those which render the body of the object, and constitute a knowledge so radical that the scientist as a scientist can scarcely understand it, and puzzles to see it rendered, richly and wastefully, in the poem, or the painting. The knowledge attained there, and recorded, is a new kind of knowledge, the world in which it is set is a new world.

5

Poetry is more complicated than an animal act, which is ordinarily a scientific sort of act; it is even more complicated than the play of an animal, though the complication of that act is one difficult for the psychologists to handle. The poetic act involves the general sensibility, with its diffusive ranging, hardly familiar to science. But it certainly involves at the same time a discipline, very like that of science. Perhaps the best way to construe a poetic labor briefly is to take it as the analogue to a scientific one (though this latter is the paragon of labors which are serious and important) and then to fill in the differences.

The poetic labors of John Milton will do for an example. He is never discovered except meditating an object which is formidable, with a scrutiny which is steady, like that of a scientist; infinitely more sensitive. Milton's poetry exceeds most poetry in its logical closeness and symmetry; the difference between his epics and Virgil's is that his are powerfully and visibly motivated at every moment, and he will not if he can recover the purity of narrative, the innocence, that marks the ancient epic. Milton is a strong man, and has intense economic persuasions, if we may bring under that term his personal, moral, and political principles. These are his precious objects; or the situations in which he finds them exercising are. But the situations in the poetry are not his actual ones; they are fancied ones which do not touch him so nearly, distant enough to inhibit the economic impulse, which would have inhibited the sensibility. The result is that Milton's poetry, broadly speaking, may be said always to deal with "important" or highly economic subjects. But the importance of the subject is not the importance of the poetry; that depends more on the sensitiveness and completeness of the experience. The subject will generally be found to have been treated more precisely or practically somewhere in his economic prose; that is, in the ethical, theological, political tracts. It pleases us to imagine, on the strength of Milton's example, that there is no prose which is incapable of becoming a poetry, no subject in his mind so urgent that he is intimidated by it, and cannot feel it, enjoy it, and spread it out; live it, in the way we might call upon some superior man to live it.

So we look briefly and definitely as we may, at the whole net accomplishment of John Milton; starting from a convenient point, which will be *Lycidas*. This poem looks backward upon a long period of minor or practice poetry, and forward to the career of the major poet; while, as I pointed out in my previous essay, it does not fail to betray the man behind the poet.

We do not find in *Lycidas* quite the proper occasion for a modern tract on communism, nor even for a contemporaneous tract on divorce; which makes it unnecessary either to regret or to be glad that Milton has not attempted a demonstration that literature is sociology, or literature is science. We do find in the death of the young clergyman the occasion for a contemporaneous tract on the degeneration of the clergy; and Milton, with some difficulty, perhaps, dismisses that temptation. For his difficulty, if we detect it, he is probably the less an artist. Yet Milton entertained strict views upon the function of the artist, and only upon strong compulsion was apostate.

Milton felt the impact of modernity which is perennial in every generation; or, if it is not, of the rather handsome degree of modernity which was current in his day. He was exposed to specific temptation because he was a man of his times and held strong views upon the contemporary ecclesiastical and political situations, in a period when the church and the political order were undergoing revolution; he was of the party of revolution. He had a natural inclination to preach, and display his zeal; to preach upon such themes as the reform of the clergy, and the reform of the government; and he tended to preach intemperately when he preached. He knew of this tendency in himself and opposed it. He went so far as to abandon that career in the church which his father had intended for him and to which he seems at first to have consented. The career which he chose instead was one which we are wrong to consider vague and indefinite, for he hardly considered it so—

the career of an artist. He has a good deal to say about this choice. If in the course of a public controversy much later he argued that he had given up the church because he could not endure its tyrannical overlords, he made no such plea in the affectionate Latin letter written to his father when the issue was hot. Here he is content to assert the superiority of the poet to other men. He is impressed with the elevation of the poet's mind, which gives him a sort of aristocracy, an attitude habitually æsthetic; and Milton has studied it, and had it, enough to know. (We must not suppose, as Milton did not, that a man has to be born in some statistical manner to this elevation. He may bring himself up to it.)

This is not quite the same as saying that Milton renounced his position as a man in order to take a position as a poet; he expected to occupy both positions, but at different times. But he did not consent to define himself as the man; that is, as the man with a profession, the economic man. As a man he was too much like any of us; if not too appetitive in the flesh, at least too zealous in intellectual action, which comes æsthetically to the same thing. He might have elected to become not an artist but a man of science; a character that is just barely not a man of action, or a professional. Science belongs to the economic impulse and does not free the spirit; its celebrated virtue is due to its position on the economic scale, well distanced from the maw and the mouth of actual red appetite, while its technique is precisely the same.

Like many other people, he had a blind spot. He could scarcely receive from ritual the æsthetic benefit which was intended for him in that dispensation. Ritual turned him suspicious and truculent; a great modernism. Yet the inhibitions lay upon the act of public participation, not so much upon his intuitive understanding of the matter, and we may easily overstate it. It is probably a common variety of Protestantism. When he came under the milder influences of poetry, he composed the kind of effects which he valued, which he constantly received in the traditional poetry of Greeks, Romans, Italians, and Englishmen—poetry nearly as ornate, mythological, religious, as a ritual itself could be. But when he was faced by the ritual, the effective thing itself, administered by priests whom he had determined to hold as hypocritical, he was roused invariably to resistance. So inveterate and passionate did this resistance become that it took him into the extremist Protestant camp to write hard doctrine, and actually to set up his own religion as a project in dialectic. All the time he "knew" better; probably no European poet exceeds him much, either for consistency or for depths of insight, in mythological sense. The same Milton appealed in a Latin exercise to Plato not to banish the myth-makers from the Republic, and some years later would have liked publicly to chase out of England the Anglican ritualists, the adherents of the then myth, as idolators. That is the Milton paradox.

He was obstinate in his idea of what the church must have been for him as a calling. His Anglo-Catholic contemporaries could have told him—probably they told him—that the priest who is charged with the performance of the ritual, and on some occasions with creating ritual on his own responsibility, is eminently in the service of the cult of æsthetic experience. His noble Italian friends certainly told him, during that triumphal tour on which he received honors incredible for a professing Puritan in Rome, except that he may have been regarded as a man not yet too openly committed, and still reclaimable. Among these friends was Manso, to whom it must have seemed a pity that a poet so prodigious, and so true to the ancient traditions of his calling, was capable of not perceiving that these had anything to do with the majestic ceremonial of a high church. We may imagine that Manso had this anomaly in mind—and not merely the havoc which the young collegiate Milton had wrought with the Catholics, or tried to wreak, in his exuberant exercise on the Gunpowder Plot—when he presented Milton with a fine Latin compliment, to which there was attached all the same an impressive qualification: "If your piety were such as your mind, your form, charm, face, and manners, then you would not be an Angle, but in sober truth an Angel." Manso was cribbing of course from the Sixth-Century Gregory, who had observed the fair-haired Anglian slaves in Rome, and hoped they might one day take their own part in the ritual of a world-wide catholic church. Gregory's hope had been realized, but now in Milton's time it seemed on the point of being deceived; and here was one of the race in question, brilliantly endowed in his mind and person, but stubborn in his barbarism; for Manso could not fail to appreciate just what it meant for a society to cast off its religious forms.

But, as I have said, Milton did know better than he acted; he made his choice and became the artist; and exercised his *métier* with an aristocratic taste that almost never failed him; though he was no more able as layman than he had been as prospective priest to apply this taste to the forms of his worship. We do not regret his decision when we have to follow him during the ten or fifteen years after 1640, the period in which he felt obliged as a citizen to drop the poet and become the preacher, the tractarian, and the economic man. During that period we remember gratefully that he shares our own view of his intractable nature, in which so much of the sin of Adam resides; that he understands his predicament. The formality of poetry sustained him, induced in him his highest nobility, and his most delicate feeling. The ding-dong of contemporary controversy brought out of him something ugly and plebeian that was there all the time, waiting. He took care that the preacher should be the Miltonic rôle for but a period;

the artist came back, and may have been the better artist for the ignominy which he had suffered; though I shall not try to argue that.

Art was his deliberate career. It is a career, precisely as science is a career. It is as serious, it has an attitude as official, it is as studied and consecutive, it is by all means as difficult, it is no less important. It may be less remunerative, it is further from offering the sort of values which are materially rewarded; today it may be so unrewarded that, if we agree to regard it like science as a career, we are not inclined to regard it like science as a profession; but so far from being at a disadvantage on that account, it may be better off, as having the more innocence because of it, and finding innocence a good condition for its peculiar process.

It would follow that Milton has been widely if not generally misunderstood, by people who define him primarily as a Puritan moralist, or a theologian, or a political thinker, or an early modern, or a scholar. Some ultra-modern critics, as was inevitable, now have turned upon him "as a man," and in that capacity as one of the damned, having an inherited disease, or a libido, or a crack in his mind—which seems at this distance unimportant if true. He was chiefly and preferably, and on a life-long scale, an artist. Those who will not undertake to gather what this involved for him will be finding themselves constantly rebuffed by the mountains of irrelevance raised against them in the body of his poetry. Milton is the poetry, and is lost to them if they do not know how to make acquaintance there. What on earth will they do with the cool flora that bloom so uselessly in the formal if somewhat tangled garden which is *Lycidas?*

Poets Without Laurels

THE poets I refer to in the title are the "moderns": those whom a small company of adept readers enjoys, perhaps enormously, but the general public detests; those in whose hands poetry as a living art has lost its public support.

Consequently I do not refer to such poets as Edna St. Vincent Millay and Robert Frost, who are evidently influenced by modernism without caring to "go modern" in the sense of joining the revolution; which is very much as if they had stopped at a mild or parlor variety of socialism, when all about them the brave, or at least the doctrinaire, were marching under the red banner. Probably they are wise in their time; they have laurels deservedly and wear them gracefully. But they do not define the issue which I wish to discuss. And still less do I refer to poets like E. A. Robinson, Sturge Moore, and John Masefield, who are even less modern; though I have no intention of questioning their laurels either. I refer to poets with no laurels.

I do not wish to seem to hold the public responsible for their condition, as if it had suddenly become phlegmatic, cruel, and philistine. The poets have certainly for their part conducted themselves peculiarly. They could not have estranged the public more completely if they had tried; and smart fellows as they are, they know very well what they have been doing, and what they are still stubborn in doing, and what the consequences are.

For they have failed more and more flagrantly, more and more deliberately, to identify themselves with the public interests, as if expressly to renounce the kind affections which poets had courted for centuries. Accordingly, they do not only encounter public indifference, they sometimes encounter active hostility. A Pulitzer committeeman, I hear, says about some modernist poet whose book is up for judgment: "He will never get the award except over my dead body." The violence of the remark seems to exceed the occasion, but it is not exceptional.

Poets used to be bards and patriots, priests and prophets, keepers of the public conscience, and, naturally, men of public importance. Society crowned them with wreaths of laurel, according to the tradition which comes to us from the Greeks and is perpetuated by official custom in England—and in Oklahoma. Generally the favor must have been gratefully received. But modern poets are of another breed. It is as if all at once they had lost their prudence as well as their piety, and formed a compact to unclasp the chaplet from their brows, inflicting upon themselves the humility of delaureation, and retiring from public responsibility and honors. It is this phenomenon which has thrown critical theory into confusion.

Sir Philip Sidney made the orthodox defense of

poetry on the ground of the poet's service to patriotism and virtue:

> He doth not only show the way, but giveth so
> sweet a prospect into the way, as will
> entice any man to enter into it.

And what was the technique of enticement?

> With a tale forsooth he cometh unto you, with a
> tale which holdeth children from play,
> and old men from the chimney corner.

The poets, therefore, told entrancing tales, which had morals. But the fact was, also, that the poets were not always content to win to virtue by indirection, or enticement, but were prepared to preach with almost no disguise, and to become sententious and repetitious, and the literature which they created is crowded with precise maxims for the moralists. There it stands on the shelves now. Sometimes the so-called poet has been only a moralist with a poetic manner. And all the poets famous in our tradition, or very nearly all, have been poets of a powerful moral cast.

So I shall try a preliminary definition of the poet's traditional function on behalf of society: he proposed to make virtue delicious. He compounded a moral effect with an æsthetic effect. The total effect was not a pure one, but it was rich, and relished highly. The name of the moral effect was goodness; the name of the æsthetic effect was beauty. Perhaps these did not have to coexist, but the planners of society saw to it that they should; they called upon the artists to reinforce morality with charm. The artists obliged.

When they had done so, the public did not think of attempting to distinguish in its experience as reader the glow which was æsthetic from the glow which was moral. Most persons probably could not have done this; many persons cannot do it today. There is yet no general recognition of the possibility that an æsthetic effect may exist by itself, independent of morality or any other useful set of ideas. But the modern poet is intensely concerned with this possibility, and he has disclaimed social responsibility in order to secure this pure æsthetic effect. He cares nothing, professionally, about morals, or God, or native land. He has performed a work of dissociation and purified his art.

There are distinct styles of "modernity," but I think their net results, psychologically, are about the same. I have in mind what might be called the "pure" style and what might be called the "obscure" style.

A good "pure" poem is Wallace Stevens' "Sea Surface Full of Clouds"—famous perhaps, but certainly not well known. I shall have to deal with it summarily. Time and place, "In that November off Tehuantepec." The poem has five uniform stanzas, presenting as many surface effects beheld at breakfast time "after the slopping of the sea by night grew still." The first surface made one think of rosy chocolate and gilt umbrellas; the second, of chophouse chocolate and sham umbrellas; the third, of porcelain chocolate and pied umbrellas; the fourth, of musky chocolate and frail umbrellas; the fifth, of Chinese chocolate and large umbrellas. Nothing could be more discriminating than these details, which induct us respectively into the five fields of observation. The poem has a calculated complexity, and its technical competence is so high that to study it, if you do that sort of thing, is to be happy. That it has not been studied by a multitude of persons is due to a simple consideration which strikes us at once: the poem has no moral, political, religious, or sociological values. It is not about "res publica," the public thing. The subject matter is trifling.

Poetry of this sort, as it was practised by some French poets of the nineteenth century, and as it is practised by many British and American poets now, has been called pure poetry, and the name is accurate. It is nothing but poetry; it is poetry for poetry's sake, and you cannot get a moral out of it. But it was to be expected that it would never win the public at large. The impulse which led readers to the old poetry was at least as much moral as it was æsthetic, while the new poetry cannot count on any customers except those specializing in strict æsthetic effects. But the modern poets intend to rate only as poets, and would probably think it meretricious to solicit patronage by making moral overtures.

As an example of "obscure" poetry, though not the most extreme one, I cite Allen Tate's "Death of Little Boys." Here are some of its verses:

Then you will touch at the bedside, torn in two,
Gold curls now deftly intricate with gray
As the windowpane extends a fear to you
From one peeled aster drenched with the wind all day. . . .

Till all the guests, come in to look, turn down
Their palms; and delirium assails the cliff
Of Norway where you ponder, and your little town
Reels like a sailor drunk in his rotten skiff.

There is evidently a wide difference between Stevens and Tate, as poets. Tate has an important subject, and his poem is a human document, with a contagious fury about it: Stevens, pursuing purity, does not care to risk such a subject. But Tate, as if conscious that he is close to moralizing and sententiousness, builds up deliberately, I imagine, an effect of obscurity; for example, he does not care to explain the private meaning of his windowpane and his Norwegian cliff; or else, by some feat, he permits these bright features to belong to his total image without permitting them to reveal any precise meaning, either for himself or for his reader. Stevens, however, is objective from begining to end; he completes all his meanings, knowing these will have little or no moral importance.

Pure or obscure, the modern poet manages not to slip into the old-fashioned moral-beautiful compound. If pure, he will not consider a subject which lends itself to moralization; that is, a subject of practical interest. It is his chief problem to find then a subject which has any interest at all. If, however, he prefers the other road, he may take the subject nearest his own humanity, a subject perhaps of terrifying import; but in treating it will stop short of all moral or theoretical conclusions, and confuse his detail to the point where it leaves no positive implications.

To be more technical: it is as if the pure poet presented a subject and declined to make any predication about it or even to start predication; and as if the obscure poet presented a subject in order to play with a great deal of important predication without ever completing any.

Personally, I prefer the rich obscure poetry to the thin pure poetry. The deaths of little boys are more exciting than the sea surfaces. It may be that the public preference, however, is otherwise. The public is inclined simply to ignore the pure poetry, because it lacks practical usefulness; but to hate the obscure poetry, because it looks important enough to attend to, and yet never yields up any specific fruit. Society, through its spokesmen the dozens of social-minded critics, who talk about the necessity of "communication," is now raging with indignation, or it may be with scorn, against the obscure poetry which this particular generation of poets has deposited. Nevertheless, both types of poetry, obscure as well as pure, aim at poetic autonomy; that is, speaking roughly, at purity.

Modern poetry in this respect is like modern painting. European painting used to be nearly as social a thing as poetry. It illustrated the sacred themes prescribed by the priests, whether popularly (Raphael) or esoterically and symbolically (Michelangelo); did the portraits of kings and cardinals, and the scenes of battles and great occasions; worked up allegorical and sentimental subjects. But more or less suddenly it asserted its independence. So we find Impressionists, doing the most innocent tricks with landscapes and mere objects; and we find Cézanne, painting so many times and so lovingly his foolish little bowl of fruits. The procedure was a strange one for the moral laity, who could detect nothing of importance there; and indeed nothing of public importance was there, only matters of technical interest to painters, and to persons who found painting sufficient. Later, and today, we find painters taking up the most heroic human material again in the most promising manner, yet arriving at no explicit meaning and, on the whole, simply playing with its powerful symbols. (Not all painters, of course.)

Apostate, illaureate, and doomed to outlawry the modern poets may be. I have the feeling that modernism is an unfortunate road for them to have taken. But it was an inevitable one. It is not hard to defend them from imputations against their honor and their logic. It is probably a question of whether we really know them, and understand their unusual purpose, and the powerful inhibitions they impose upon themselves.

But let us approach the matter from a slightly different angle. Poets have had to become modern because the age is modern. Its modernism envelops them like a sea, or an air. Nothing in their thought can escape it.

Modern poetry is pure poetry. The motive behind it cannot be substantially different from the motive behind the other modern activities, which is certainly the driving force of all our modernism. What is its name? "Purism" would be exact, except that it does not have the zealous and contriving sound we want. "Platonism" would do, provided there were time to come to an agreement about the essential meaning of Plato's act. I think the name "Puritanism" will describe this motive, if I may extend a little a term whose application in history has been mostly religious and moral.

Our period differs outwardly from other periods because it first differs inwardly. Its spiritual temper is puritanical; that is, it craves to perfect the parts of experience separately or in their purity, and is a series of isolated perfections. These have often been brilliant. But perhaps the modern program, on the whole, is not the one under which men maintain their best health and spirits. A little fear to that effect is beginning to cloud the consciousness of the brilliant moderns.

And here I conclude my defense of the modern poet. He is a good workman, and his purpose is really quite orthodox in its modernism. But it is no better.

The development of modern civilization has been a grand progression in which Puritanism has invaded first one field and then another.

The first field perhaps was religion. The religious impulse used to join to itself and dominate and hold together nearly all the fields of human experience; politics, science, art, and even industry, and by all means moral conduct. But Puritanism came in the form of the Protestant Reformation and separated religion from all its partners. Perhaps the most important of these separations was that which lopped off from religion the æsthetic properties which simple-hearted devotees and loving artists had given it. The æsthetic properties constituted the myth, which to the temperamental Protestants became superstition, and the ceremonial, which became idolatry. Under the progressive zeal of the Reformation the being of God has become rarefied in the degree that it has been purified, until we find difficulty in grasping it, and there are people who tell me, just as there are people who tell the reader, that religion as a living force here in the Western world is spent. Theology is purer or more abstract than ever before, but it would seem to belong exclusively to theologians, and it cannot by itself assemble together all those who once delighted in the moral precepts, the music and the pomp, the social communion, and the concrete Godhead, of the synthetic institution which was called religion.

Next, or perhaps at the same time, Puritanism applied itself to morality. Broad as the reach of morality may be, it is distinct enough as an experience to be capable of purification. We may say that its destiny was to become what we know as sociology, a body of positivistic science. It had to be emancipated from its religious overlords, whose authority, after all, was not a moral one. Then it had to be emancipated from the dictates of taste, or æsthetic, and this latter emancipation was the harder, and perhaps the more needless. The Greeks, though they were incipient Puritans, scarcely attempted it. They had a compound phrase meaning "beautiful-good," which even their philosophers used habitually as the name of something elemental and indissoluble. Suspicion was aroused in Greeks by a goodness which could not produce beauty, just as to a man like Spenser the idea of virtue was incomplete until it flowered into poetic form, and just as to the sympathetic French artist our new American liberty was not quite won until identifiable with an able-bodied demi-goddess lifting a torch. The splitting up of the moral-beautiful compound for the sake of the pure moral article is visibly at work in the New Testament, and in the bourgeois cult of plainness in seventeenth-century England, and in the finicky private life of a Puritan moralist like Kant, and today in moral or sociological treatises (and authors) which neither exhibit nor discuss charm. Now, it is true that we moralize with "maximum efficiency" when we do it technically, or abstractly, but when that comes to be the rule we no longer approach a moral discussion with anything but a moral interest. To be moral is no longer to be "decent," and it looks as if moral appeal had become something less wide and less instant than it was.

Then Puritanism worked upon politics. I am not prepared to go deeply into this, but it is evident that purification consisted in taking the state away from the church, from the monarch, from the feudal aristocracy, from any other concrete attachments, in order that it might propel itself by the force of pure statecraft. Progress in this direction meant constitutionalism, parliamentarianism, republicanism. A modern state like ours is transparent in the perfection of its logic. But that does not make it the more realistic. It is obliged to count upon a universal and continuous will on the part of the citizens to accept an abstract formula of political action. But such a will may not be there. The population, not being composed exclusively of politicians, is inclined to delegate statecraft to those who profess it. The old mixed states had a greater variety of loyalties to appeal to.

Puritanism is an ideal which not all persons are strong enough to realize, but only those with great power of concentration. Its best chance of success lies in individual projects. Accordingly, Puritanism fairly came into its own in the vast multitude of private enterprises which go together to make modern science. Galileo and Kepler found science captive to religious dogma. America, the paradise of Puritanism, was not yet in being, but England was; and there presently, while other Puritanisms were going on, Lord Bacon was able to anticipate the complete emancipation of science by virtue of its adoption of the pure experimental method. Now, there have been other incubi besides religion resting upon science at one time or another; and chiefly the tendency of poetry to haunt its deliberations. Poetry is a figurative way of expression, science is a technical or abstract way; but since science employs language, the figurative associations are hard to keep out. In earlier days poetry kept close to science, and it did not seem so strange if Lucretius wanted to set forth the body of accepted science in verse. But poetry now cannot attend science into its technical labyrinth. The result is greater success for scientists, but not necessarily their greater happiness as men; and the general understanding on our part that we will follow science if we are scientists, but otherwise will leave it to the scientists.

It was but one step that Puritanism had to go from there into the world of business, where the material sciences are systematically applied. The rise of the modern business world is a development attendant upon the freedom which it has enjoyed; upon business for business' sake, or pure business, or "laissez faire," with such unconditioned principles as efficiency, technological improvement, and maximum productivity. If I wished to attack the record of business, I should by now have been long anticipated. It is common opinion that business as a self-contained profession has created business men who are defective in their humanity; that the conduct of business has made us callous to personal relations and to social justice; and that many of the occupations which business has devised are, in the absence of æsthetic standards, servile.

All these exclusions and specializations, and many more, have been making modern life what it is. It is significant that every specialization on the list has had to resist the insidious charms of æsthetic experience before its own perfection could arise. (Evidently the æsthetic interest is remarkably catholic among our faculties in its affinities; ready to attach itself easily to almost any sort of moment; a ubiquitous element in experience, it might be thought, which it would be unhealthy to cast out.) But the energy of so deep an impulse as Puritanism had to flow through all the channels, and to come to its last outlet in a pure art, a pure poetry. Those who have not observed the necessity may choose to hold its predestined agents the poets in contempt, or in amazement. The poets are in the spirit of their time. On the one hand, they have been pushed out of their old attachments, whereby they used to make themselves useful to public causes, by the specialists who did not want the respective causes to be branded with amateurism. On the other hand, they are moved by a universal tendency into their own appropriate kind of specialization, which can be, as they have been at pains to show, as formidable as any other.

Considerations of this kind, I feel sure, have been more or less precisely within the intuition of all modern poets, and have motivated their performance. Technically, they are quite capable of writing the old compound poetry, but they cannot bring themselves to do it; or rather, when they have composed it in unguarded moments, as modern poets still sometimes do, they are under the necessity of destroying it immediately. There is no baffling degree of virtuosity in the old lines,

> Roll on, thou deep and dark blue Ocean, roll!
> Ten thousand fleets sweep over thee in vain:
> Man marks the earth with ruin, his control
> Stops with the shore.

The modern poet can accomplish just as elegant a rumination as this; but thinks it would commit him to an anachronism, for this is the style of an older period. In that period, though it was a comparatively late one, and though this poet thought he was in advance of it, the prophets of society were still numbering and tuning their valuable reflections before they saw fit to release them; and morality, philosophy, religion, science, and art could still meet comfortably in one joint expression, though perhaps not with the same distinction they might have gained if they had had their pure and several expressions. A passage of Byron's if sprung upon an unsuspecting modern would be felt immediately as "dating"; it would be felt as something that did very well for those dark ages before the modern mind achieved its own disintegration and perfected its faculties serially.

Even as readers, we must testify readily to the force of this time-principle. We sometimes pore over an old piece of poetry for so long that we fall under its spell and forget that its spirit is not our spirit. But we began to read it in a peculiar manner; by saying to ourselves, This is early Greek epic, This is seventeenth-century English drama. By means of one of the ripest and subtlest powers in us, that is, the historical sense, we made an adaptation of our minds to its mind, and were able to suspend those centuries which had intervened. Those centuries had made our minds much more knowing and at the same time, it is to be feared, much less suggestible. Yet it is not exactly with our own minds that we are reading the old poetry; otherwise we could not read it. For when we come back to our own world there begins to function in us a different style of consciousness altogether. And if we had begun to read a poetry of this old sort by saying, This was written last night by the poet around the corner, we could not have put up with it. If we throw away impatiently a contemporaneous poetry which displays archaisms of diction, what will we do with that which displays archaisms of temper? It looks spurious; for we require our art, and the living artists require it too, to be as contemporaneous as our banking or our locomotion.

What, then, is the matter with a pure poetry? The question is really more theoretical than practical. A school, an age, is involved by such a question, not merely some small poem or poet. And there is nothing the matter with this particular branch of purity which is not the matter with our other modern activities. All are affected by Puritanism, just as the vegetation is affected, generally and indifferently, by the climate.

It is impossible to answer the question categorically because the items are intangible. But we find ourselves reasoning about it as well as we can, which is as follows.

You may dissociate the elements of experience and exploit them separately. But then at the best you go on a schedule of small experiences, taking them in turn, and trusting that when the rotation is complete you will have missed nothing. And at the worst you will become so absorbed in some one small experience that you will forget to go on and complete the schedule; in that case you will have missed something. The theory that excellence lies in the perfection of the single functions, and that society should demand that its members be hard specialists, assumes that there is no particular harm in missing something. But I do not see why. A maniac with a fixed idea is a variety of specialist, and an absorbing specialty is a small mania.

As for poetry, it seems to me a pity that its beauty should have to be cloistered and conventual, if it is "pure," or teasing and evasive, if it is "obscure." The union of beauty with goodness and truth has been common enough to be regarded as natural. It is the dissociation which is unnatural and painful.

But when we talk about simple and compound experiences, we are evidently employing a chemical mode of speech to represent something we cannot quite make out. Units of consciousness are hard to handle scientifically; it takes more science than we have. Max Eastman thinks the future of literary criticism is bound up with the future of psychology, and very likely it is; but it is difficult to share his sanguine expectations of that science. It cannot become as effective a science as chemistry.

Nevertheless, I shall make a tentative argument from the analogy of chemistry. Lemonade is only a mechanical mixture, not very interesting to chemists. Aside from the water, a drop of lemonade contains lemon and sugar in no standard proportions. If it tastes too sour, add sugar, and if it tastes too sweet, add lemon. (And do not forget to stir the mixture.) No matter what the final proportions, you can still detect in the lemonade the sweet taste and the sour; though this is too abstract a matter to bother about if the lemonade is satisfactory, for in that case you simply drink it.

Table salt, however, is a true chemical compound; a molecule of it is NaCl. Understanding this, you do not claim to know the taste either of sodium or of chlorine when you say you are acquainted with the taste of salt. Whatever the Na was and however it tasted by itself, it gave up that identity when it compounded with Cl; and *vice versa.*

NaCl is found in the state of nature, where it is much commoner than either of its constituents. But suppose the chemists decided to have nothing to do with NaCl because of its compoundness, and undertook to extract from it the pure Na and Cl to serve on the table. Suppose they made war on all the natural compounds, broke them down into the hundred or so atomic elements, and asked us to live on these alone. The beneficiaries would regard this service as well-meaning but mistaken.

But we provide the necessities for our minds and affections with more harshness than we dare use on our stomachs and bodies—so inferior in precision is our knowledge of minds to our knowledge of bodies. Poets are now under the influence of a perfectly arbitrary theory which I have called Puritanism. They pursue A, an æsthetic element thought always to have the same taste and to be the one thing desirable for poets. They will not permit the presence near it of M, the moral element, because that will produce the lemonade MA, and they do not approve of lemonade. In lemonade the A gets itself weakened and neutralized by the M.

But it is possible that MA is not a drop of lemonade after all, but a true molecule, into which the separate M and the separate A have disappeared and out of which an entirely new taste is born. The effects which we attribute to a poet like Virgil, or Milton, are on the following order: pious, philosophical, imaginative, sonorous, and the like. But perhaps the effect which we actually receive from the poetry is not that of an aggregate or series or mechanical mixture of distinct properties but only the single effect of a compound. In that event the properties will exist separate only in our minds, by a later act of qualitative analysis, and they will not really be in the poetry in their own identities.

Is the old-fashioned full poetry a mechanical mixture like lemonade or a chemical compound like table salt? That is probably the most important question which the modern critics have opened up to speculation. There are many corollary questions along with it, like these: When does the display of doctrine in poetry incur the charge of didacticism? And must the poet also bear arms—that is, like the economist and the social reformer, view his performance in the light of a utility rather than an end?

Now some poetry, so-called, is not even lemonade, for the ingredients have not been mixed, much less compounded. Lumps of morality and image lie side by side, and are tasted in succession. T. S. Eliot thinks that this has been the character of a great deal of English poetry since the age of Dryden. Such poetry occupies some of the best room in the library, and takes up some of the best time of the earnest student of literature. It is decidedly one of the causes of that revulsion of feeling on the part of the modern poet which drives him away from the poetic tradition.

When our critical theory is complete, perhaps we shall be able to distinguish various combinations of elements passing for poetry; thus, poetry by assemblage, poetry by mixture, and poetry by composition. The last of these sounds the best.

I suggest that critics and philosophers fix their most loving attention upon certain natural compounds in human experience. But I say so diffidently, and not too hopefully. It will take a long time to change the philosophical set which has come over the practice of the poets. The intellectual climate in which they live will have to be altered first.

The Poet as Woman[1]

MISS ATKINS has published an exuberant and extended critical biography of Miss Millay. It is an apologia. To read it is to have a mounting inclination to try a little dialectic upon the poet's poetry and the critic's criticism. I have tried it, and offer some observations resulting from the exercise, which has been honest, if not complete and systematic.

Perhaps it is best to begin with the kind of general remark about Miss Millay's place in literature which might be more expected at the conclusion. Actually, after a fresh reading of this poet, it turns out to be very much the same remark that I would have offered before commencing. Very well: Miss Millay is the best of the poets who are "popular," and loved by Circles and Leagues of young ladies; perhaps as good a combination as we can ever expect of the "literary" poet and the poet who is loyal to the "human interest" of the common reader. She can nearly always be cited for the virtues of clarity, firmness of outline, consistency of tone within the unit poem, and melodiousness. Her career has been one of dignity and poetic sincerity. She is an artist.

She is also a woman. No poet ever registered her-

[1]*Edna St. Vincent Millay and Her Times*, by Elizabeth Atkins. University of Chicago Press. 1936.

self more deliberately in that light. She therefore fascinates the male reviewer but at the same time horrifies him a little too. He will probably swing between attachment and antipathy, which may be the very attitudes provoked in him by generic woman in the flesh, as well as by the literary remains of Emily Dickinson, Elizabeth Barrett, Christina Rossetti, and doubtless, if we only had enough of her, Sappho herself. I shall simulate perfect assurance in speaking to that point. A woman lives for love, if we will but project that term to cover all her tender fixations upon natural objects of sense, some of them more innocent and far less reciprocal than men. Her devotion to them is more than gallant, it is fierce and importunate, and cannot but be exemplary to the hardened male observer. He understands it, from his "recollections of early childhood," or at least of youth, but he has lapsed from it; or rather, in the best case, he has pursued another line of development. The minds of man and woman grow apart, and how shall we express their differentiation? In this way, I think: man, at best, is an intellectualized woman. Or, man distinguishes himself from woman by intellect, but he should keep it feminized. He knows he should not abandon sensibility and tenderness, though perhaps he has generally done so. But now that he is so far removed from the world of the simple senses, he does not like to impeach his own integrity and leave his business in order to recover it; going back, as he is often directed, to first objects, the true and tried, like the moon, or the grass, or the dead girl. He would much prefer if it is possible to find poetry in his study, or even in his office, and not have to sit under the syringa bush. Sensibility and tenderness might qualify the general content of his mind, if he but knew the technique, however "mental" or self-constructed some of that content looks. But the problem does not arise for a woman. Less pliant, safer as a biological organism, she remains fixed in her famous attitudes, and is indifferent to intellectuality. I mean, of course, comparatively indifferent; more so than a man. Miss Millay is rarely and barely very intellectual, and I think everybody knows it.

I will try to express this by a more literary locution. The age may perhaps be defined with respect to its characteristic plunge into poetry. It is the age which among other things has recovered the admirable John Donne; that is the way to identify its literary taste. Therefore it is hardly the age of which it may be said that Miss Millay is the voice. Donne is the poet of intellectualized persons; he always was. Since he lived, intellectual development has had a great acceleration, and the mind has travelled far in a hundred directions, all tangential; so that the task of a Donne today would be rather harder than when he undertook it; perhaps also it must be conceded that few Donnes, or men of that poetic stature, are now living. For whatever reason, the poetry of the intellectuals today is probably something less than completely successful, but the reassimilation of the split fragments of the world of thought by poetry, even if it rates as a partial accomplishment, is brilliant. There is little relation between such half-successes and Miss Millay's triumphs in the treble.

A critic must be scrupulous. He is limited to making a few citations as evidence; perhaps some of the worst poems, certainly some of the best. He may note many of the poet's scattering features, here and there, yet that does not seem to be quite the job which he must define and undertake. The most general and staple considerations will be on the following order. Is the experience comprehensive or "expressive" of the whole personality? (The reviewer's masculine and contemporary personality, not Miss Millay's personality, which may have to be assumed as perfectly expressing itself.) Is it up to his mental age or general level of experience? And is there any nonsense in it? The last question concerns the competence of the poet to carry out her intention consistently whatever the limits of the intention. For the devoted critic must maintain that poetry on whatever level must make as consistent sense as prose, and he does not like being committed in it to nonsense; it cannot be the idea of poetry to make us foolish, if that is not our habit, even though it must sometimes try to render something that is elusive and hard to render.

Miss Atkins, the biographer, does not ask these questions exactly of her poet. She is a woman critic, satisfied with the effects of a woman poet, and almost ignores or almost resents the intellectual effects of other poets. Ignores them when they are effects of some standard, authorized, and old poet, whom she does not please to challenge, and resents them when they are effects of a new, contemporary, and well-challenged poet. If the poet is Donne, she believes, or half-believes, or pretends, that Miss Millay is his own daughter. If the poet is Eliot, she remarks that the paths of Millay and Eliot have diverged, and it is unfortunate for Eliot, though she knows this young man is well spoken of and she does not propose to say any unnecessary thing against the force of his mind and of his character.

I feel like examining the Donne-Millay relation, because it bears upon both my objects, the poetess and the critic. Miss Atkins makes many direct references to Donne because Miss Millay makes many indirect ones, as in placing the title *Fatal Interview* over her sonnet sequence. Now Donne is an intellectualist poet, in the first place, and therefore he is fooling with a kind of content which is not to her taste and is not sympathetically induced into her work; there is no danger of her discrediting herself with the Drydens by "perplexing the minds of the fair sex with nice speculations of philosophy, when he should engage their hearts, and entertain them with the softnesses of love." This is despite the fact that her sonnets represent perhaps the highest intellectual plane of her poetry; their intellectualism is not the exciting kind that is in Donne's metaphysical work but the mild and dilute variety which appears in the Petrarchan and Elizabethan sonnet tradition. But there is still another thing about Donne, not necessarily implied in his intellectualism. He is just as great an original for his realism, which makes him a pattern for any poet, even a perfectly unaspiring love-poet. If the love-poet is also a woman-poet, his lesson is still available. But I must try to define it. What he teaches is strength; or directness, and in that sense realism; a kind of shortness of speech, when there is in every poet an evil spirit persuading him to elaborate, prettify, ritualize everything that he approaches in love; an unprettiness. Miss Atkins is somewhat aware of this virtue of Donne's, and therefore it is really a disservice to Miss Millay to say too much about Donne; for why should not the reader pick up his Donne and make some parallel readings to Miss Millay's hurt? Miss Atkins even goes before the reader to cite the parallels. When Miss Millay cries,

> I burn my candle at both ends,
> It will not last the night,
> But ah, my foes, and oh, my friends,
> It gives a lovely light!

Miss Atkins proudly points to Donne's line,

> We are tapers too, and at our own cost die.

But the gulf is too wide. The last two lines of the quatrain Donne could not have endured for their foolish ejaculations, so twinned yet laboriously varied, and for the poverty of the vulgar *lovely*. This is overwriting. To wish to make a thing look pretty or look smart is to think poorly of it in itself and to want it more conventional, and to try to improve it is to weaken and perhaps destroy it.

I should like to make some comparisons on a more extended scale. Behind the *Fatal Interview*, as I have said, Miss Atkins indicates the Donne influence, which as she knows is far from thoroughgoing. Yet these sonnets represent the mature work of Miss Millay, not her little-girl things. They vary in power, in something like inverse proportion to the prettiness. Here is one which certainly begins like Donne:

Heart, have no pity on this house of bone:
Shake it with dancing, break it down with joy.
No man holds mortgage on it; it is your own;
To give, to sell at auction, to destroy.
When you are blind to moonlight on the bed,
When you are deaf to gravel on the pane,
Shall quavering caution from this house instead
Cluck forth at summer mischief in the lane?
All that delightful youth forbears to spend
Molestful age inherits, and the ground
Will have us; therefore, while we're young, my friend—
The Latin's vulgar, but the advice is sound.
Youth, have no pity; leave no farthing here
For age to invest in compromise and fear.

I must undertake the rather pretentious task of showing how a genuine Donne influence would have rejected or modified parts of this sonnet. It would have said that *blind to moonlight* and *deaf to gravel* are slightly overdone and inferior to the direct *see not the moonlight* and *hear not the gravel;* that caution personified is pretty but perhaps weak, though its quality might well be *quavering* and *clucking;* that the predication furnished for this caution, the line 8, bearing the whole emphasis of the quatrain, is trifling; and that even if *cluck* or *cluck up* or *cluck out* might do, *cluck forth* is a miscegenation, from which issue is unlikely; that the passage from the Latin is "literary" and impeaches the genuineness of the passion; that *farthing* is ditto, in this American idyll; that *fear* is better alone than compounded with *compromise,* and that the last line might conceivably read, if nothing better should turn up,

> For age to invest it, and in what but fear.

The glory of the entire sequence, for Miss Atkins, and many other reviewers, and the anthologists, seems to be the concluding sonnet, the Endymion one. The lover, a woman, seeing the beloved depart, apostrophizes the well known Man in the Moon with a scorn that her own ungallant gentleman is expected to take to himself. A promising conception. As the man is the perfect analogue of Endymion, so the woman, harried by love and unable as the man is to outdie it, is another Moon goddess.

> Oh, sleep forever in the Latmian cave,
> Mortal Endymion, darling of the moon!

> Her silver garments by the senseless wave
> Shouldered and dropped and on the shingle strewn,
> Her fluttering hand against her forehead pressed,
> Her scattered looks that trouble all the sky,
> Her rapid footsteps running down the west—
> Of all her altered state, oblivious lie!
> Whom earthen you, by deathless lips adored,
> Wild-eyed and stammering to the grasses thrust,
> And deep into her crystal body poured
> The hot and sorrowful sweetness of the dust:
> Whereof she wanders mad, being all unfit
> For mortal love, that might not die of it.

Of which sonnet Miss Atkins writes:

> What future generations will think of this sonnet, I cannot guess, but I can read it beside any of the other poems that have been written about the moon and like it best of all. The eerie quality of cloud-dappled moonlight on a windy night by the sea is evoked here so magically that one is scarcely aware that words are the source of the vision, and the picture of the wavering, distracted moonlight is so shot through with the tragic mood of heartbreak that it seems unthinkable that the feeling could have been expressed in other terms.

It had not occurred to me that the moon's cast-off garments in the story were intended to be represented by the white clouds in the sky, as Miss Atkins seems to think; but another reader gives me her oral testimony to having the same impression. And if we are to see the moon fleeing desperately down the western sky, as Miss Millay bids us in line 7, we may as well assimilate the cloud-garments to the picture. But it was one part of Donne's technique to observe the limits beyond which with all his daring he must not push his figure, or his myth. The moon is a celestial body, travels westward, may be attended by silver clouds. But likewise any configuration on the moon's surface, as for instance the so-called man; their relation is simply that of part to whole, part sharing in the acts of whole. On the other hand, there is the Moon, a personification, having a relation to the Man, who is another one; and entering that field of impressions we are within a perfectly ideal kingdom of events, and out of astronomy. Moon may do what any other maiden would for love, and Man may be as fickle as he likes. It is when we try to identify the details of their story with the details of the visible heavens that we get into ridiculous difficulties. And for example, how is the Moon to be observed fleeing any more than the Man? And how are the garments hers rather than his? But this is so absurd that I prefer to say it seems impossible to know what Miss Millay meant.

In style the last two lines are Donne, and possibly the sixth. The others conflict with this style or are indifferent. *Hand against her forehead pressed* is a significant item spoiled by *fluttering*, which is either contradictory or excessive. The *all* which qualifies *altered state*, and the one which qualifies *unfit* also, are needed for the metre, but among the enemies to poetic strictness and economy the first and last is the consent of the poet to accept the determination of some metrical necessity. The third quatrain would only have revolted Donne, and I do not mean in his professional capacity of Dean. The *by deathless lips adored* is pure obstruction, though it is to be expected that something pretty will turn up in a romantic poem. The three following lines are rude in substance, deficient in grammar, and flowing in musical effect. The poet cannot really be impressed by the integrity of a Donne who, even beyond any actual need to chop up the music in order to keep the logic significant and delicate, seemed usually to aim at a little of musical discontinuity on principle, as a promise of good faith, for the reader and himself to go by. It is a pity that the nineteenth century reversed this practice and chose to sacrifice the logic to the music. In lines like these the music must be supposed to act as an anesthetic, inhibiting normal good sense, so violently are the pretty words put together; a parody of honest poetry. The model is Keats. Miss Millay has simply gone for Endymion in the early Keats manner, which he himself handsomely repented a very few years after.

Miss Millay has many literary sources for her more studied verse. The most valuable contribution which Miss Atkins makes to our understanding of her is in tracking down a surprising multitude of first-class origins for the fine phrases—the same labor of love which many scholars have performed for John Milton. Miss Millay has gone faithfully to school. She could not possibly lapse into a merely popular poet and yet bear so many distinguished derivations; or cherish her Virgil, for example, as we learn that she does, her husband reporting of her, "For years she has not travelled anywhere without a book of Latin poetry in her suitcase; this goes in as automatically as her toothbrush." The information is endearing. In one general division which we might make of her verse she is a traditionalist with the highest literary standards in her consciousness. But they apply principally to her detail, to her phrasing, and a promiscuous eclecticism of this kind does not guarantee a Miltonic success though Milton also was eclectic. The fact is, in my judgment, that it is in the other division of her verse, where she is entirely or nearly original and contemporary, and less pretentious, that she is decidedly the more considerable as a poet.

Miss Atkins, closely acquainted with the literary tradition, performs well the labor which I have indicated. She also permits herself to generalize, and to write critical essays, and there her thinking is not distinguished. Working at large topics of discourse, she has the innocence of the amateur who tries too early to be ingenious, which under the circumstances is to be ingenuous. She is particularly at pains to show that nearly every published work of Miss Millay's serves as a reproach and corrective against some wayward school of thought which was in vogue at the respective moment. But it is too hard to make out the pattern for every instance, and Miss Atkins has to do some contriving. Spengler himself was not such an abritrary historian. Incidentally, Spengler's sense of philosophy was not superficial.

Miss Atkins devotes a chapter to each book and proposes a subtitle upon which she elaborates. Examples are: "I. Renascence: Poetry of a Child's Certainties"; "III. The Reedy's Mirror Sonnets: In a Time of Free Verse"; "V. Aria da Capo: Tragedy in the Jazz Age"; "VI. Second April: In a Time of Self-Doubt"; "VII. The Harp-Weavers: In the Heyday of Behaviorism"; "XI. Wine from These Grapes: In a Time of Foreboding." I shall illustrate the method from Chapter VI. Early in the chapter we read:

> T. S. Eliot was leading a flock of followers straight on into the desert of nihilism, among the cacti and Joshua trees of symbolism, marquetry, obscurantism, and caricature, whereas Millay was walking the Maine seacoast of her childhood, finding in her unshaken love of earth and ocean and the noble aspirations of past ages an impregnable defense against the disintegrating forces of her time; and she was meeting all the devastating logic of nihilism with the proud cry, rather like that of Descartes, "I care, therefore I am!"

Nihilism. And continuing with her study of the malady of the age—which within a year was to change to an Age of Behaviorism—Miss Atkins goes right back and lays the child at the doorstep of David Hume. Hume's dissociationism had waited a hundred and eighty years to find its way into the hearts of the poets; but there it suddenly appeared at last.

It may or may not amount to the same thing, but presently Miss Atkins is saying that the poets fell into "our terrible devil-worship of time as the sole reality." And in this connection, unless it is in some other, we learn that they were convinced of two things only: that cynical irony was the mood for poetry, and that deliberate incoherence, reflecting the meaninglessness of life, was its method. But, a corollary perhaps—they also felt that the method should be a hit-or-miss mingling of scraps of older literature with comments on the contemporary world. Hence Joyce, and Eliot—who, "by the way," is a sort of literary Einsteinian relativist. But speaking of incoherence again she discovers that "the cult of intentional obscurity owes most to Gerard Manley Hopkins," first published in 1918, whose influence upon Eliot she attempts to document. After twenty pages of this, enter Miss Millay with *Second April:*

> This was the world in which Millay's *Second April* appeared. Can anyone who read it in 1922 ever forget the bewilderment with which one met the simplicity of its old right ways of saying things? This poetry was pre-symbolist, pre-vorticist, pre-Dada, pre-jazz, pre-imagist, pre-vers-librist. One stammered, "But poetry can't be like this any more!" And then one stammered again, "But it is!" For *Second April* was no bouquet of strawflowers, dusty with disintegrated metaphors and sentiments . . . These poems were the irrepressible emotions of a human being drinking in the world of 1921.

Certainly there is something to what Miss Atkins says, but it is not well defined, and to whom is it addressed? Hardly to the intellectual enemy, for she does not speak his language.

I should like to refer to one of the specific judgments expressed in this passage, because it seems to me an error, and its correction would bear upon the quality of Miss Millay's poetry. Miss Atkins thinks that the influence of Father Hopkins has been dominating upon Eliot and others, but she is evidently partial to Hopkins as a vicious example because he committed himself to a half-formal theory about the effect of intellectual poetry being that of a delayed "explosion." She remarks: "To Hopkins' admirers among twentieth-century poet cynics it seemed that in the heyday of the crossword puzzle, this device of tantalizing obscurity was poetry's only hope of appealing to the gnawing restlessnes of the modern mind." What Miss Atkins calls obscurity may be real obscurity, which life is quite too short to defend, but it may equally be a poetic intellectualism which communicates well enough to intellectual persons. In any case I doubt if Hopkins' influence at any time has been dominating, and still more if it dominated at the time of *Second April.* I prefer the more usual opinion, which is represented by Edmund Wilson and others, that the principal influence upon Eliot, and directly or indirectly upon those who followed him, was that of the French Symbolists. The French Symbolists were intellectual and romantic like Baudelaire and Rimbaud, and they influenced poets like Hart Crane and Allen Tate, or they were intellectual and witty, like LaForgue, and then they influenced poets like Eliot (in his early phase). But with or without the French Symbolists went two other influences, one or both of which have affected many poets. One was John Donne's kind of performance, and the other was Ezra Pound's kind of preaching and teaching: an example of manly honesty rescued from a perishing tradition, and a living monitor. These influences came to precisely the same thing. No dead man has purified modern poetry of adventitious and meretricious decoration as has John Donne, no living man has done it as has Ezra Pound. French Symbolists may have caused our poets to try to assimilate a very much wider range of knowledge than they might otherwise have dared. Donne and Pound, between them, have caused poets to consider technique as a charge upon their conscience. Under their influence many poets now are willing to subordinate verbal and metrical effects to real imagination.

As to Miss Millay's musicianship. Sometimes her preoccupation with it seduces her poetic invention into acts of mere fancy, as we have seen. But it is pleasant to testify that she has an accomplished ear, and that means among other things, I should think, an intelligent one, without foolish ambition, which in order to secure its own delights does not have to set up in opposition to imagination. It is also pleasant to believe that she does not for a moment attach to her sound-patterns such powers as Miss Atkins attributes to them. In nearly every chapter Miss Atkins would show us that the Millay sound-patterns are peculiarly descriptive of their logical contents. There is a fallacy here which is common, and unquestionably of hoary lineage. We may say that Miss Millay's arrangement of vowels and consonants, runs and rests, suits the particular sense she would convey, if we mean simply that it is not unsuitable. Very little more can be said for any poet. If Miss Atkins seems to me to make absurd claims for Miss Millay's ability to suggest the thing by sounds, and apart from the logical associations of the words, my criticism is of Miss Atkins, not of Miss Millay, who does everything that is possible, but hardly that. Miss Millay is said at one place to have

> the fluent pentameter line that had seemed to belong to Shakespeare alone, a line in which the syllables are like leaves springing from a twig, so subtly are their vowels and consonants varied and repeated. Such a line as the dying Hamlet's
>
> Absent thee from felicity awhile,
>
> with its panting *f*'s, its languid *l*'s, and its darker vowels around the three short *i*'s together in one climactic word, so that "felicity" seems lifted into a glimmer of sunlight in a gloom, such a line seems to have as much living oneness as a green branch has.

But it is far from clear whether, and how, she is the sole inheritor of Shakespeare's pentameter line; and it hardly defines that line to liken it to a green branch. The variation of the vowels and consonants may be very intricate, but so is that in a weather report, and it is a question if it is subtle, or deliberate, for it would probably obtain anyway. The quoted line from Shakespeare is a famous one, but why? We use *f*'s too freely (as in *philosophy, fluffy ruffles, fortify, falsify*) to identify them with panting, and *l*'s too freely (as in *syllable, golly, laughable, Lilliput*) to identify them with languidness. *Felicity* is climactic, but the climax has little to do with the short *i*'s, for *lubricity* or *acidity* would not work at all. It is easy to imagine an occasion on which the line might stand intact and yet have no poetic effect, least of all the effect of sunlight in gloom. For example, if a graduate English student were urging a friend to stay and discuss metres with him awhile, and not rush off to the beer party. Then

> Absent thee from felicity awhile

becomes a euphuism, a piece of university diction, faintly facetious. And so it may have been for Shakespeare's Hamlet, who was an incorrigible alumnus of Wittenberg, as some of Shakespeare's colleagues were of Oxford and Cambridge, and who in his dying speech said to his best friend,

> If thou didst ever hold me in thy heart,
> Absent thee from felicity awhile,
> And in this harsh world draw thy breath in pain,
> To tell my story.

The line in question is the odd thing about the speech, but this is due to logical and not phonetic causes: *felicity* is its oddest word, because the least emphatic, but *absent thee* is nearly as odd, because nearly as weak. Lines 1, 3, and 4 are in strong monosyllabic Saxon diction, but line 2, our line, is Latinistic, foppish, and amazing. That may be why it is memorable, and in that case it has accidentally, and not in its own right, become the eternal expression of a thought which might be paraphrased

> Seek not thy Heav'n's bliss quickly, stay awhile.

Poor as this version is, it suits an earnest sentiment better than the other; it would serve Moody and Sankey better, if they needed a line. The phonetic quality is trifling in either case.

If Miss Atkins has made out a pretty case for Shakespeare, she does at least as well for Miss Millay, who, I hope, will consider the service slightly ill-advised. Syllables and words, even elementary phrases, are language units which phonetically have very little more color of their own than chameleons. The character which they take on so instantly and display so positively is that of the logical meanings. (Central or marginal, denotative or connotative meanings.) The phonetic elements would not be serviceable for language if they were not indefinitely negotiable; that is, able to be dissociated quickly and cleanly from given meanings and reassociated with fresh ones. But many critics, especially if they are not themselves composers, confuse cause and effect. The poetic image, let us say, is of green grass, but the oversubtle critic discovers a green chameleon that hides there and points out that the chameleon has colored the grass, and not *vice versa* as ignorant persons suppose. The critics do not see how modest are the limits within which poets seek rhythm, which should not be at all foreign to the common genius of the language, and some degree of euphony, which is easily obtained, and otherwise have no great concern with phonetic projects. Miss Atkins is one of the critics, indefatigable in making illusory discoveries. The topic seems worth examination, and I quote one of her many extended passages upon it:

> Sometimes Millay gives an effect of spaciousness to pentameter by a double stress before a pause, as in
>
> On the wíde heáth, by évening óvertáken.
>
> Something of the same effect of space is in the first part of another line,
>
> Dówn, dówn, dówn, into the dárkness of the gráve,
>
> in contrast with the second half of the line, wherein the clusters of many unaccented syllables give an effect of fumbling bewilderment. But she gets many different effects with clusters of unaccented syllables. With the many *f*'s and *r*'s and *th*'s a fine feeling of fluffiness is given to one line by the many unaccented syllables:
>
> Cómfort, sófter than the feáthers of its bréast,
>
> sounds as soft as the bird's downy breast feels. In another line,
>
> I stánd, remémbering the íslands and the séa's lóst sóund,

the three unstressed syllables before and after the stressed *isl* isolate that syllable as the island is isolated in the sea, and the three strong stresses together at the close of the line suggest the strong pounding of the tide. One of the biggest lines which yet keeps the effect of being pentameter is

O Ápril, full of bloód, full of breáth, have mércy upón us,

where almost every foot is a full phrase, set off by caesuras.

I remark: (1) As to the effect of spaciousness caused by a double stress before a pause. Too startling is the coincidence that *on the wide heath* means spaciousness, whether its action describes spaciousness or not. If the phrase were *in the strict tomb*, I think Miss Atkins would be saying that the double stress indicated crowdedness. What would be really significant would be a double stress in nonsense syllables, and an agreement on the part of disinterested listeners that the effect was of spaciousness. (2) Clusters of unaccented syllables are said to furnish many different effects. They really do. They are meek things, and furnish nearly any effects required, but it is the meanings of the clusters which determine what effects. Why else should the effect be fumbling bewilderment in the second example, but nothing of the kind in others? (3) In the third example the effect is a fine feeling of fluffiness and a softness as of the bird's downy breast, while the cause is said to be the many unaccented syllables, assisted by the many *f*'s, *r*'s, and *th*'s. But I will substitute a line which preserves all these factors and departs from the given line mainly by rearrangement:

> Crúmpets for the fóster-fáthers of the bráts.

Here I miss the fluffiness and the downiness. (4) In the fourth example the three straight stresses are said to indicate the pounding of the tide. Substitute for the phrase *sea's lost sound* the phrase *sea's white death;* it is a picture of antarctic ice. The stresses remain but the pounding of the tide has vanished. (5) A line may become bigger, and perhaps better, yet remain a pentameter line; but this is not so marvellous, it is a simple case of graduating out of syllabic verse, where every syllable is counted, into stress verse, where only the stressed ones are counted; and it is entirely within Miss Millay's right. Miss Millay has tried that frequently and successfully. Latterly, she has become still more informal and written a good deal of free verse. The descriptiveness manifested by the sounds in a free line is still slight if the line has much logical finesse, but I imagine it becomes more conspicuous there, by the absence of other complication. The complication which is lacking for the reader's attention is metre. It is Miss Millay's problem to determine whether the apparent improvement in the descriptiveness of the sounds, or any other benefit that free verse may offer, is enough to compensate for the loss of the metrical effect. But I should trust her to take a perfectly intelligent advantage of her metrical experiments. She knows her metres.

But I return to the topic which is more difficult than the errors of Miss Atkins, and that is—the limitation of Miss Millay. If I must express this in a word, I still feel obliged to say it is her lack of intellectual interest. It is that which the male reader misses in her poetry, even though he may acknowledge the authenticity of the interest which is there. I used a conventional symbol, which I hope was not objectionable, when I phrased this lack of hers: deficiency in masculinity. It is true that some male poets are about as deficient; not necessarily that they are undeveloped intellectually, but that they conceive poetry as a sentimental or feminine exercise, themselves as under a strange compulsion to practise it. Not deficient in it are some female poets, I suppose, like Miss Marianne Moore; and doubtless many women are personally developed in intellect without having any idea that poetry can master and use what the intellect is prepared to furnish. For that matter, intellectual poverty has limited most poetry in all periods, whatever the gender of the authors, an evidence which would indicate that poetry has not really been the completely expressive art it is said to be. But the exceptional poetry which may properly be called expressive, but which is popularly called intellectual, is not so rare but that we may know the real capacity of poetry as an instrument. It is a piano, a well-tempered clavier, and does not have to stick to the rules of the violin.

It is not reduced to the picturization of simple and pleasant objects, though it is valuable when poets discover them, and especially at the back door, where Miss Millay found the pear tree blossoming

> Like the waste-man's little daughter
> In her first communion dress.

Nor is it reduced to the display of the generous human passions, like the love of earth and God, as when she writes:

> About the trees my arms I wound;
> Like one gone mad I hugged the ground;
> I raised my quivering arms on high;
> I laughed and laughed into the sky,
> Till at my throat a strangling sob
> Caught fiercely, and a great heart-throb
> Sent instant tears into my eyes;
> O God, I cried, no dark disguise
> Can e'er hereafter hide from me
> Thy radiant identity!

These are earlier bits of poetry. It is with something of a feeling of guilt that the intellectual adult male participates in them. His heart wants to be in it but is not. This is because his intellect is not in it. And not entirely in it when Miss Millay is less juvenile, and appears as the adult but unintellectual woman. But, for that matter, the male reader feels some shame even at going with Wordsworth, feeling it monstrous that he should flee the humanized world which he actually inhabits and breathe exclusively the innocence of external nature. Without fundamental difference are the two passages of Miss Millay's and the following one:

> O blessed Bird! the earth we pace
> Again appears to be
> An unsubstantial faery place;
> That is fit home for Thee!

Or this one:

> At eve the beetle boometh
> Athwart the thicket lone:
> At noon the wild bee hummeth
> About the mossed headstone:
> At midnight the moon cometh
> And looketh down alone.

Or perhaps,

> Oh, to be in England,
> Now that April's there!

Miss Millay has exhibits not particularly inferior to these. The love of natural effects, the worship of Nature, the delight of the senses, the concerns of the elemental passions, and even, if we can get it more felt than primly moralized, the guilt of civilized man: these themes invite, or at least permit, a very simple treatment, and then we have a real poetry but probably not one that furnishes a satisfactory expression, unless we are abandoned to corruption and despair, and have to try for a radical regeneration.

Intellect in the special sense is supposed to be pure

thought engaged in a series of technical or abstract processes. The greatest impulse behind them doubtless is the systematic one known as science. Yet the categories and predicates they arrive at are common properties, frequently negotiable. To be intellectual is to be disciplined in technique and stocked with learning, a very great advantage for every purpose, and even for fertilizing the pleasures of imagination. It is only from pedantry, which is the result of bad education, or, behind that, of dulness, that we do not know how to escape from the copybook routine of intellect. We ought to be able to focus at any instant the learning we have acquired. There need not be an incompatibility between the man of intellect and the man of imagination, and I shall prove this quickly by citing, first,

> Where we went in the boat was a long bay
> A sling-shot wide, walled in by towering stone—
> Peaked margin of antiquity's delay
> And we went there out of time's monotone,

where, as for the third line, we would have been informed by the title that the excursion is in a region still storied with the deeds of Greeks and of Romans. Then I would cite:

> The body dies; the body's beauty lives.
> So evenings die, in their green going,
> A wave, interminably flowing.
> So gardens die, their meek breath scenting
> The cowl of Winter, done repenting.
> So maidens die, to the auroral
> Celebration of a maiden's choral.

Then a short one, but I think sufficient,

> I should have been a pair of ragged claws
> Scuttling across the floors of silent seas.

And this:

> O weary mariners, here shaded, fed,
> Dull as the wave, old hostages to sleep,
> Well-bearded, eloquent, the world's hands,
> Take what the kind sea brings to your feet—
> Shells, rays, tributes of the unsparing deep.

And finally:

> [She] lived as 'twere a king
> That packed his marriage day
> With banneret and pennon,
> Trumpet and kettledrum,
> And the outrageous cannon,
> To bundle time away
> That the night come.

They are not the most ambitious efforts of their authors, who are of the living intellectualist poets; I have hit upon them hurriedly. But it is my impression that Miss Millay has done no such passages as these. Intellectual power, with some of the skills that come from the intellectual disciplines, is written on them. The treasures too, for the field of reference is too wide to be commanded by the innocent woman-mind, or for that matter the man-mind which is not flexible enough to be at ease with its intellectual attainments.

Such are Miss Millay's limits. I suppose I have been teased by Miss Atkins' foolish adoration, and even, it may be, by a vague sense that too much of that sort of thing has been going on, into giving a disproportionate space to telling what Miss Millay's poetry is not. We come finally to her quite positive talent or, as I like to think, genius. But I still have to identify by restriction the field in which I find it displayed.

The formal, reflective, or "literary" poems fall for the most part outside this field. She is not a good conventional or formalist poet, and I think I have already suggested why: because she allows the forms to bother her and to push her into absurdities. I imagine there are few women poets of whom this is not so, and it would be because they are not strict enough and expert enough to manage forms,—in their default of the disciplines under which men are trained.

Then, the young-girl poems fall outside it; and I am afraid I refer to more poems than were composed in the years of her minority. This charming lady found it unusually difficult, poetically speaking, to come of age. *Renascence* is genuine, in the sense that it is the right kind of religious poem for an actual young girl of New England, with much rapture, a naïve order of images, and a dash of hell-fire vindictiveness. *God's World* is a painful reading, in execrable taste, but adolescent taste is declared by authorities to be really unsure. The volume *A Few Figs from Thistles* is well known as a series of anti-religious and Bohemian shockers, and that stage should have been behind her when she published the work at the age of twenty-eight. The college plays were exactly right for their occasions, but *Aria da Capo* comes long afterward and still suggests the prize-winning skit on the Senior Girls' Stunt Night of an unusually good year. And then come the poems of *Second April*, whose author at twenty-nine is not consistently grown up. For instance, there is the longest poem of the volume, a narrative of the Day of Judgment, telling how the narrator witnessed the burning up of the earth, and had to run back at great risk to rescue a poor blue-flag in a bog, but took God's hand and got his special permission to set the plant out and make a little private garden for it in Heaven. I do not think any obligation can lie upon the male adult requiring him to assist at this sort of thing, or, if he must, to smile other than untenderly though God's smile was tender. But gradually the affectations of girlhood in Miss Millay disappear.

When they are absent, she has a vein of poetry which is spontaneous, straightforward in diction, and excitingly womanlike; a distinguished objective record of a natural woman's mind. The structures are transparently simple and the effects are immediate. There are few poems, I think, that do not fumble the least bit, unless they are very short, but she has the right to be measured as a workman by her excellent best. Her best subjects are death, which she declines like an absolute antiphilosopher to accept or gloze, a case of indomitable feminine principle; personal moods, which she indulges without apology, in the kind of integrity that is granted to the kind of mind that has no direction or modulation except by its natural health; and natural objects which call up her love or pity. I have to except from this list the love of a woman for a man, because, in her maturity at least, she has reserved that subject for the sonnets, and they are rather unconventional in sentiment, but literary, and corrupted by verbal insincerities.

Though I cannot do much quoting, there is *Elegy*, from which I must offer a fragment. The dead friend is gone, and the poet inconsolable, but on a peculiar and, to a man, arbitrary ground. The poet cherishes an auditory and not a visual image. Other visions will replace the dead girl's beauty but no sound will compensate for the voice. I have the feeling that this is a legitimate and rather exquisite fixation though I had not encountered it.

> Let them bury your big eyes
> In the secret earth securely,
> Your thin fingers, and your fair,
> Soft, indefinite-colored hair . . .
>
> But your voice,—never the rushing
> Of a river underground,
> Not the rising of the wind
> In the trees before the rain,
> Not the woodcock's watery call,
> Not the note the white-throat utters,
> Not the feet of children pushing
> Yellow leaves along the gutters
> In the blue and bitter fall,

Shall content my musing mind
For the beauty of that sound
That in no new way at all
Ever will be heard again.

The Poet and His Book is another charming feminism. Many poets must have hoped that their verse will confer immortality upon them, but I believe only Miss Millay sees such a vague consummation in a series of precise and living actions. For example:

When this book is mold,
And a book of many
Waiting to be sold
For a casual penny,
In a little open case,
On a street unclean and cluttered,
Where a heavy mud is spattered
From the passing drays,

Stranger, pause and look;
From the dust of ages
Lift this little book,
Turn the tattered pages,
Read me, do not let me die!
Search the fading letters, finding
Steadfast in the broken binding
All that once was I!

The most ambitious single work of Miss Millay's would be her operatic play, *The King's Henchman;* ambitious, but suited to her powers, and entirely successful. It has a tenth-century English story, and the following unusual principle of language: the words used in it are all of the Anglo-Saxon branch of English, never of the Latin; or so at least Miss Atkins finds, and I have found nothing to the contrary. Operatic drama lends itself to Miss Millay's scope. Its action is a little brief and simple, and it permits the maximum number of lyrical moments and really suits Poe's idea of the long poem as a series of short poems rather than a single consecutive whole. The work does not prove Miss Millay to be a dramatist, but it shows what an incessant fountain of poetry is a woman's sensibility in the midst of simple human and natural situations. It should be remarked that, being tenth century, the properties have the advantage of being a little picturesque, and the tone of the language slightly foreign, like a Scottish or Irish idiom perhaps. But these are the arrangements of the artist, of whom it cannot so fairly be said that she is in luck as that she is a competent designer.

The poem of all Miss Millay's work which I like best is *The Return.* It pictures Earth in a sort of Mother Hubbard character, receiving back the sons she sent forth to failure, but too busy to give them much attention, and unaware of any reason why they should have failed. This version of mortality is tender, and characteristic of Miss Millay's most mature phase. By way of contrast it suggests the ironic or cynical images of another poet of simplicity, but a man; Housman, who likewise is always giving new forms to the generalization of death. The poem for me is nearly perfect.

> Earth does not understand her child,
> Who from the loud gregarious town
> Returns, depleted and defiled,
> To the still woods, to fling him down.
>
> Earth cannot count the sons she bore:
> The wounded lynx, the wounded man
> Come trailing blood unto her door;
> She shelters both as best she can.
>
> But she is early up and out,
> To trim the year or strip its bones;
> She has no time to stand about
> Talking of him in undertones
>
> Who has no aim but to forget,
> Be left in peace, be lying thus
> For days, for years, for centuries yet,
> Unshaven and anonymous;
>
> Who, marked for failure, dulled by grief,
> Has traded in his wife and friend
> For this warm ledge, this alder leaf:
> Comfort that does not comprehend.

This is almost effortless, like the grave speech of a woman with beautiful intonations of a voice which she does not raise. I have only one small grievance: the last line ought to be clear and memorable but it is weak, and even uncertain of meaning, and has bothered me a great deal. I believe it intends to define what the grave, that same felicity which Hamlet coveted, means to the sons of Earth; and apparently it means that they obtain there her loving comfort but not her understanding. There are two ambiguous words. *Comfort* may mean the abstract thing or the personal comforter; and *comprehend* may mean include or understand. It is but one line, but I think for the sake of criticism it is worth a moment's moralizing. The poet, it seems to me, is not sure whether she is saying: A comforter who does not understand, or: A comfort that does not comprehend (or include) understanding. It is by a verbal accident that *comprehend* is ambiguous, and it is only by some wrenching that *comprehend* in the sense of *understand* (for which it substitutes poorly) can be predicated of the abstract term *comfort*. But under what circumstances do poets adopt combinations of words that do not quite fit into perfect meanings? I know too well one way to answer that: when the combination offers the uncertain possibility of two meanings rather than the certainty of one meaning, and when at the same time it fits perfectly into the metrical pattern. The finish of the metre gives the illusory sense of an equal finish in the sense, and if there comes any doubt about the sense it may be argued to be even better because the range of its possibilities is wider. A poet is sometimes like a maker of gentlemen's pipes in preferring the knot to the straight grain; unlike in that he has not sought the knot, it has been thrust upon him.

Such calculations on my part are a laboratory exercise, oversimplifying the delicate problem, surely tedious, perhaps invidious, in which I try to weigh the situation and the fitness of the poetic act. Here the act seems inadequate, and I look for the trouble, saying confidently: Metre. I think that is the trouble. Let us remember Procrustes, who will symbolize for us the mechanical determinism of metrical necessity, a tyrant against whom only pure-hearted and well-equipped champions will consistently prevail. Procrustes, let us say with absurd simplicity, finds the good word *comforter* too long for the bed. So he lops off her feet.

Poetry: A Note in Ontology

A POETRY may be distinguished from a poetry by virtue of subject-matter, and subject-matter may be differentiated with respect to its ontology, or the reality of its being. An excellent variety of critical doctrine arises recently out of this differentiation, and thus perhaps criticism leans again upon ontological analysis as it was meant to do by Kant. The recent critics remark in effect that some poetry deals with things, while some other poetry deals with ideas. The two poetries will differ from each other as radically as a thing differs from an idea.

The distinction in the hands of critics is a fruitful one. There is apt to go along with it a principle of valuation, which is the consequence of a temperament, and therefore basic. The critic likes things and intends that his poet shall offer them; or likes ideas and intends that he shall offer them; and approves him as he does the one or the other. Criticism cannot well go much deeper than this. The critic has carried to the last terms his analysis of the stuff of which poetry is made, and valued it frankly as his temperament or his need requires him to value it.

So philosophical a critic seems to be highly modern. He is; but this critic as a matter of fact is peculiarly on one side of the question. (The implication is unfavorable to the other side of the question.) He is in revolt against the tyranny of ideas, and against the poetry which celebrates ideas, and which may be identified—so far as his usual generalization may be trusted—with the hateful poetry of the Victorians. His bias is in favor of the things. On the other hand the critic who likes Victorian verse, or the poetry of ideas, has probably not thought of anything of so grand a simplicity as electing between the things and the ideas, being apparently not quite capable of the ontological distinction. Therefore he does not know the real or constitutional ground of his liking, and may somewhat ingenuously claim that his predilection is for those poets who give him inspiration, or comfort, or truth, or honest metres, or something else equally "worth while." But Plato, who was not a modern, was just as clear as we are about the basic distinction between the ideas and the things, and yet stands far apart from the aforesaid conscious modern in passionately preferring the ideas over the things. The weight of Plato's testimony would certainly fall on the side of the Victorians, though they may scarcely have thought of calling him as their witness. But this consideration need not conclude the hearing.

I. PHYSICAL POETRY

The poetry which deals with things was much in favor a few years ago with the resolute body of critics. And the critics affected the poets. If necessary, they became the poets, and triumphantly illustrated the new mode. The Imagists were important figures in the history of our poetry, and they were both theorists and creators. It was their intention to present things in their thinginess, or *Dinge* in their *Dinglichkeit;* and to such an extent had the public lost its sense of *Dinglichkeit* that their redirection was wholesome. What the public was inclined to seek in poetry was ideas, whether large ones or small ones, grand ones or pretty ones, certainly ideas to live by and die by, but what the Imagists identified with the stuff of poetry was, simply, things.

Their application of their own principle was sufficiently heroic, though they scarcely consented to be as extreme in the practice as in the theory. They had artistic talent, every one of the original group, and it was impossible that they should make of poetry so simple an exercise as in doctrine they seemed to think it was. Yet Miss Lowell wrote a poem on "Thompson's Lunch Room, Grand Central Station"; it is admirable if its intention is to show the whole reach of her courage. Its detail goes like this:

> Jagged greenwhite bowls of pressed glass
> Rearing snow-peaks of chipped sugar
> Above the lighthouse-shaped castors
> Of gray pepper and gray-white salt.

For most of us as for the public idealist, with his "values," this is inconsequential. Unhappily it seems that the things as things do not necessarily interest us, and that in fact we are not quite constructed with the capacity for a disinterested interest. But it must be noted even here that the things are on their good behavior, looking rather well, and arranged by lines into something approaching a military formation. More technically, there is cross-imagery in the snow-peaks of sugar, and in the lighthouse-shaped castors, and cross-imagery involves association, and will presently involve dissociation and thinking. The metre is but a vestige, but even so it means something, for metre is a powerful intellectual determinant marshalling the words and, inevitably, the things. The *Dinglichkeit* of this Imagist specimen, or the realism, was therefore not pure. But it was nearer pure than the world was used to in poetry, and the exhibit was astonishing.

For the purpose of this note I shall give to such poetry, dwelling as exclusively as it dares upon physical things, the name Physical Poetry. It is to stand opposite to that poetry which dwells as firmly as it dares upon ideas.

But perhaps thing *versus* idea does not seem to name an opposition precisely. Then we might phrase it a little differently: image *versus* idea. The idealistic philosophies are not sure that things exist, but they mean the equivalent when they refer to images. (Or they may consent to perceptions; or to impressions, following Hume, and following Croce, who remarks that they are pre-intellectual and independent of concepts. It is all the same, unless we are extremely technical.) It is sufficient if they concede that image is the raw material of idea. Though it may be an unwieldy and useless affair for the idealist as it stands, much needing to be licked into shape, nevertheless its relation to idea is that of a material cause, and it cannot be dispossessed of its priority.

It cannot be dispossessed of a primordial freshness, which idea can never claim. An idea is derivative and tamed. The image is in the natural or wild state, and it has to be discovered there, not put there, obeying its own law and none of ours. We think we can lay hold of image and take it captive, but the docile captive is not the real image but only the idea, which is the image with its character beaten out of it.

But we must be very careful: idealists are nothing if not dialectical. They object that an image in an original state of innocence is a delusion and cannot exist, that no image ever comes to us which does not imply the world of ideas, that there is "no percept without a concept." There is something in it. Every property discovered in the image is a universal property, and nothing discovered in the image is marvellous in kind though it may be pinned down historically or statistically as a single instance. But there is this to be understood too: the image which is not remarkable in any particular property is marvellous in its assemblage of many properties, a manifold of properties, like a mine or a field, something to be explored for the properties; yet science can manage the image, which is infinite in properties, only by equating it to the one property with which the science is concerned; for science at work is always *a science*, and committed to a special interest. It is not by refutation but by abstraction that science destroys the image. It means to get its "value" out of the image, and we may be sure that it has no use for the image in its original state of freedom. People who are engrossed with their pet "values" become habitual killers. Their game is the images, or the things, and they acquire the ability to shoot them as far off as they can be seen, and do. It is thus that we lose the power of imagination, or whatever faculty it is by which we are able to contemplate things as they are in their rich and contingent materiality. But our dreams reproach us, for in dreams they come alive again. Likewise our memory; which makes light of our science by recalling the images in their panoply of circumstance and with their morning freshness upon them.

It is the dream, the recollection, which compels us to poetry, and to deliberate æsthetic experience. It can hardly be argued, I think, that the arts are constituted automatically out of original images, and arise in some early age of innocence. (Though Croce seems to support this view, and to make art a pre-adult stage of experience.) Art is based on second love, not first love. In it we make a return to something which we had wilfully alienated. The child is occupied mostly with things, but it is because he is still unfurnished with systematic ideas, not because he is a ripe citizen by nature and comes along already trailing clouds of glory. Images are clouds of glory for the man who has discovered that ideas are a sort of darkness. Imagism, that is, the recent historical movement, may resemble a naïve poetry of mere things, but we can read the theoretical pronouncements of Imagists, and we can learn that Imagism is motivated by a distaste for the systematic abstractedness of thought. It presupposes acquaintance with science; that famous activity which is "constructive" with respect to the tools of our economic role in this world, and destructive with respect to nature. Imagists wish to escape from science by immersing themselves in images.

Not far off the simplicity of Imaginism was, a little later, the subtler simplicity of Mr. George Moore's project shared with several others, in behalf of "pure poetry." In Moore's house on Ebury Street they talked about poetry, with an after-dinner warmth if not an early-morning discretion, and their tastes agreed almost perfectly and reinforced one another. The fruit of these conversations was the volume *Pure Poetry*. It must have been the most exclusive anthology of English poetry that had yet appeared, since its room was closed to all the poems that dallied visibly with ideas, so that many poems that had been coveted by all other anthologists do not appear there. Nevertheless the book is delicious, and something more deserves to be said for it.

First, that "pure poetry" is a kind of Physical Poetry. Its visible content is a thing-content. Technically, I suppose, it is effective in this character if it can exhibit its material in such a way that an image or set of images and not an idea must occupy the foreground of the reader's attention. Thus:

> Full fathom five thy father lies
> Of his bones are coral made.

Here it is difficult for anybody (except the perfect idealist who is always theoretically possible and who would expect to take a return from anything whatever) to receive any experience except that of a very distinct image, or set of images. It has the configuration of image, which consists in being sharp of edges, and the modality of image, which consists in being given and non-negotiable, and the density, which consists in being full, a plenum of qualities. What is to be done with it? It is pure exhibit; it is to be contemplated; perhaps it is to be enjoyed. The art of poetry depends more frequently on this faculty than on any other in its repertory; the faculty of presenting images so whole and clean that they resist the catalysis of thought.

And something else must be said, going in the opposite direction. "Pure poetry," all the same, is not as pure as it is claimed to be, though on the whole it is Physical Poetry. (All true poetry is a phase of Physical Poetry.) It is not as pure as Imagism is, or at least it is not as pure as Imagism would be if it lived up to its principles; and in fact it is significant that the volume does not contain any Imagist poems, which argues a difference in taste somewhere. Imagism may take trifling things for its material, presumably it will take the first things the poet encounters, since "importance" and "interest" are not primary qualities which a thing possesses but secondary or tertiary ones which the idealist attributes to it by virtue of his own requirements. "Pure poetry" as Moore conceives it, and as the lyrics of Poe and Shakespeare offer it, deals with the more dramatic materials, and here dramatic means human, or at least capable of being referred to the critical set of human interests. Employing this sort of material the poet cannot exactly intend to set the human economists in us actually into motion, but perhaps he does intend to comfort us with the fleeting sense that it is potentially our kind of material.

In the same way "pure poetry" is nicely metred, whereas Imagism was free. Technique is written on it. And by the way the anthology contains no rugged anonymous Scottish ballad either, and probably for a like reason; because it would not be technically finished. Now both Moore and De La Mare are accomplished conservative artists, and what they do or what they approve may be of limited range but it is sure to be technically admirable, and it is certain that they understand what technique in poetry is though they do not define it. Technique takes the thing-content and meters and orders it. Metre is not an original property of things. It is artificial, and conveys the sense of human control, even if it does not wish to impair the thinginess of the things. Metric is a science, and so far as we attend to it we are within the scientific atmosphere. Order is the logical arrangement of things. It involves the dramatic "form" which selects the things, and brings out their appropriate qualities, and carries them through a systematic course of predication until the total impression is a unit of logic and not merely a solid lump of thing-content. The "pure poems" which Moore admires are studied, though it would be fatal if they looked studious. A sustained effort of ideation effected these compositions. It is covered up, and communicates itself only on a subliminal plane of consciousness. But experienced readers are quite aware of it; they know at once what is the matter when they encounter a realism shamelessly passing for poetry, or a well-planned but blundering poetry.

As critics we should have every good will toward Physical Poetry: it is the basic constituent of any poetry. But the product is always something short of a pure or absolute existence, and it cannot quite be said that it consists of nothing but physical objects. The fact is that when we are more than usually satisfied with a Physical Poetry our analysis will probably disclose that it is more than usually impure.

2. PLATONIC POETRY

The poetry of ideas I shall denominate: Platonic Poetry. This also has grades of purity. A discourse which employed only abstract ideas with no images would be a scientific document and not a poem at all, not even a Platonic poem. Platonic Poetry dips heavily into the physical. If Physical Poetry tends to employ some ideation surreptitiously while still looking innocent of idea, Platonic Poetry more than returns the compliment, for it tries as hard as it can to look like Physical Poetry, as if it proposed to conceal its medicine, which is the idea to be propagated, within the sugar candy of objectivity and *Dinglichkeit.* As an instance, it is almost inevitable that I quote a famous Victorian utterance:

> The year's at the spring
> And day's at the morn;
> Morning's at seven;
> The hill-side's dew-pearled;
> The lark's on the wing;
> The snail's on the thorn:
> God's in his heaven—
> All's right with the world!

which is a piece of transparent homiletics; for in it six pretty, co-ordinate images are marched, like six little lambs to the slaughter, to a colon and a powerful text. Now the exhibits of this poetry in the physical kind are always large, and may take more of the attention of the reader than is desired, but they are meant mostly to be illustrative of the ideas. It is on this ground that idealists like Hegel detect something unworthy, like a pedagogical trick, in poetry after all, and consider that the race will abandon it when it has outgrown its childishness and is enlightened.

The ablest arraignment of Platonic Poetry that I have seen, as an exercise which is really science but masquerades as poetry by affecting a concern for physical objects, is that of Mr. Allen Tate in a series of studies recently in *The New Republic.* I will summarize. Platonic Poetry is allegory, a discourse in things, but on the understanding that they are translatable at every point into ideas. (The usual ideas are those which constitute the popular causes, patriotic, religious, moral, or social.) Or Platonic Poetry is the elaboration of ideas as such, but in proceeding introduces for ornament some physical properties after the style of Physical Poetry; which is rhetoric. It is positive when the poet believes in the efficacy of the ideas. It is negative when he despairs of their efficacy, because they have conspicuously failed to take care of him, and utters his personal wail:

> I fall upon the thorns of life! I bleed!

This is "Romantic Irony," which comes at occasional periods to interrupt the march of scientific optimism. But it still falls under the category of Platonism; it generally proposes some other ideas to take the place of those which are in vogue.

But why Platonism? To define Platonism we must remember that it is not the property of the historical person who reports dialogues about it in an Academy, any more than "pure poetry" is the property of the talkers who describe it from a house on Ebury Street. Platonism, in the sense I mean, is the name of an impulse that is native to us all, frequent, tending to take a too complete possession of our minds. Why should the spirit of mortal be proud? The chief explanation is that modern mortal is probably a Platonist. We are led to believe that nature is rational and that by the force of reasoning we shall possess it. I have read upon high authority: "Two great forces are persistent in Plato: the love of truth and zeal for human improvement." The forces are one force. We love to view the world under universal or scientific ideas to which we give the name truth; and this is because the ideas seem to make not for righteousness but for mastery. The Platonic view of the world is ultimately the predatory, for it reduces to the scientific, which we know. The Platonic Idea becomes the Logos which science worships, which is the Occidental God, whose minions we are, and whose children, claiming a large share in His powers for patrimony.

Now the fine Platonic world of ideas fails to coincide with the original world of perception, which is the world populated by the stubborn and contingent objects, and to which as artists we fly in shame. The sensibility manifested by artists makes fools of scientists, if the latter are inclined to take their special and quite useful form of truth as the whole and comprehensive article. A dandified pagan worldling like Moore can always defeat Platonism; he does it every hour; he can exhibit the savor of his fish and wines, the fragrance of his coffee and cigars, and the solidity of the images in his favorite verse. These are objects which have to be experienced, and cannot be reported, for what is their simple essence that the Platonist can abstract? Moore may sound mystical but he is within the literal truth when he defends "pure poetry" on the ground that the things are constant, and it is the ideas which change—changing according to the latest mode under which the species indulges its grandiose expectation of subjugating nature. The things are constant in the sense that the ideas are never emancipated from the necessity of referring back to them as their original; and the sense that they are not altered nor diminished no matter which ideas may take off from them as a point of departure. The way to obtain the true *Dinglichkeit* of a formal dinner or a landscape or a beloved person is to approach the object as such, and in humility; then it unfolds a nature which we are unprepared for if we have put our trust in the simple idea which attempted to represent it.

The special antipathy of Moore is to the ideas as they put on their moral complexion, the ideas that relate everything to that insignificant centre of action, the human "soul" in its most Platonic and Pharisaic aspect. Nothing can darken perception better than a repetitive moral earnestness, based on the reputed superiority and higher destiny of the human species. If morality is the code by which we expect the race to achieve the more perfect possession of nature, it is an incitement to a more heroic science, but not to æsthetic experience, nor religious; if it is the code of humility, by which we intend to know nature as nature is, that is another matter; but in an age of science morality is inevitably for the general public the former; and so transcendent a morality as the latter is now unheard of. And therefore:

> O love, *they* die in yon rich sky,
> *They* faint on hill or field or river;
> *Our* echoes roll from soul to soul,
> And grow forever and forever.

The italics are mine. These lines conclude an otherwise innocent poem, a candidate for the anthology, upon which Moore remarks: "The Victorian could never reconcile himself to finishing a poem without speaking about the soul, and the lines are particularly vindictive." Vindictive is just. By what right did the Laureate exult in the death of the physical echoes and call upon his love to witness it, but out of the imperiousness of his savage Platonism? Plato himself would have admired this ending, and considered that it redeemed an otherwise vicious poem.

Why do persons who have ideas to promulgate risk the trial by poetry? If the poets are hired to do it, which is the polite conception of some Hegelians, why do their employers think it worth the money, which they hold in public trust for the cause? Does a science have to become a poetry too? A science is the less effective as a science when it muddies its clear waters with irrelevance, a sermon becomes less cogent when it begins to quote the poets. The moralist, the scientist, and the prophet of idealism think evidently that they must establish their conclusions in poetry, though they reach these conclusions upon quite other evidence. The poetry is likely to destroy the conclusions with a sort of death by drowning, if it is a free poetry.

When that happens the Platonists may be cured of Platonism. There are probably two cures, of which this is the better. One cure is by adversity, by the failure of the ideas to work, on account of treachery or violence, or the contingencies of weather, constitution, love, and economics; leaving the Platonist defeated and bewildered, possibly humbled, but on the other hand possibly turned cynical and worthless. Very much preferable is the cure which comes by education in the fine arts, erasing his Platonism more gently, leading him to feel that that is not a becoming habit of mind which dulls the perceptions.

The definition which some writers have given to art is: the reference of the idea to the image. The implication is that the act is not for the purpose of honest comparison so much as for the purpose of proving the idea by the image. But in the event the idea is not disproved so much as it is made to look ineffective and therefore foolish. The ideas will not cover the objects upon which they are imposed, they are too attenuated and threadlike; for ideas have extension and objects have intension, but extension is thin while intension is thick.

There must be a great deal of genuine poetry which started in the poet's mind as a thesis to be developed, but in which the characters and the situations have developed faster than the thesis, and of their own accord. The thesis disappears; or it is recaptured here and there and at the end, and lodged sententiously with the reader, where every successive reading of the poem will dislodge it again. Like this must be some plays, even some play out of Shake speare, whose thesis would probably be disentangled with difficulty out of the crowded pageant; or some narrative poem with a moral plot but much pure detail; perhaps some "occasional" piece by a Laureate or official person, whose purpose is compromised but whose personal integrity is saved by his wavering between the sentiment which is a public duty and the experience which he has in his own right; even some proclaimed allegory, like Spenser's, unlikely as that may seem, which does not remain transparent and everywhere translatable into idea but makes excursions into the territory of objectivity. These are hybrid performances. They cannot possess beauty of design, though there may be a beauty in detailed passages. But it is common enough, and we should be grateful. The mind is a versatile agent, and unexpectedly stubborn in its determination not really to be hardened in Platonism. Even in an age of science like the nineteenth century the poetic talents are not so loyal to its apostolic zeal as they and it suppose, and do not deserve the unqualified scorn which it is fashionable to offer them, now that the tide has turned, for their performance is qualified.

But this may be not stern enough for concluding a note on Platonic Poetry. I refer again to that whose

Platonism is steady and malignant. This poetry is an imitation of Physical Poetry, and not really a poetry. Platonists practise their bogus poetry in order to show that an image will prove an idea, but the literature which succeeds in this delicate mission does not contain real images but illustrations.

3. METAPHYSICAL POETRY

"Most men," Mr. Moore observes, "read and write poetry between fifteen and thirty and afterwards very seldom, for in youth we are attracted by ideas, and modern poetry being concerned almost exclusively with ideas we live on duty, liberty, and fraternity as chameleons are said to live on light and air, till at last we turn from ideas to things, thinking that we have lost our taste for poetry, unless, perchance, we are classical scholars."

Much is conveyed in this characteristic sentence, even in proportion to its length. As for the indicated chronology, the cart is put after the horse, which is its proper sequence. And it is pleasant to be confirmed in the belief that many men do recant from their Platonism and turn back to things. But it cannot be exactly a *volte-face*, for there are qualifications. If pure ideas were what these men turn from, they would have had no poetry at all in the first period, and if pure things were what they turn to, they would be having not a classical poetry but a pure imagism, if such a thing is possible, in the second.

The mind does not come unscathed and virginal

out of Platonism. Ontological interest would have to develop curiously, or wastefully and discontinuously, if men through their youth must cultivate the ideas so passionately that upon its expiration they are done with ideas forever and ready to become as little (and pre-logical) children. Because of the foolishness of idealists are ideas to be taboo for the adult mind? And, as critics, what are we to do with those poems (like *The Canonization* and *Lycidas*) which could not obtain admission by Moore into the anthology but which very likely are the poems we cherish beyond others?

The reputed "innocence" of the æsthetic moment, the "knowledge without desire" which Schopenhauer praises, must submit to a little scrutiny, like anything else that looks too good to be true. We come into this world as aliens come into a land which they must conquer if they are to live. For native endowment we have an exacting "biological" constitution which knows precisely what it needs and determines for us our inevitable desires. There can be no certainty that any other impulses are there, for why should they be? They scarcely belong in the biological picture. Perhaps we are simply an efficient animal species, running smoothly, working fast, finding the formula of life only too easy, and after a certain apprenticeship piling up power and wealth far beyond the capacity of our appetites to use. What will come next? Perhaps poetry, if the gigantic effort of science begins to seem disproportionate to the reward, according to a sense of diminishing returns. But before this pretty event can come to pass, it is possible that every act of attention which is allowed us is conditioned by a gross and selfish interest.

Where is innocence then? The æsthetic moment appears as a curious moment of suspension; between the Platonism in us, which is militant, always sciencing and devouring, and a starved inhibited aspiration towards innocence which, if it could only be free, would like to respect and know the object as it might of its own accord reveal itself.

The poetic impulse is not free, yet it holds out stubbornly against science for the enjoyment of its images. It means to reconstitute the world of perceptions. Finally there is suggested some such formula as the following:

Science gratifies a rational or practical impulse and exhibits the minimum of perception. Art gratifies a perceptual impulse and exhibits the minimum of reason.

Now it would be strange if poets did not develop many technical devices for the sake of increasing the volume of the percipienda or sensibilia. I will name some of them.

First Device: metre. Metre is the most obvious device. A formal metre impresses us as a way of regulating very drastically the material, and we do not stop to remark (that is, as readers) that it has no particular aim except some nominal sort of regimentation. It symbolizes the predatory method, like a sawmill which intends to reduce all the trees to fixed unit timbers, and as business men we require some sign of our business. But to the Platonic censor in us it gives a false security, for so long as the poet appears to be working faithfully at his metrical engine he is left comparatively free to attend lovingly to the things that are being metered, and metering them need not really hurt them. Metre is the gentlest violence he can do them, if he is expected to do some violence.

Second Device: fiction. The device of the fiction is probably no less important and universal in poetry. Over every poem which looks like a poem is a sign which reads: This road does not go through to action; fictitious. Art always sets out to create an "æsthetic distance" between the object and the subject, and art takes pains to announce that it is not history. The situation treated is not quite an actual situation, for science is likely to have claimed that field, and exiled art; but a fictive or hypothetical one, so that science is less greedy and perception may take hold of it. Kant asserted that the æsthetic judgment is not concerned with the existence or non-existence of the object, and may be interpreted as asserting that it is so far from depending on the object's existence that it really depends on the object's non-existence. Sometimes we have a certain melancholy experience. We enjoy a scene which we receive by report only, or dream, or meet with in art; but subsequently find ourselves in the presence of an actual one that seems the very same scene; only to discover that we have not now the power to enjoy it, or to receive it æsthetically, because the economic tension is upon us and will not indulge us in the proper mood. And it is generally easier to obtain our æsthetic experience from art than from nature, because nature is actual, and communication is forbidden. But in being called fictive or hypothetical the art-object suffers no disparagement. It cannot be true in the sense of being actual, and therefore it may be despised by science. But it is true in the sense of being fair or representative, in permitting the "illusion of reality"; just as Schopenhauer discovered that music may symbolize all the modes of existence in the world; and in keeping with the customary demand of the readers of fiction proper, that it shall be "true to life." The defenders of art must require for it from its practitioners this sort of truth, and must assert of it before the world this dignity. If jealous science succeeds in keeping the field of history for its own exclusive use, it does not therefore annihilate the arts, for they reappear in a field which may be called real though one degree removed from actuality. There the arts perform their function with much less interference, and at the same time with about as much fidelity to the phenomenal world as history has.

Third Device: tropes. I have named two important devices; I am not prepared to offer the exhaustive list. I mention but one other kind, the device which comprises the figures of speech. A proper scientific discourse has no intention of employing figurative language for its definitive sort of utterance. Figures of speech twist accidence away from the straight course, as if to intimate astonishing lapses of rationality beneath the smooth surface of discourse, inviting perceptual attention, and weakening the tyranny of science over the senses. But I skip the several easier and earlier figures, which are timid, and stop on the climactic figure, which is the metaphor; with special reference to its consequence, a poetry which once in our history it produced in a beautiful and abundant exhibit, called Metaphysical Poetry.

And what is Metaphysical Poetry? The term was added to the official vocabulary of criticism by Johnson, who probably took it from Pope, who probably took it from Dryden, who used it to describe the poetry of a certain school of poets, thus: "He [John Donne] affects the metaphysics, not only in his satires, but in his amorous verses, where nature only should reign. . . . In this Mr. Cowley has copied him to a fault." But the meaning of metaphysical which was common in Dryden's time, having come down from the Middle Ages through Shakespeare, was simply: supernatural; *miraculous.* The context of the Dryden passage indicates it.

Dryden, then, noted a miraculism in poetry and repudiated it; except where it was employed for satire, where it was not seriously intended and had the effect of wit. Dryden himself employs miraculism wittily, but seems rather to avoid it if he will be really committed by it; he may employ it in his translations of Ovid, where the responsibility is Ovid's and not Dryden's, and in an occasional classical piece where he is making polite use of myths well known to be pagan errors. In his "amorous" pieces he finds the reign of nature sufficient, and it is often the worse for his amorous pieces. He is not many removes from a naturalist. (A naturalist is a person who studies nature not because he loves it but because he wants to use it, approaches it from the standpoint of common sense, and sees it thin and not thick.) Dryden might have remarked that Donne himself had a change of heart and confined his miraculism at last to the privileged field of a more or less scriptural revelation. Perhaps Dryden found his way to accepting Milton because Milton's miraculism was mostly not a contemporary sort but classical and scriptural, pitched in a time when the age of miracles had not given way to the age of science. He knew too that Cowley had shamefully recanted from his petty miraculism, which formed the conceits, and turned to the scriptural or large order of miraculism to write his heroic (but empty) verses about David; and had written a Pindaric ode in extravagant praise of "Mr. Hobs," whose naturalistic account of nature seemed to render any other account fantastic if not contrary to the social welfare.

Incidentally, we know how much Mr. Hobbes affected Dryden too, and the whole of Restoration literature. What Bacon with his disparagement of poetry had begun, in the cause of science and protestantism, Hobbes completed. The name of Hobbes is critical in any history that would account for the chill which settled upon the poets at the very moment that English poetry was attaining magnificently to the fullness of its powers. The name stood for common sense and naturalism, and the monopoly of the scientific spirit over the mind. Hobbes was the adversary, the Satan, when the latter first intimidated the English poets. After Hobbes his name is legion.

"Metaphysics," or miraculism, informs a poetry which is the most original and exciting, and intellectually perhaps the most seasoned, that we know in our literature, and very probably it has few equivalents in other literatures. But it is evident that the metaphysical effects may be large-scale or they may be small-scale. (I believe that generically, or ontologically, no distinction is to be made between them.) If Donne and Cowley illustrate the small-scale effects, Milton will illustrate the large-scale ones, probably as a consequence of the fact that he wrote major poems. Milton, in the *Paradise Lost*, told a story which was heroic and miraculous in the first place. In telling it he dramatized it, and allowed the scenes and characters to develop of their own native energy. The virtue of a long poem on a "metaphysical" subject will consist in the dramatization or substantiation of all the parts, the poet not being required to devise fresh miracles on every page so much as to establish the perfect "naturalism" of the material upon which the grand miracle is imposed. The *Paradise Lost* possesses this virtue nearly everywhere:

> Thus *Adam* to himself lamented loud
> Through the still Night, not now, as ere man fell,
> Wholsom and cool, and mild, but with black Air
> Accompanied, with damps and dreadful gloom,
> Which to his evil Conscience represented
> All things with double terror: On the ground
> Outstretcht he lay, on the cold ground, and oft
> Curs'd his Creation, Death as oft accus'd
> Of tardie execution, since denounc't
> The day of his offence. Why comes not Death,
> Said hee, with one thrice acceptable stroke
> To end me?

This is exactly the sort of detail for a large-scale metaphysical work, but it would hardly serve the purpose with a slighter and more naturalistic subject; with "amorous" verses. For the critical mind Metaphysical Poetry refers perhaps almost entirely to the so-called "conceits" that constitute its staple. To define the conceit is to define small-scale Metaphysical Poetry.

It is easily defined, upon a little citation. Donne exhibits two conceits, or two branches of one conceit in the familiar lines:

> Our hands were firmly cemented
> By a fast balm which thence did spring;
> Our eye-beams twisted, and did thread
> Our eyes upon one double string.

The poem which follows sticks to the topic; it represents the lovers in precisely that mode of union and no other. Cowley is more conventional yet still bold in the lines:

> Oh take my Heart, and by that means you'll prove
> Within, too stor'd enough of love:
> Give me but yours, I'll by that change so thrive
> That Love in all my parts shall live.
> So powerful is this my change, it render can,
> My outside Woman, and your inside Man.

A conceit originates in a metaphor; and in fact the conceit is but a metaphor if the metaphor is meant; that is, if it is developed so literally that it must be meant, or predicated so baldly that nothing else can be meant. Perhaps this will do for a definition.

Clearly the seventeenth century had the courage of its metaphors, and imposed them imperially on the nearest things, and just as clearly the nineteenth century lacked this courage, and was half-heartedly metaphorical, or content with similes. The difference between the literary qualities of the two periods is the difference between the metaphor and the simile. (It must be admitted that this like other generalizations will not hold without its exceptions.) One period was pithy and original in its poetic utterance, the other was prolix and predictable. It would not quite commit itself to the metaphor even if it came upon one. Shelley is about as vigorous as usual when he says in *Adonais:*

> Thou young Dawn,
> Turn all thy dew to splendour. . . .

But splendor is not the correlative of dew, it has the

flat tone of a Platonic idea, while physically it scarcely means more than dew with sunshine upon it. The seventeenth century would have said: "Turn thy dew, which is water, into fire, and accomplish the transmutation of the elements." Tennyson in his boldest lyric sings:

> Come into the garden, Maud,
> For the black bat, night, has flown,

and leaves us unpersuaded of the bat. The predication would be complete without the bat, "The black night has flown," and a flying night is not very remarkable. Tennyson is only affecting a metaphor. But later in the same poem he writes:

> The red rose cries, "She is near, she is near";
> And the white rose weeps, "She is late";
> The larkspur listens, "I hear, I hear";
> And the lily whispers, "I wait."

And this is a technical conceit. But it is too complicated for this author, having a plurality of images which do not sustain themselves individually. The flowers stand for the lover's thoughts, and have been prepared for carefully in an earlier stanza, but their distinctness is too arbitrary, and these are like a schoolgirl's made-up metaphors. The passage will not compare with one on a very similar situation in *Green Candles*, by Mr. Humbert Wolfe:

> "I know her little foot," gray carpet said:
> "Who but I should know her light tread?"
> "She shall come in," answered the open door,
> "And not," said the room, "go out any more."

Wolfe's conceit works and Tennyson's does not, and though Wolfe's performance seems not very daring or important, and only pleasant, he employs the technique of the conceit correctly: he knows that the miracle must have a basis of verisimilitude.

Such is Metaphysical Poetry; the extension of a rhetorical device; as one of the most brilliant successes in our poetry, entitled to long and thorough examination; and even here demanding somewhat by way of a more ontological criticism. I conclude with it.

We may consult the dictionary, and discover that there is a miraculism or supernaturalism in a metaphorical assertion if we are ready to mean what we say, or believe what we hear. Or we may read Mr. Hobbes, the naturalist, who was very clear upon it: "II. The second cause of absurd assertions I ascribe to the giving of names of 'bodies' to 'accidents,' or of 'accidents' to 'bodies,' as they do that say 'faith is infused' or 'inspired,' when nothing can be 'poured' or 'breathed' into anything but body . . . and that 'phantasms' are 'spirits,' etc." Translated into our present terms, Hobbes is condemning the confusion of single qualities with whole things; or the substitution of concrete images for simple ideas.

Specifically, the miraculism arises when the poet discovers by analogy an identity between objects which is partial, though it should be considerable, and proceeds to an identification which is complete. It is to be contrasted with the simile, which says "as if" or "like," and is scrupulous to keep the identification partial. In Cowley's passage above, the lover is saying, not for the first time in this literature: "She and I have exchanged our hearts." What has actually been exchanged is affections, and affections are only in a limited sense the same as hearts. Hearts are unlike affections in being engines that pump blood and form body; and it is a miracle if the poet represents the lady's affection as rendering her inside into man. But he succeeds, with this mixture, in depositing with us the image of a very powerful affection.

From the strict point of view of literary criticism it must be insisted that the miraculism which produces the humblest conceit is the same miraculism which supplies to religions their substantive content. (This is said to assert the dignity not of the conceits but of the religions.) It is the poet and nobody else who gives to the God a nature, a form, faculties, and a history; to the God, most comprehensive of all terms, which, if there were no poetic impulse to actualize or "find" Him, would remain the driest and deadest among Platonic ideas, with all intension sacrificed to infinite extension. The myths are conceits, born of metaphors. Religions are periodically produced by poets and destroyed by naturalists. Religion depends for its ontological validity upon a literary understanding, and that is why it is frequently misunderstood. The metaphysical poets, perhaps like their spiritual fathers the mediæval Schoolmen, were under no illusions about this. They recognized myth, as they recognized the conceits, as a device of expression; its sanctity as the consequence of its public or social importance.

But whether the topics be Gods or amorous experiences, why do poets resort to miraculism? Hardly for the purpose of controverting natural fact or scientific theory. Religion pronounces about God only where science is silent and philosophy is negative; for a positive is wanted, that is, a God who has his being in the physical world as well as in the world of principles and abstractions. Likewise with the little secular enterprises of poetry too. Not now are the poets so brave, not for a very long time have they been so brave, as to dispute the scientists on what they call their "truth"; though it is a pity that the statement cannot be turned round. Poets will concede that every act of science is legitimate, and has its efficacy. The metaphysical poets of the seventeenth century particularly admired the methodology of science, and in fact they copied it, and their phrasing is often technical, spare, and polysyllabic, though they are not repeating actual science but making those metaphorical substitutions that are so arresting.

The intention of Metaphysical Poetry is to complement science, and improve discourse. Naturalistic discourse is incomplete, for either of two reasons. It has the minimum of physical content and starves the sensibility, or it has the maximum, as if to avoid the appearance of evil, but is laborious and pointless. Platonic Poetry is too idealistic, but Physical Poetry is too realistic, and realism is tedious and does not maintain interest. The poets therefore introduce the psychological device of the miracle. The predication which it permits is clean and quick but it is not a scientific predication. For scientific predication concludes an act of attention but miraculism initiates one. It leaves us looking, marvelling, and revelling in the thick *dinglich* substance that has just received its strange representation.

Let me suggest as a last word, in deference to a common Puritan scruple, that the predication of Metaphysical Poetry is true enough. It is not true like history, but no poetry is true in that sense, and only a part of science. It is true in the pragmatic sense in which some of the generalizations of science are true: it accomplishes precisely the sort of representation that it means to. It suggests to us that the object is perceptually or physically remarkable, and we had better attend to it.

A Psychologist Looks at Poetry

It is the age of psychology. When we observe how different are our philosophical questions from those that harassed the Greeks, we mean, I think, that we have psychology and the Greeks had not. It is on the whole a burden, but that does not mean that we shall ever get rid of it. In philosophy our insistent psychological sense is an embarrassing self-consciousness always reminding us that when we think we have a knowledge of the objective world it may be only a projection of our own feelings and wishes. The spontaneous acceptance of knowledge as an objective record is an early capacity that has passed from our power.

A peculiar thing has happened in this connection. When Kant and his successors, bringing to a head the tendencies which had been in action since Descartes, emphasized the dual constitution of knowledge, with special emphasis on a subjective element that determined it, the scientists (as it were through their constitutional lawyers the Positivists) conceded with pleasure that this consideration turned theology and metaphysics into no-knowledge; they quite failed to think it necessary to remark that it scarcely left science whole and untouched. There cannot often have been an exception taken by professional thinkers more naïvely than this one. It has done duty for the better part of a century, with all but unanimous consent. Only in our own time have scientists themselves begun to discover and to testify officially that the world which they have appropriated is a world which they have created, precisely like the world of the religionists; that their own world also is myth. But even while this discovery was being published, the professional psychologists themselves so failed to partake of the enlightenment as to announce that they would not be concerned with anything psychic, which would be admittedly subjective, but with the objective gray matter that aggregated in skulls and spinal columns and filiated through flesh; in other words, they demanded seats in the same car with physical science, as if that vehicle were very much more substantial though less picturesque than any God, or poem, or dream.

And now the psychologists, having for some time disposed of religion as an illusory or bogus knowledge, proceed to the disposition of poetry in the same manner. Poetry is an illusion like superstition, and based on the same subjective need of expression.

Of that presently. But first it may be observed that the arts, including poetry, will have to be a little different in an age of psychology, with or without the connivance of the professional psychologists. Romantic arts, I think, are the ones which suit a self-conscious age. The artists indulge frankly in make-believe, inventing the object to suit their own happiness, as if delivered from the responsibility of knowledge. They express themselves rather than an object.

And here is a modernism in art which does not exactly identify itself with romantic, but is another application of the same self-consciousness; perhaps it calls itself a realism. Recording actual experience the artists are interested principally in expressing what is near the subject-pole of the subject-object relation. This is very obvious in fiction, which occupies itself as nearly as possible with the pure state of consciousness. I suppose this sort of art reflects what good biologists might regard as the paralysis of animal will; for I do not know what the vital animal intends if not to translate the animal feelings incessantly into terms of objective environment; into knowledge and action. Animal life presupposes knowledge.

2

Mr. I. A. Richards is a British psychologist devoted to a very special career, which is the application of his science to poetry. He has certainly improved the public reception of poetry, but it would not follow that he has yet perfected the apparatus. Put together the analytic power of modern psychology (he says in effect) and the healing yet obscure and today not quite reputable influence of poetry upon the mind, and the future of poetry will be indeed immense, and you will have a revolution of Copernican importance for our happiness. This is good news. Certainly we need to know what poetry does to us when we receive it, and to know that we need the aid of psychology. In many of his own psychological analyses of what certain poems mean, Mr. Richards himself has come to our aid. Since we are self-conscious and analytic about everything else that goes through our heads, there is no reason why we should stop short of the analysis of poetry; or rather, it is impossible to stop short. If it is not Mr. Richards, it will be Mr. Eastman, or some other psychologist.

Mr. Richards is already a voluminous author, but in describing his doctrine I shall not attend to all the volumes; saving for a conclusion a late one, "Coleridge on Imagination," because it seems to show an author breaking with his own past; and not drawing on the very early one, "The Meaning of Meaning," because I have not the heart, though I have the documentary notes. It is a book which does not justify its pretentiousness, but it is an early book. Its interest for us primarily is that it shows the psychological bias from which Mr. Richards started, and has never worked free; this is contained in his jaunty faith in what "modern psychology" says, his denial of metaphysics and formal philosophy, and his occasional impression that psychology is a branch of physics.

He is a sort of behaviorist. I quote from *Principles of Literary Criticism*, the most comprehensive of his books:

> That the mind is the nervous system, or rather a part of its activity, has long been evident, although the prevalence among psychologists of persons with philosophic antecedents

has delayed the recognition of the fact in an extraordinary fashion. . . . It is true that as our knowledge of the nervous system stands at present much of the detail of the identification is impenetrably obscure, and the account which we give must frankly be admitted to be only a degree less fictitious than one in terms of spiritual happenings.

And this:

Some relation [among the mental phenomena] at present hidden from us in the jungles of neurology.

And this:

The joy which is so strangely the heart of the experience is not an indication that "all's right with the world" or that "somewhere, somehow, there is Justice"; it is an indication that all is right here and now in the nervous system.

The effect of these passages is to say that the author regards spiritual happenings as unsatisfactory for the purpose of scientific data, and wishes that neural or physical happenings might be substituted; which is an expression, I believe, of behavioristic attitude. He talks as if neurology will eventually make this possible; though "at present" the neurological account is "only a degree less fictitious" than the account it wants to replace. Most readers will retort, of course, that in the very large majority of cases the spiritual happenings are the only happenings we have observed, and the neural happenings are simply what the behaviorists would like to observe. At present the mental datum is the fact and the neural datum is the inference.

This is very debonair of Mr. Richards. Probably

behaviorism has its uses but it is a strange profession of faith for a psychologist, particularly for one reporting poetry. It looks like the sign of a scientist who has got into the wrong science, and is seeking effects that belong to some other science—such as objectivity of data, certainty of generalization, precision rather than delicacy of judgment. At the risk of being very commonplace I feel like repeating a well-known gradation of the sciences which goes back to Aristotle or perhaps further. At the bottom is placed physical science, concerned with masses, their composition out of other masses, and their motions; very simple qualitatively, very precise quantitatively, very binding, very useful; a gross science, in a usual way of speaking, but otherwise the perfect example of effectiveness. Next comes biological science, concerned with the form, genetics, growth, and physiology of the living being. We observe that the living being is composed of physical masses and is therefore responsive to the laws of physical science; but that, beyond this, it is governed by biological, not physical, laws. The relation of the oak to the acorn is not one that physical science can define or predict. But the laws which operate here are less exact and determining than those of physics and inorganic chemistry. Finally we come to psychology, with the associated anthropological sciences, concerned with the mind of man. Man is a physical being, therefore under physical science; a living being, therefore under biological science; but also a mind, and to that extent not understood by either of those sciences. The data of psychology are mental data, and the science is the hardest and least definitive of all. It is a great pity, but there it is. I blush to tell all this.

Mr. Richards treats of mental data, on the whole, but not without many a look backward into the simpler orders of data. He brings into the account of poetry an unusual set of terms; and their principle seems to be that, if they are not quite physical terms, they will not be so very spiritual. I suppose they are orthodox terms in the new psychology. The analysis of a poetic experience given in *Science and Poetry* reads like the study of a brain. We encounter a surface—the impression of the printed words on the retina—and an agitation which goes deeper and deeper and involves images; then two streams, the bigger one composed of rushing feelings and emotions, the smaller one being the intellectual stream; then a great many "interests" clashing and balancing; and finally the attitudes, or outward-looking adjustments which complete the response to the original stimulus. Some of these terms are physical, some are physiological, and others are barely psychological. The importance of the term *intellectual* is played down. Mr. Richards partakes of the behavioristic aversion to the concept of thought. He writes that man "is not in any sense primarily an intelligence; he is a system of interests." The common conception of man as primarily an intelligence is a mistake, of which Mr. Richards writes:

The whole traditional analysis of the working of the

mind has been turned upside down. It is largely as a remedy from the difficulties which this mistake involves that poetry may have so much importance in the future.

Mr. Richards emphasizes the complexity of a poetic experience. It is great, and he is right; his rightness is a reproach against many highly connnected critics who have thought poetry was simple, and have been prepared to recite very promptly and in a few words what they define as the "meaning" of a poem. (It turns out to be only the moral meaning, or other single meaning. Mr. Richards has a valuable doctrine about the meaning of poetry which amounts to a Doctrine of Multiple Meanings.) But what is this complexity like? He is not the man to let it reside in the object experienced, he has to have the complexity in the head of the subject experiencing; that is, it is not constitutional to nature but to the mind. This is arbitrary and unnatural; it is a psychologism. It is difficult not to wonder whether he finds it all there, or puts some of it there; plants it, as they say of gentlemen with faked gold mines to sell. He starts out to show how elaborate is the experience of reading Wordsworth's "Sonnet on Westminster Bridge"; but after a good start he discovers that he is reciting not at all the detail of the reader's mind but the detail of the poem; and gives up that project and resorts to an impressive metaphor about the wonderful organization of the "interests" in the mind:

Suppose that we carry a magnetic compass about in the neighborhood of powerful magnets. The needle waggles as we move and comes to rest pointing in a new direction whenever we stand still in a new position. Suppose that instead of a single compass we carry an arrangement of many magnetic needles, large and small, swung so that they influence one another, some able only to swing horizontally, others vertically, others hung freely. As we move, the perturbations in this system will be very complicated. But for every position in which we place it there will be a final position of rest for all the needles into which they will in the end settle down, a general poise for the whole system. But even a slight displacement may set the whole assemblage of needles busily readjusting themselves.

One further complication. Suppose that while all the needles influence one another, some of them respond only to some of the outer magnets among which the system is moving. The reader can easily draw a diagram if his imagination needs a visual support.

The mind is not unlike such a system if we imagine it to be incredibly complex. The needles are our interests, varying in their importance, that is, in the degree to which any movement they make involves movement in the other needles. Each new disequilibrium, which a shift of position, a fresh situation, entails, corresponds to a need; and the wagglings which ensue as the system rearranges itself are our responses, the impulses through which we seek to meet the need.

Mr. Richards has a tricky explanation somewhere of the business of metaphor. It brings in a fresh object when there is not enough to the original object, feeding the interests when they are not getting their sustenance out of the given straightforward account. I wonder if that is not the purpose of Mr.

Richards' own metaphor here. He cannot identify, at least he has not yet identified, as many as several of the little magnetic needles that go through such agitations and finally come to rest. They are probably not there. If in one line of the sonnet,

> Ships, towers, domes, theatres and temples lie,

Wordsworth conveys five separate objects for the mind to feed upon, does it follow that there are five separate little interests clamoring there, the first one for ships, the second one for towers, the third one for domes, and so on? I suspect that Mr. Richards' zeal on behalf of the little interests contains some pious fraud. His interests are going to be very tiny, very many, and very private, and the fact is that Mr. Richards will never know they are there until a poet arrives with little details that seem pleasant, and therefore, he supposes, must be tickling some corresponding little entities inside us.

Mr. Richards will have to reduce his idea of the number of organic interests, and then name a few of them independently to show his good faith. They will be quite general and classifiable interests, and each will have an immense flexibility, enough to function over a very wide range of particulars. But he might as well refer the particularity to external nature.

3

What is the value of a poetic experience to Mr. Richards? He has many statements about that.

Sometimes he finds a social value, being a sociologist as well as a psychologist. It is the usual one. We are all aware that poetry has charms to soothe the savage breast. The poets, says Mr. Richards, offer us their charming myths and create a Nature that is not the same as the soulless one given by the physical sciences:

> It is such a Nature that the religions in the past have attempted to provide for man. And it is with such a Nature that the political mythologizing of the more cramped sections of humanity—a Nature including Nordic destinies and Japanese "missions"—is endeavoring to direct world affairs.

If the races can be persuaded by myths into programs and actions, then they should have nothing but good myths that will safely bring them to World Peace. I do not know of any objection to this. But the harder and more important question is about the value of poetry to the mind that entertains it; the intrinsic æsthetic value, not the extrinsic or utilitarian value.

It is certainly this question which Mr. Richards prefers to discuss. But he is defeated, as I think, by his characteristic rejection of the cognitive element of the poetic experience. The cognitions offered in poetry are constantly scorned, now on the ground that they are false, again on the ground that they are of no importance. He conceives that poetry, without having recourse to any knowledge, can somehow serve the emotions, or interests, or attitudes. It makes the magnetic needles oscillate, and we suppose that the oscillation makes them happy. But he emphasizes very strongly the conclusion of the experience, which is balance, poise, and peace. As if to escape from holding the experience as too cheap, he proposes that it is a gigantic feat of ordering and organizing the system of clashing interests, setting a valuable example for the human economy to follow when it has real business to pursue. But he makes no effort to show how a poem can perform this ordering. It is inevitable in his account that the poem should simply agitate the interests, and that the interests should then fight it out and order themselves automatically by the law of the survival of the strongest. There seems to be again a little fraud, as Mr. Richards imputes magic to the poet in the following manner:

> He uses these words because the interests which the situation calls into play combine to bring them, just in this form, into his consciousness *as a means of ordering, controlling and consolidating* the whole experience.

The italics are his. He nowhere offers the least circumstantial account of this matter. Unless I am mistaken, Mr. Richards is not himself a poet, and I think the fact bears on some of his strange utterances.

The theory of poetry as agitation gives us a muscular or gymnastic view of poetry: the poem resembles a gymnasium with plenty of dumb-bells and parallel bars for all the member interests; and what the member interests obtain from it is pure or abstract exercise, which does not pretend to have any relation to affairs. Now emphasize the gratifications and the pleasures they receive from it, and we obtain a hedonistic view. But think how imaginary and unreal are the objects that engage them, and we come to a view of poetry as a form of self-abuse. Then talk about the inalienable right of the little interests to "function" just as freely as the big public ones, and it becomes a doctrine of expressionism. Mr. Richards does not sponsor these various views, but he is not far off; they are proper corollaries to his view.

I cannot see how the interests can function if they are not interested, and I do not believe they can be interested in something which they persuade the imagination to invent for them *ad hoc*, or for the express purpose of interesting them. The psychic "healer" puts his disordered patient on a chaise longue, induces relaxation, and then repeats a lot of words until some one word makes the patient jump, because it has a reference to his special or secret interest; but the rigmarole of the healer does not constitute a poem. Mr. Richards has an almost infinite number of little interests to satisfy; his problem is a good deal harder. But the one thing they would have in common is that they all are, must be, interests in external reality. *Inter-esse* means to be environed, and interest means sensitiveness to environment. To be interested is to try to obtain a cognition, to do what Mr. Richards wickedly denies to poetic experience and grants exclusively to science: to seek the truth. I think the biologist would justify only this conception of the function of our interests.

The imagination supplies the form of knowledge

for poetry. I should hardly define imagination as Mr. Richards does, hardly even as Coleridge is represented in Mr. Richards' latest book as having done. I should say that imagination is an organ of knowledge whose technique is images. It presents to the reflective mind the particularity of nature; whereas there is quite another organ, working by a technique of universals, which gives us science. The image presented by the imagination ordinarily means to be true. The poet ordinarily is sincere and means his images to be true, and I do not think that readers of my acquaintance will put up with a poet's imagery long if it is not true. It is probably true in the commonest sense of true: verifiable; based on observation.

4

Mr. Richards has not stood still. His progress as an æsthetician consists in his reluctant and gradual adoption of the view that cognition is the essential element in a poetic experience. (Poetry is a form of knowledge.) He is increasingly concerned over the fact that the poet makes assertions; but unfortunately they seem to be only mythical: "pseudo-statements" which science has to reject. He comforts himself somewhere with the remark that the "greatest poets" will be found not to make many assertions. He evidently considers that when they offer only images they are not making assertions. But their images are perceptions, and perceptions are assertions; perceptions are as true and as false as propositions. Mr.

Richards' readers will not suggest that he read the stock philosophers, for he has read them all, but that he ought to read them more humbly. The Neo-Hegelians, for instance; it is from them that I have the impression of having received my fullest understanding of what is implied in a perception. Or even the Greek æstheticians, with their doctrine of imitation—a term meant to confer upon the artistic images at least the dignity of truthfulness.

Poets make plenty of assertions; if the predication is not overt, so that grammar can recognize it, it is implicit. ("The oak, ancient, moaning its splendors gone," commits the poet as much as if he had said, "The oak moans in pain.") But these assertions (the one just cited, for example) may be "mythical" ones, and what will be their status as cognition? They are supposed not to appear in science. Are we to believe them, and in what sense? It is one of the hardest problems in the theory of poetry. And no modern writer has wrestled with it more manfully and more continuously than has Mr. Richards.

We cannot believe these assertions at all, Mr. Richards says; but we can ignore them and make use of the accompanying details (or images) to feed the interests; or we can "suspend" our disbeliefs, forget them, and enjoy what is offered us. He feels that poetry can now be saved to the world only by a new and cunning technique of suspended disbelief. He does not venture to give much instruction in it, though he concedes that it will be a difficult technique for the public to acquire. It will; the public is given to taking its poetry more seriously than Mr. Richards does; in fact, the public expects not only the statements in the poetry but even the images to be true ones.

An account of poetry as knowledge by images, reporting the fulness or particularity of nature, would hardly be acceptable to Mr. Richards. But it permits us to do what Mr. Richards, with all his argument about the mythiness of poetry, has never tried to do: to classify with respect to their verifiability or scientific standing the kinds of assertion which poets make. It need not take long to do it roughly.

A great deal of poetry is analogous to ordinary painting; it simply presents its objects in detail without ever exceeding actual observation:

> The trees stood up against the sky.

Of course the context is diffuse; that is, it contains some pure and perfectly contingent details, enough to stand for an inexhaustible particularity, and distinguishes itself from a scientific study in the fact that no single detail is abstracted out of it. It is a context made of images, and the images are attended to and dwelt on without removal from context.

This is poetry of a primary or simplest order. It does not give us scientific truth, for that is the abstracted or universal aspect of the picture. But every detail in it is accurate detail, or it should be. If poetry did no more than this, it would still be eternally distinct as a form of knowledge, and it would be needless to ask what we wanted it for. It views the world as particularity, and we have to have the world in that sense.

The poetic impulse is much too insistent to stop there. The poet proceeds next to assert properties and behaviors in the object which are not verifiable, or not sufficiently so to be approved by the strict canon of science. It animates nature. It confers mentality upon the rock, the tree, the star, which do not discoverably have it, nor the organs for it; it makes the mountain brood protectively over the mountaineer, and the Easter bird sing carols. Poetry does this by virtue of what we call the pathetic (sympathetic) fallacy. The poet invests the lower forms of animal life, or even the inorganic body, with his own mentality. (His procedure in elevating an object to a higher classification is opposite to that of the behaviorist, who degrades it into a lower classification.)

There is still another variety of this bolder sort of poetic assertion. The poet now takes up the purely instrumental terms which the sciences have arrived at, which do not have even the lowest degree of objective existence, and animates them too; abstract qualities, abstract collective or quantitative terms; and gives them body, life, and mind. The poet in Plato did this for certain handsome terms, like truth, goodness, and beauty, capitalizing their names as if they were persons, and giving them a residence in the sky as if they were personages; but being guarded about the detail because he had trained himself to love universals and despise particularity. There are terms so valuable as instruments for the human society that they receive political and ecclesiastical honors like persons. There is the State; a pure abstraction, but clothed with countless images, and in various personalities, such as Leviathan, Fatherland, John Bull. The terms good and evil fall into the hands of poets and become first, perhaps, Forces, then Spirits, then Gods, then God and Satan, and the work is not finished until each is invested with a kingdom, a court, and a host of ministering angels. The doctrines of religion are poetry in this sense, and certainly religion cannot outlast poetry; the religion that surrenders its images to the scientific censors is about to go out of business as religion and become Social Service, or Rotarianism, or Humanism—with a capital letter as the last ikon it has preserved.

Society in the past has been prodigiously hospitable to these systems of imagery. Now, however, the iconoclasts are in power, and the weapon they employ is the charge of falsity, superstition, and weakmindedness. Mr. Richards expresses his concern over this situation:

> Countless pseudo-statements—about God, about the universe, about human nature, the relations of mind to mind, about the soul, its rank and destiny—pseudo-statements which are pivotal points in the organization of the mind, vital to its well-being, have suddenly become, for sincere, honest and informal minds, impossible to believe. For cen-

> turies they have been believed; now they are gone, irrecoverably; and the knowledge which has killed them is not of a kind upon which an equally fine organization of the mind can be based.

If such pseudo-statements are contradictory to knowledge I think their case is indeed lost, and poetry of this kind—all poetry except the primary and simpler kind—will have to cease to be written. It is quite possible that they will disappear, and that poetry will reduce itself to a transcript of the mere visible natural world, and become an art of about the same scope as painting. But their case is not quite like this, and not quite so desperate, I hope, as Mr. Richards thinks.

I prefer to think that these images or assertions which exceed observation are the form that certain cognitions take with us because of our natural propensities as knowers; perhaps that is a Kantian sort of position. The poet wants to particularize his objects in order to understand them fully, and images of this sort are habitual to our particularization. This argument makes them natural, and therefore makes them stubborn.

The æsthetic doctrine of empathy, which circulates widely, has an application here that seems more important than the one generally ascribed. The empathists look at paintings of objects and even at buildings and report that they—the generic spectators—read into the physical objects their own muscular tensions; read consciousness into them. But of course the painter and the architect (or the poet of the primary order) do not exactly write the consciousness in by some sort of objective record. The spectator supplies it; and so the doctrine of empathy seems to claim that it has discovered the psychological law that in reading objects as particulars we involuntarily observe them under the forms with which our own minds are familiar. If the doctrine is correct, the poet who ascribes mentality to the lower orders and even to purely instrumental and abstract terms is doing no more than we all do without being aware of what we do. It seems very likely. Perhaps it is just as hard for a higher being to understand a lower as for the lower to understand the higher. Perhaps intelligent beings are the only ones intelligible to us. A pure mechanical cause is certainly too simple for us; for instance, the pull of objects toward each other by gravitation, or the pushing of one object away from another; if we care to make images of these operations, probably we are forced to construe them in the terms of "spiritual happenings." The existence of a stone is incredible to us, because we are forbidden to call it the life of a stone; it is therefore abstract, and abstractions cannot be existents. But Kant said that the world of living things, at least, looks purposive, which means that we cannot but attribute purpose to it. Imagination, the organ by which we secure the particularity of objects, is hardly going to be prohibited from certain fields on the ground that they offer less particularity than it likes, or offer none at all.

5

Suspended disbelief is the formula of the writer whom I have been representing as the author of certain earlier books. But he is now the author of the volume on Coleridge, and voids much of the criticism which I have made of him. The new work is an attempt to recover, defend, and recommend to the modern critics the doctrine of imagination which Coleridge propounded. That would be no ordinary project for any man's book; but Coleridge, a not always intelligible adapter of German idealism, cloudy and rhetorical and insistently metaphysical, is the last influence which would have been expected to bear upon Mr. Richards. I do not know enough of his private history to understand how this attachment arose, and it would not be the business of a critic to know anyhow; certainly Mr. Richards in the other books has been citing Coleridge with increasing frequency. Now he has adopted what most people will call the idealist philosophy, though he himself is inclined to quibble over the term. His doubts of the truth of the poetic assertions disappear, and poetry becomes for him nearly as strong as science.

Following Coleridge, Mr. Richards comes finally to the doctrine which has either one of two versions:

1. The mind of the poet at moments, penetrating "the film of familiarity and selfish solicitude," gains an insight into reality, reads Nature as a symbol of something behind or within Nature not ordinarily received.
2. The mind of the poet creates a Nature into which

his own feelings, his aspirations and apprehensions, are projected.

But it does not matter, Mr. Richards says, which version you accept; they are one doctrine. The knowledge of Nature is either something you read out of Nature or something you read into Nature, but the point is that the poet and the physicist obtain it in the same way. You cannot treat one set of assertions as objective and the other set as subjective. They are exposed to the same hazard, and they come out with equal success. (The mind is in the ambiguous position of an observer of a moving body under the hypothesis of relativist physics: he cannot tell whether the motion is his or that of the thing observed.)

So all knowledge is equally real, or all is equally mythical. We find Mr. Richards talking with a pretty easiness about the myths of physics, but we also find him relieving his vocabulary, perhaps forever, of such phrases as "pseudo-statements," in which he used to offer his apologies for the untruthfulness of poetry. His change is like what the evangelists call a "conversion."

I applaud the regeneration; but now—I hope it is not contrariness—I find myself wanting it not to be too sweeping. It is philosophical to say that all knowledge is an impure product, or compound, of two factors, a subjective constitution and an external object, but in having said that we have not settled any æsthetic problems. We have laid down a proposition which governs all our knowledges, and governs them equally whether they appear in poems or in sciences. But a good many things happen after that. The primary order of poetry—the one that does not go beyond the data of an inscrutable world which must at least offer its data—seems to be in precisely the same predicament as ordinary science, or the same dignity; the poetry being faithful to the profusion and fullness of the data as they cluster in some local unit, and the science abstracting very carefully from the data for its much more focussed and practical intention. But what of the other poetry?

Poetry, I think, must be much more "creative" than science is, or at least much more spiritedly, incessantly so. It is such an eager cognitive impulse that it overreaches its object. That is its glory, and one of the causes of its delightfulness perhaps, and certainly the source of its bad reputation. It goes where science hardly cares to set foot. But its reputation may be improved if poetry will watch closely after its own innocence; that is, be careful not to pervert by positive misrepresentation this world's data; though it is elemental, and essential to all acts of mind, to assume the validity of the data. Even so, poetry is inclined to make very free in its path through the world, and to pass fróm the presence of its actual data. It makes its own version, a new and not clearly authorized one, of the world. (So do scientists too, when they compound their data; but cautiously.)

Mr. Richards will have to do what Coleridge did, and recommend to poets eternal vigilance.

A Cathedralist Looks at Murder

T. S. ELIOT's latest is *Murder in the Cathedral.* A snappy title. (Mildly embarrassing association: "Murder in Mesopotamia," detective serial running in the world's most popular weekly.) A drama that starts religious, but reverts, declines, very distinctly towards snappiness. Can Eliot sustain the religious tone? As critic, as prose man, yes, for anybody can sustain any tone, by main strength; as poet, you do it only if the tone is you, or is grace of God implanted in you. Literary evidence is that Eliot is religious more by conviction than by grace. Pertinent reflection, that Eliot's seriousness has always been in his criticism and in his critical manner, which is sometimes pontifical, while his poetry has with the very greatest difficulty, and hardly ever, managed to suppress modernity and snappiness; just reversing the order of things we probably believe in. Perhaps a thousand lines of verse in this play, and two scenes in prose besides: enough to take some sustaining. But before remark seems to sound too disparaging, do him the honor to compare him with the former generations of poets, the men who were as giants before the flood; not with his contemporaries, whom for the most part he exceeds easily, who are incapable of remarkable

[1]This .paper is excerpted from an omnibus review of the season's poetry several years ago in *The Southern Review.*

catharses, who make the little and precious effects their virtue, who are without dimensions; this is his due. By the old standards, then, what of this poem? By old standards it quickly appears that *sostenuto* is the one signal lack in Eliot's equipment. His strongest effects are not by sustaining the note but by juxtaposing incongruous notes, by brilliant discords; modernism itself. That was the single effect in his early satirical verses. Call it irony, it is disruptive still. It comes, it must come, out of a personal disintegration and unfaith. Unless it is fairer to say it comes out of an age of unfaith. But leave that. The play's the thing. And the cue to the criticism: to compare it with something similar in the big creative epochs. Our election is almost certain; it falls on the *Samson Agonistes* of Milton. (I am sorry that Eliot dislikes Milton, but that is perfectly fortuitous. The present comparison need have nothing to do with such deficiency as Eliot finds in Milton.) Now Milton, at a certain stage in his spiritual history, was like Eliot, one of a diminishing party of adherents to an old faith, out of touch in his deepest interests with the "spirit of his times." And *Samson* is like *Murder* in being first a drama, then a historical drama, then a loving religious historical drama. Samson's immolation like Becket's martyrdom, too; a pair of fine occasions for the religio-poetic faculties of two accomplished poets; equally appealing to the imagination. But, as histories, documented bodies of data for dramatic arrangement, the Becket material greatly exceeding the Samson material in voluminousness, and much closer in contemporaneity and acquaintance; so that Eliot's play should be denser, fuller, Milton's play the one pieced-out and briefer. It is just the contrary. Milton's is longer yet much more severely unified, and it is Eliot who has to make use of skits and fireworks. The fundamental difference which I am afraid of: in the respective original poetic energies themselves. Milton, always a thorough workman, tackling his occasions like a professional, challenging any occasion, giving always more than the occasion's decent minimum requirement; see *Comus* and *Lycidas,* and a dozen prose affairs. The distinguished modern, a brilliant amateur, whose performance will have stimulating novelties but will not keep you long. Even—if I may be impertinent—when there is a rare occasion, like this: "The Chapter would like very much to present in the Cathedral an original drama having to do with its own history, and such as Mr. Eliot might care to write." (Against misunderstanding, once more; the limitations not personal to T. S. E., or at least not necessarily; generic to his age. The late Mr. Robinson could have done a big thing with this subject, but not a powerful thing, nothing Miltonic; the power of his effects not being proportionate to his ability to sustain them.) The best thing that Milton had, looked at from this distance, was *copia,* God's plenty, unlimited wealth in poetic stock; it did not give out, nor need reinforcements, nor require dilution. Thus in the Samson play, a chorus of wise old men but not for decoration. Their lines not only lyrical but religious, and not only religious but hammering incessantly on Samson's own religious agony, discussing and emphasizing the truth which is the truth of the play. So has the Becket play a chorus, but of silly old women, who are picturesque and lyrical but very aimless and repetitive, garrulous old women, going on about life and presently going on about death; above all, knowing nothing in the world about poor Becket's inner tragedy. Are they in the play to repel the thought that this is a stiff Cathedral play? Certainly Becket proceeds nobly and with full understanding to his martyrdom, and it is all clearly communicated to us, but a great deal of the action does not concern this although it is a small play. And as for poetries of the two poets. The poetry never flags in the *Samson*, it engages in every situation, it flows through every mind; but that in the *Murder* gives way twice to prose, and one of these times to a prose more than usually anomalous in a poetic drama. Becket preaches a last sermon, and the author provides him with a very fine one; but could not the poetry assimilate this occasion and produce a poetic homily? If the poet's denial of poetry is out of ecclesiastical considerations (saying here is an historical archbishop in his pulpit), this is a personal but not literary scruple. The other prose passage seems as freakish and insubordinate as anything ever in competent drama. It breaks in the first place with dramatic propriety. The four knights are just assassins, villains, nameless fellows, forces of evil, agents with a bad job to do. Suddenly, after the job is done, when the play is really about over, and the mind of the audience full of its central meaning, the author softens on behalf of his villains, or he wearies of his strictness in drama—at any rate he decides to characterize them, to make them somebodies, to give them a big scene; a gross disrespect to a dead archbishop, to say the least. And it breaks with the tone. The murderers convene the people and defend their act. Their speeches are not just prose, but actually modern mock-parliament hustings stuff, clever—if we were not rather too bewildered to understand it—and probably satirical.

> . . . In what we have done, and whatever you may think of it, we have been perfectly disinterested. (*The other Knights:* 'Hear! hear!') *We* are not getting anything out of this. We have much more to lose than to gain. We are four plain Englishmen who put our country first. I dare say we didn't make a very good impression when we came in. The fact is that we knew we had taken on a pretty stiff job; I'll only speak for myself, but I had drunk a good deal—I am not a drinking man ordinarily—to brace myself up for it. When you come to the point, it does go against the grain to kill an Archbishop, especially when you have been brought up in good Church traditions. So, if we seemed a bit rowdy, you will understand why it was; and for my part I am awfully sorry about it. We realized that it was our duty, but all the same we had to work ourselves up to it. And, as I said, *we* are not getting a penny out of this.

The note of this is like a note that Auden sounds, that most witty and far-gone modern poet; and a surprising, disconcerting note for this play, or for anything that is not by intention cynical and desperate. But now, and finally, even supposing the proses were out, what of the quality of the poetry? The proses don't exactly spoil a great poem, for the poetry itself is not quite sure and consistent. The poetry breaks. I won't quote from the song and dance which the drunken knights stage; that is beneath criticism. Take the choral passages, which run on to great length. Obviously, the women must be stopped from falling into a singsong, into a rigmarole of grief or terror; so there are times when the poet must increase the pace. (This poet would never tolerate monotony, he makes a point of variety, and rising and falling motions, he understands poetic composition.) The women have a sudden prescience of evil, and when they go to register it, it turns out that their force is just violence, not really poetic force. Like this:

I have smelt
Death in the rose, death in the hollyhock, sweet pea,
hyacinth, primrose and cowslip. I have seen
Trunk and horn, tusk and hoof, in odd places;
I have lain on the floor of the sea and breathed with the
breathing of the sea-anemone, swallowed with
ingurgitation of the sponge.
I have lain in the soil and criticized the worm. In the air
Flirted with the passage of the kite, I have plunged with
the kite and cowered with the wren. I have felt
The horn of the beetle, the scale of the viper, the mobile
hard insensitive skin of the elephant, the evasive flank
of the fish. I have smelt
Corruption in the dish, incense in the latrine, the sewer in

> the incense, the smell of sweet soap in the woodpath, a hellish sweet scent in the woodpath, while the ground heaved.

Which is only a part of a passage full of astonishing items in the listed or categorical manner, suggesting the wisdom of Pliny's natural history and the vocabulary of the King James Bible, and closing not at all prettily:

> What is woven on the loom of fate
> What is woven in the councils of princes
> Is woven also in our veins, our brains,
> Is woven like a pattern of living worms
> In the guts of the women of Canterbury.

This is a striking assemblage of poetic ingredients, at the best, and short of the highest poetry in the same degree perhaps as its loose metric is short of the firm work of the *Samson* chorics. And so to bed. On the conclusion, that there are features of Eliot's play not worthy of the analogues in the older tradition. That this comparison, which would be too hard on other moderns, is not kind even to Eliot. That the play might be very good by common modern standards, but Eliot knows how weak are modern standards. That with its "features" it might have done well even for the Elizabethan stage, but Eliot knows what a fatal turn for vaudeville that stage had.

The Cathartic Principle

It is mortifying when the critic finds himself hunting an excuse for talking about poetics, which are general, rather than about some poetry, which is particular.

I suppose our modern critics have learned to talk more closely about poems than their predecessors ever did. The closeness of Mr. Eliot in discussing a text may well be greater than anybody's before him, and he in turn may now be even exceeded in closeness by Mr. Blackmur, and perhaps others. These are close critics, and define our age as one of critical genius.

Mr. Blackmur, however, and even Mr. Eliot, had to change the style of their criticism, insensibly it may be, as they went along. Looking if possible ever more closely at their texts, at the same time they have seemed to find bigger and harder and more theoretical questions always being forced upon their attention. And why not? The good critic cannot stop with studying poetry, he must also study poetics. If he thinks he must puritanically abstain from all indulgence in the theory, the good critic may have to be a good little critic. Actually, it seems reasonable to suppose that no such critic exists. Theory, which is expectation, always determines criticism, and never more than when it is unconscious. The reputed condition of no-theory in the critic's mind is illusory, and a dangerous thing in this occupation, which demands the utmost general intelligence, including perfect self-consciousness.

I seem to feel that it is unfashionable for the critic to talk about theory by itself; I know that the time comes when he is obliged to do it. I think the taboo may have originated with Mr. Eliot, who speaks with what I take to be a Socratic irony about his own disinterest in theory; or in some narrow trades-unionism that the guild has adopted, perhaps by treaty with the professional æstheticians who resent poaching on their trade. At any rate, I seem to find my occasion in Sir Arthur Quiller-Couch's volume, "The Poet as Citizen, and Other Papers," and especially in the paper on the *Poetics* of Aristotle. It is evidently one of his lectures to the Cambridge undergraduates. It is indeed far from being a fresh examination of the thinking of Aristotle, being the act of a decent and never obstreperous guildsman. But it is the only contemporary piece of writing I can find to initiate some talk on a venerable but highly unsettled pair of questions: the question of catharsis, and the question of mimesis. They are unsettled even though they were handled in a matter-of-fact manner by the eminent Stagyrite—as he might easily have been called by Sir Arthur in the complacent prose which does refer to him as the Master.

I am advertising a certain impertinence on my part, thinking I have everything to gain if it turns out that I have overemphasized this tone in advance. But Sir Arthur is a great Victorian; rather, to try a more current name for a man of his robust temper and easy accomplishments, a great Liberal. Butcher is his authority for what Aristotle really said; Butcher could not endure to believe that Aristotle meant what he said. For Aristotle sounded cynical in his way of treating poetry, but there couldn't be anything really anti-poetic in his doctrine, since he was wise with all of human wisdom, and must have loved his poetry as he loved his sciences, and there are no real oppositions between them anyhow, and the good the true the beautiful are one, and we should all be happy. This sounds confused, but it may not be more than slightly in caricature of a cross-section of the academic Liberal mind.

Possibly it will not matter very much that Sir Arthur's view of Aristotle is so entirely suited to a certain handsome academic background; or that Butcher's view, upon which Sir Arthur's is based, is only a little more Aristotelian; nor will it matter even that Aristotle's view itself, construed this way or that, has been canonical ever since it was resurrected several centuries ago, if it is not a view that accords to art the dignity and meaning to which it is entitled.

Aristotle laid down two fundamental propositions, perhaps equally startling to each subsequent generation that has really looked at them. First, that art in form is a mimesis or imitation of reality; and, second, that at least one variety of art, or tragedy, has for its function the catharsis, or elimination from the mind by purging, of the emotions of pity and terror.

But catharsis is an ugly term, and pity if not terror is a noble thing, of which surely the more the better; and what sort of doctrine can this be? I shall follow Sir Arthur's order and examine the second proposition first.

The description of a work of art as a cathartic pill, by a philosopher who was son to the King's physician, has always been a stumbling-block. On the one hand, the name of Aristotle behind this remark is revered beyond any earthly name that Europe knows how to spell. On the other hand, there could not well be the occasion for a cathartic without there being a nasty and toxic excrement somewhere, and a state of disease resulting from its presence within the system; nor can the joy of art be anything but the pleasure that attends an act of elimination; and all the fine notions which Europeans have entertained so easily about their arts and artists must be dissipated. By this view poetry is not a pretty business; the best that can be said is that it takes the place of something worse.

A choice is indicated between the authority of Aristotle and the inherited European notions of art. But as a rule it is a choice which the academic authorities have not cared to make. They have preferred to saddle upon Aristotle certain "interpretations" which have for their object to make his view, which was explicit, cover and authorize their views, which are scarcely explicit and certainly very different. They have wanted to keep both their Aristotle and their art.

Sir Arthur derives from Butcher, and Butcher derives from a whole series of German writers, which would include Lessing, Schiller, Goethe, and Bernays. Another German series, which is related to this series as professionals are related to amateurs, would include Kant, Schelling, and Hegel. But when we run into a professional system of æsthetics we incline to stop; it is not entirely a gesture of cowardice. The critic can hardly run the risk of deferring to the professional philosopher. A professional philosophy tends to rise a little crazily upon its base, and after it has got a certain distance from the ground to collapse like Babel in a confusion of jargon. It has happened again and again in the history of thought. A school tumbles, and then thinking can begin all over again; and philosophy is cyclic in action, like business, and like civilization. It has to be renewed every generation or so; and it is not likely anyway that one generation can live on another's philosophy. We do well to go back to Aristotle, who was a pioneer in æsthetic theory, and a plain-talking workman. And to do this we must deliberately disrespect our Butchers and our literary and even professional Aristotelians.

The late Professor Bosanquet, whose *History of Æsthetic* is both learned and scrupulous, agreed with Bernays that Aristotle's view of catharsis was simply that of an act of elimination, and in the preface to the edition of 1894 remarked drily: "Professor Butcher has developed a modification of this view, which the student should learn from Professor Butcher's work." The student will probably think of Professor Butcher's view in these terms: Professor Butcher's modification of Aristotle.

This is Butcher:

> Tragedy, then, does more than effect the homeopathic cure of certain passions. Its function on this view is not merely to provide an outlet for pity and fear, but to provide for them a distinctively æsthetic satisfaction, to purify and clarify them by passing them through the medium of art.

It sounds as if an æsthetic outlet for the passions were nobler than an outlet in action, and a very fine thing in itself; but the æsthetic outlet was, for Aristotle, an outlet through representations or fictions, and therefore the most innocuous private backyard outlet that could be devised, much simpler and less expensive than an outlet through action. As for the purification and clarification, these are euphemistic terms, and when applied to the passions themselves, and not to the mind from which they are expelled, they read into the act of purging some grotesque complications.

Butcher again:

> The tragic catharsis requires that suffering shall be exhibited in one of its comprehensive aspects; that the deeds and fortunes of the actors shall attach themselves to larger issues, and the spectator himself be lifted above the special case, and brought face to face with universal law and the divine plan of the world.

The sentence occurs late in Butcher's chapter on "The Function of Tragedy"; by this time he has brought in all the Liberal ideology which Aristotle had spurned. There is not a passage in all the *Poetics* so pious and noble as this; so the tone is false. And the argument too, for Aristotle's emphasis on the probable and typical as the subject of tragedy was not for the purpose of talking about divine law, but for the purpose of explaining how the illusion of reality must be built up. On that topic he speculated like an expert; and it tickles anybody's ingenuity. Aristotle had in mind, I should think, that basic look or attitude of poetry which German æstheticians have called Schein (or semblance, or transparency), and which some æstheticians today refer to when they talk of æsthetic distance: you must see clearly that the work of art is fiction, not reality; yet you must be able to pretend it is reality; you must find its events and characters likely.

And here is Sir Arthur:

> Tragedy, by its doses of pity and terror, showing him [the man in the audience] overweening pride, ambition, lust, exaggerated in a spectacle of kings and princes, will teach him to discharge these accretions of self-pity, vaulting ambition, unreasonable terrors from his soul, and dismiss him with "calm of mind, all passion spent."

With the exception of the unreasonable terrors (which couldn't be too unreasonable, or they would not be likely) the accretions here consigned to the catharsis are gratuitous. By this account tragedy becomes the elimination of everything bad from the will, and the agent of general moral improvement. But this is not Aristotle's point; it was pity and terror that had to be eliminated, and for reasons which were not technically moral at all. Aristotle must have considered that pity and terror, if not periodically eliminated, would clog the system, produce paralysis, or "auto-intoxication" as we would say; for he approved tragedy in a doctor's terms.

Here is Sir Arthur on the catharsis that might be predicated of another art:

> Music, if I may use the illustration, corrects the sort of vocality to which unbridled man gives way in his bath.

The lecturer is being jolly here, so that perhaps it is not quite fair to suggest that he is off the point. Cathartic music was also approved by Aristotle, precisely like tragedy; we have this pronouncement in the *Politics*. It is a permitted indulgence, possibly an orgy, to which unbridled man is invited to give way, and in which certain passion will be got rid of so that it will not remain to trouble the routine of his life. Just as the matter of tragedy must be frightful if the passions of pity and fear are really to be purged, so the "enthusiasm" or mystical frenzy put into the music has to be extreme; the experience will then leave him relieved and easy, and permit the expectation that he will not sing in his bath at all.

These are typical of the passages, both oral and written, in which Aristotle's theory of tragedy is expounded in the English-speaking universities; though I know nothing of how it is done elsewhere. The feeling is, perhaps, that Aristotle expressed himself very sternly about the poor playwrights' function, but there is a scientific quality about it that is praiseworthy, while the expositors for their part must not let the poor playwrights down as these were noble men, and their works uplifting, and in short that everybody concerned must be all right. The expositors are not to be reproached because they want to present favorable views of an art, except so far as the views are muddled and not referred to basic principles, but because they ascribe to these views the paternity of Aristotle, whose teaching was quite otherwise.

Aristotle was temperamentally a naturalist, was in fact the first complete naturalist, and the father of the natural sciences. (This is not a private nor revolutionary judgment.) His system is positive; if examined comparatively it might yield a great deal of spiritual affinity with such nineteenth-century systems as that of Comte, or Spencer. He undertook to examine all the fundamental sciences, and to place them in precise relations with each other so that they would form a hierarchy of knowledge. Knowledge was of one kind essentially: the scientific. All individuals were subject to the law of classification under ascending types of universals; to receive their classifications, and therein to perish as individuals, was the honor which he was prepared to bestow upon them.

"Ascending types." For Aristotle's God is nothing miraculously revealed, and nothing discovered by some mystical communion; he is an entity inferentially established—the top of the hierarchy of substances. There is Nature (physical, vegetable, animal), and Man, and therefore God; it is a matter of completing your series. Aristotle was a magnificent naturalist but not much of a lover of nature. Now it seems probable that one of the consequences of a love of nature is that you imitate or represent it in some tangible forms, and in the works of imitation you have your arts. Another consequence might well be that you worship its Creator, and Prime Mover, and then you have your religion. Aristotle, the comprehensive schematizer, treats both arts and religion. But in the former treatment his method is reportorial and classificatory; the method of the naturalist. It is done with so little feeling that at this moment I, and perhaps my patient reader, are pondering the question whether he really had any particular liking for the thing he was handling. If the reader says that naturally he liked it, for who wouldn't, then I object that there is little sign of it in the tone of the performance; and if I claim that probably he cared little for it, or even disliked it, I cannot find that feeling registered in the tone either, though I make a point of a certain cynicism in his use of the figure of catharsis to describe it. And as for his treatment of God, and the absence of any trace of religious feeling in it, it might be instructive to superpose Lambda, the twelfth book of the *Metaphysics*, upon any of the source-books of the world's great religions. Capacious as Aristotle's mind is reputed to have been, there was no religious genius in it. He observes that men are enthusiasts, or filled with God-passion, and coolly gives them Phrygian music to eliminate it.

The limitations of Aristotle's mind are so apparent, if we look at it searchingly, that a curious thought will probably occur to us: the peculiar sentiment in which his name is held must have some special and indeed accidental cause. And so it has; the tender glow in which it is bathed is due to the act of the Roman Church, so warm and catholic in its humanity, so rich by its long accumulation of romantic dogmas, in taking that name into its keeping and sanctifying it. Hard as it is to view any world-event critically after it has come actually to pass, it still strikes us as one of the strange things in human history that the Church should have swallowed so greedily the *Summa Theologica* of Thomas. That work may be thought of as simply a very great *tour de force* and monument of learning, but it may also be regarded as a monument of naïveté; for in it the naturalism fathered by Aristotle and the dogma of Christianity seek to enter into a formal partnership. The principle of faith and the principle of science are wedded. It is rather like saying, The hospitable principle of true Catholicism and the rejective principle of Protestant Dissent. But it is a handsome alliance; perhaps a destinate one. Its consequences are difficult to discover precisely, I suppose, but I seem to have remarked as one of them that it has involved brilliant Roman intellectuals in considerable bewilderment ever since. It explains how, even today, you cannot have a complete discussion with a Roman; he shifts at will back and forth between reason and revelation. But surely another consequence has been that Aristotle, a rationalist, of low æsthetic and religious interest, has been substantially relieved of having to appear before the world in his true colors.

I have mentioned what Aristotle thought of enthusiasm, or religious frenzy, or, I think it may be called, mysticism. He detested it; and perhaps this might be expected, for it is not the sort of display that a natural scientist, reporting his own species, would be happy to find. Yet he found it natural, in the simple sense that the Greeks, much nearer to the Oriental than any modern Europeans, were powerfully given to it. He was therefore in the position of many doctors today who have to deal with ungovernable propensities. Enthusiasm was too strong and too common to be suppressed; therefore let it be authorized, and let the Greeks have their orgiastic rites periodically, in order to work it off and pass at least the interval periods in decency.

Closely associated with this technique for religion was the technique for art. (How close were religion and art with the Greeks is probably very well reflected by Nietzsche in his *Birth of Tragedy*.) There was not necessarily a religious frenzy enacted on the Greek stage, but there were at least scenes of secular horror, which could be described as inspiring pity and terror. Why did Greeks attend upon such scenes?

Because Greeks had another weakness: they were addicted to pity and terror. But it was so important that they should be delivered of this weakness that they might as well have their drama and get rid of it there; with the understanding that they would be the better citizens after such a debauch, or between debauches.

Aristotle's disapproval of pity and terror was deliberate and, I think, carefully sustained; for after discussing other matters he is careful to keep coming back to mention this again as the fundamental consideration; as if it were a text written on a blackboard to which he could point. The other matters here, of course, are the various features of drama, with which he shows a somewhat better than distinterested acquaintance. He is not only a penetrating critic of technique of all sorts, but a great admirer of good technique, even if I argue that he was theoretically cold to the general project to which this technique is working. I think we shall hardly find much more there than can be accounted for under the head of the love of a good scientist for a good job. Or we might express it this way. He has a sort of addiction to the drama, and is like some sober modern thinker, a scientist, let us say, who permits himself one single indulgence for relaxation, namely, the reading of detective stories, but while he is about it makes himself an authority on the subject, knowing all the good murder novels and the tricks of all the authors.

We go back and ask in what light precisely he

regarded pity and terror, then, if he did not want them. To determine this we must go beyond the letter of any of the texts in which he has mentioned them. Terror (or rather fear, the genus) is treated at great length in the *Nichomachean Ethics*, as well as courage, which is the proper conditioning of the mind between too much and too little fear. Both fear and pity are treated descriptively, with many examples, in the *Rhetoric*, where we are shown that the occasions of the two are the same. But the occasion discussed in the *Poetics* as found in the tragic plot is something very special: the spectacle of a fine and, ordinarily, royal man, with just enough human weakness to remind us of ourselves, suffering such ruin as no human contrivance can save him from and no sense of justice can allow. The commentary which the spectator is forced to make upon such a sight as this will have to do with the nature of God's world, the impotence of the moral order, and the fact of evil. If this is true, it is clear why pity and terror are distasteful to Aristotle. For he believes in his sciences, that is, in the acquisition of systematic knowledges and theoretical techniques, and in dutiful and effective living; these will fill up the whole of life if the citizen will allow them; nothing more is needed. But the sense of evil, if he indulges that, will paralyze him; the citizen of Aristotle's state has no business with brooding. We imagine Aristotle, on his part, doing little of this brooding; such a perfect and undeviating scientist he was, so firmly in possession of the secret of happiness. Nevertheless, he observed that men at large did plenty of it, and therefore he was prepared to give them public tragedies, or imitative spectacles, in which the injustice of the world-order might be concentrated for especial horror, on the theory that under such an administration the thing would hurt them least.

So music was to purge Greeks of their enthusiasm, and tragedy was to purge them of their sense of cosmic evil. But there were other arts, and even other literary arts. Did Aristotle intend these to be cathartic too?

The only literary art which Aristotle specifically describes as cathartic is tragedy; the only non-literary art is Phrygian music. Is the list arbitrary, and could it be expanded? I cannot think Aristotle at any point attends to the making of a true or inclusive list; he simply remarks about the cathartic function of tragedy when he is on that topic, and of Phrygian music in another connection.

In the *Politics* Aristotle plans his educational system in the tone of a sober thinker whose principal business is to work out the useful studies, but who then obliges himself to remember that his citizens will not be working all the time, and had better also be "educated for leisure"—the same argument which sober educators are using today. The dualism of work and play: that feels like a very modern idea, dating decidedly after the industrial revolution, yet it is as old as civilization, and states the whole misfortune of civilization, from which it does not occur to Aristotle that we shall ever be delivered, or for that matter that we need to be. (Civilization *is* an industrial revolution.) Nor will we be delivered, unless we shall be educated again into the kind of work that occupied our putative ancestors in a Golden Age: a work that rejected maximum efficiency as servile, and tempered itself constantly with play; a science that never forgot to be a poetry. Aristotle adopts the play-forms without much remark; they were all standardized in the life of well-bred young Greek gentlemen. But when he comes to Phrygian music, and to tragedy, he stops as if to say that here the violence hardly consists with mere pastime, but the violence may as well be conceded as indicating the existence of dangerous passion, and the arts in question will pass it off during the play-period, and leave the citizen ready for his business.

He must have come to the same conclusion about any art that threatened to take itself too seriously—if this threat had been raised in the discussion with his pupils, or if he himself had had more strength to think of it, and could have rounded off these late chapters in his philosophical system more completely.

And so, comedy, a spirited and possibly dangerous art. It is easy, on Aristotle's own principles, to discover the cathartic effect of comedy. But we have to remember that Greek comedy was devoted peculiarly to satire and lampoon. The romantic comedy which moderns know is simply the drama which begins as tragedy, by exciting the worst apprehensions, but weakens and at length permits the happy ending. Aristotle paid his respects to that as incompetent tragedy which produces no true catharsis. In comedy proper the subject was the ridiculous, and it exercised in the spectator the sense of the ridiculous. But this sense is analogous to pity and terror, in that it unfits a man for his duty; for there is implied in the citizen, if he goes about finding everything ridiculous, the belief that he is witnessing an irrational universe. Hence the need of catharsis through comedy. We are assisted in attributing this sort of reasoning to Aristotle because we know that Plato had discussed the habit of ridicule, or being a buffoon, and speculated on the effect that attendance on comedy might have upon it.

Of course his conclusion here, as with other forms of imitation, is very different from Aristotle's. Plato did not believe that any catharsis was effected by art, but that the passions affected by it were only encouraged. It was the view of a literal and uncompromising moralist. The Sunday-school superintendent is opposed to the doctor. Aristotle's opinion we have seen; it was that of a man with a medical training; it amounted to saying that people had better make the best of a delicate situation, and it was precisely like the point of view of a modern military authority legalizing prostitution in the neighborhood of the camp.

Then there was epic. It happens that Aristotle

discusses epic at some length in the *Poetics*, as a form which involves all the important features of tragedy, with certain characteristic or formal differences. The tragic sufferings are there, and the same sorts of occasion; that is, occasions that produce pity and terror, with the reservation that the action does not need to be so literally realistic, so immediately representative of the actual world, as the eye-witness effects in drama. We wonder why he does not talk about its cathartic action, and I think that theoretically there is no reason. But practically, epic poetry does not matter so much; the population does not rush to attend upon it as upon drama. Popular drama is the doctor's prescription for attending to pity and terror, but for anybody who takes his epic poetry seriously enough the doctor will certainly prescribe more epic poetry—provided the doctor knows where his prescription can be filled.

And what about that purest and slightest and most innocent form of poetry, the lyric? In his discussion of tragedy Aristotle insists that the songs and meters must be of the highest excellence, and he must have known that there were likely to be perfectly untragical songs in any tragedy, such as those in the *Œdipus at Colonus*. Did he think that, from his natural-scientist point of view, there was no possible harm in them? Or rather, conceived as cathartic agents, no possible good in them, no passion from which they would help to deliver the Greeks? It hardly seems possible to think he was so blind when we think of his sitting before Plato for twenty years and hearing Plato agitating himself over poetic performances of all kinds. He must have come to the conclusion that the passion of lyric poetry, the lyricism of it, was either dangerous to citizens or not dangerous; and that, if dangerous, as Plato said it was, it would best be handled by the liberal provision of lyric poetry. (For he and Plato might diagnose the disease the same way, and prescribe for it differently.)

Not Plato nor the Greek language had such a word as lyricism. But the passion behind the lyric poem is the pure act of mimesis, or imitation; that is all Plato says about it, but for a person with his metaphysical preferences that is saying enough. Poets and their audiences imitated persons, and then the art was drama, or epic. But they imitated even things; they indulged in the most unbecoming raptures of sympathy not only with the prince and the shepherd, but with the mountain and the sea, the sheep, the olive tree, and the nightingale. Then the art was the lyric. It may have looked like the last abdication of human dignity; mimesis in its most promiscuous application. It was for metaphysical reasons that Plato disapproved such imitations; he preferred to go behind the imitations to the actuals, and even behind the actuals to the Pure Ideas, which good and fortunate men by virtue of their divine nature were able to make out, and which were superior for their contemplation. Aristotle did not inherit all the detail of this prejudice but he probably inherited the prejudice: he must have disapproved of imitations where people became so addicted to them that it interfered with their labors.

So we shall have to look at the general doctrine of mimesis, or imitation: the passion or impulse that lies behind the very purest forms of art when no other impulses are discoverable there. There could not be a topic more important in the re-examination of æsthetic theory.

The Mimetic Principle

THE Greeks were not provided with a technical vocabulary with which to philosophize. Probably that is the attainment of races quite advanced in their linguistic. One of the consequences of this deficiency must have been that a well-spoken Greek could always feel free to do a little philosophizing as he passed. But another consequence was that you could never be sure at first sight just how philosophically some term was being employed. Did it bear a popular figurative racy sense, as if intending just to make the most of the single occasion, or did it intend to be used definitively and systematically in a close piece of reasoning? You had to have a good deal of the context to decide.

Catharsis was such a term—a medical word adapted by Aristotle to the description of the effect of tragedy. It is a hard word for the lovers and respecters of art to have to come to. It reflects the patronizing view of certain natural scientists, who have strenuous programmes in view for humanity, and tolerate the arts only for medical or sanitary reasons, and in consideration for the present weak state of the racial mind. (In the same way we have seen systems of legalized and regulated prostitution, meant to take charge of an excess of certain primitive energies; and systems of legalized and restricted liquor dispensaries.) It is tempting to think that Aristotle in springing his famous term upon the doctrinaires of poetry might have been only remarking something like this: "Tragedy certainly brings out the terror and the pity, no matter how hard the spectator is; it acts on these emotions as a dose of cathartic acts on the contents of the long intestine." And that would be all there was to it, though we might raise a question of his good taste. But no; Aristotle keeps using the word, returning to it, till we are obliged to concede that it has become a deliberate and technical term in his theory. He means it.

Even so, the ingenious interpreter—Butcher, Quiller-Couch, or one of hundreds of our professors of literature—will undertake to save tragedy, by the curious process of saving Aristotle from being a disparager of tragedy. For instance, by claiming that Aristotle never meant by catharsis to purge the soul of the terror and pity that were in the soul, but to purge these emotions of certain unholy elements (unspecified) which were in the emotions. But the harder we try to figure what this interpretation can mean, the more comical the image becomes; and, whatever the intellectual character of the interpreters may be, we know that Aristotle was not silly. Furthermore, he was fairly explicit. He justified tragedy and certain forms of music because they purged the soul of the noxious emotions fear, pity, and enthusiasm; and we know from many other contexts that he wanted the soul to be purged and clean, so that it might be up and doing, having in fact very splendid things before it to do.

The other great term in the Aristotelian æsthetic is likewise strange-sounding; it is mimesis, which certainly means imitation. It is not Aristotle's own term for the artistic act; he inherited it from Plato, and perhaps Plato took it out of the air. The identification of art with mimesis, the imitation of nature, was so fixed that the Greeks could not quite admit architecture into the company of the fine arts; on the ground that it was too industrial, not wanting simply to imitate nature, which would be to respect it, but to improve upon nature and use it.

I imagine mimesis was not such an obvious discovery, not a disaparaging one, and not without extreme significance for theory. We are told that the human infant up to a certain age is like the beasts in being unable to read painting, or photography: he cannot conceive that in addition to the natural object itself there may also be its artificial imitation; he has no functional need of the imitation as long as he has the original, and therefore cannot approve it or even attend to it. Our infant later makes acquaintance with imitations, as a matter of course; but with what intention? At first, it is likely, he employs the imitation for the sake of its illusion, as giving him in imagination the same satisfaction as the original might have given him in fact; that is, as a substitute for an original which he cannot have. This leads to the idea which even some adults nurse, that an artist is a man who makes an imitation because it is portable, and inexpensive; he can manage with it when he cannot have access to the original. The playwright can hardly arrange for a murder to be enacted as a public spectacle, for the sake of moral edification, but he may have one imitated on the stage. Many persons think it ought to be as "realistic" there as possible, with screams and gore, so that the spectator may forget it is only an imitation; whereas the Greeks, and the sophisticated populations generally, though not necessarily the modern ones, have liked their plays produced under severe restrictions which did not permit the spectator to be so stupid even if he wanted to; plays that were imitations undisguised.

And as for the painting: it perhaps does not occur to naïve persons that some painter from his window will command permanently his view of the city roofs, and yet be impelled to paint the imitation of it on a canvas beside the window, and to return again and again to the canvas in preference to the window as the occasion of his æsthetic experience. The studied æsthetician will admit to this fact, but will contend perhaps that the painting is better for the purpose than the view from the window, because the painting has suppressed something, or added something, or distorted something; being quite unable to conceive that its superiority may lie in the simple fact that it is the imitation of something rather than the original. An imitation is better than its original in one thing only: not being actual, it cannot be used, it can only be known. Art exists for knowledge, but nature is an object both to knowledge and to use; the latter disposition of nature includes that knowledge of it which is peculiarly scientific, and sometimes it is so imperious as to pre-empt all possibility of the former.

Unanimously, when the world of Greek art had come into being, and the age of reflection had arrived, the Greeks looked at the rich profusion and said, "This looks like imitation." If any testimony was lacking, Aristotle, colder and more objective in his views than most, was ready to supply it; he concurred with the other witnesses. The doctrine of mimesis was the foundation of the Greek æsthetic; it is probably the best foundation for any æsthetic. If it is dwelt upon, it will prompt within a little while all the important questions. Thus: What is the ontological status of an imitation as compared with original nature? What is its motive in terms of the will and affections? How does it contrast with the peculiar treatment which science gives to nature? What degree of accuracy and fidelity to detail is required in an imitation? Does the theory of imitation consist with our impression that a work of art is a work of "imagination" or "creation"? Finally (though these are not necessarily all the questions) there is a characteristic Aristotelian question: what good does it do to man, the lord of nature, the intelligence which is so much higher than nature? Some of the problems immediately suggested by mimesis are carefully formulated by Bosanquet in the Third Chapter of his *History of Æsthetic.*[1] But the Greeks, in failing to develop these problems, seem to be a disappointment to him. I think he goes too fast, and fails to receive the simple or commonsense meaning which the thing had for them.

Aristotle was an honest natural scientist, ambitious for the perfection of the human mind in reason, yet prepared to countenance whatever was common; he for his part looked over the Grecian artifacts, and round him like a shrewd anthropologist at human nature everywhere, and remarked that the love of imitation must be one of the universal human traits.

[1]About Bosanquet's admirable work: it is a history with a thesis. Bosanquet is just and patient in all his considerations, and his view of art is that of a perfect order of knowledge in which the object exhibits not only what is typical or universal (the aspect to which science attends) but also what is characteristic or private. He ignores, I think, the first of all the questions: why the laborious work of art at all? For nature, the original of art, invites of us the perfect act of knowledge, it is ready to exhibit both typical and characteristic. Hegelians, including even Bosanquet, have no real use for imitations and fine arts, because in their piety they expect the race to recover the power of perfect knowledge, and in this expectation they are deceived because they cannot read history. In all human history the dualism between science and art widens continually by reason of the aggressions of science. As science more and more completely reduces the world to its types and forms, art, replying, must invest it again with body. The one technical process requires the other. The artist resorts to the imitation because it is inviolable, and it is inviolable because it is not real. In strict theory it might be said that his purpose is to exhibit the typical along with the characteristic, but in view of his actual occasion it may be said much more simply to be: to exhibit the characteristic. He has no fear that the typical at this late date will be obscured.

We need not imagine that he regarded it as a fine one. But everybody liked to imitate; it was one of the specific marks of human nature, not found among the lower animals. And apparently the encounter with a good imitation gave pleasure, analogous perhaps to the pleasure given by a good scientific demonstration. A person recognized the object—in a painting, for example—and exclaimed, "This is the very man." Aristotle does not tell us what the speaker would have said upon making a corresponding identification in the work of science. But since the work of science is a work of classification in terms of universals, not a work of imitation in terms of particulars, Aristotle would certainly have found the speaker exclaiming, "This is the sort of person he is," or, "This is the very class for such an object." The Ἐκεῖνος (*ekeinos*) recognized in the imitation would become the οἷος (*hoios*) of the scientific description.

The distinction is one to be made and sensed powerfully; without it there is no difference between the characteristic activities of science and art. One of the features of Platonism, as in a different way of Aristotelianism, is its passionate preference for universals over particulars. It was because art was concerned with particulars that Plato rejected it, in those moments when he had the courage of his convictions, and banished the poets from his Republic. But Aristotle does not reject art; he is merely cold to it.

Idealism, the passion for universals, is so strong that it does not mind trying to appropriate art for its own purpose; the purpose being the communication of the ideas; of ideas and ideality in general, or of those special ideas which have a regulative or moral value in the determination of the persons who will receive them. Plato is a good example of the idealist surveying art with respect to both these uses.

He was interested first in a system of archetypal and ruling ideas which he contemplated with a fervor that was religious, or metaphysical, or both at once. He objectified his universals into gods, and thought of particulars as little creations thrown off by these splendid first causes. Aristotle was not so polite as this to the universals; he regarded them as only immanent in the particulars, yet, for practical purposes, as the indispensable instruments by which the mind acquired its hold of natural law and ordered the universe. Plato, Aristotle, the Hegelians, and many others related and unrelated, are quite alike in being unable to attach their interest to mere particulars, and disposed always to use them as the beginnings of a process destined to go "higher," "behind," or "further"; accordingly rather resentful of the seeming acquiescence of artists in particulars as something crude and philistine. Plato was an aggressive idealist with a head full of Big Ideas, and he could see no sense in the artist's imitation of natural objects as if that were something to do. And he could not discover that the artist was doing anything else. I suggest that the artist is not necessarily doing anything else.

Plato was also a moralist; but what is a moralist? A moralist is a valuable but pedestrian species of idealist; his interest is not in the private, particular, and characteristic, but in one variety of the standard, universal, and ideal. What Plato as moralist would have asked of the artist seemed not to involve any fatal concession. Let him imitate decent things and moral persons, in order to induce moral interests in the public audience. Plato could have used some good moral art in his Republic, when he is tinkering with its educational scheme. So can Aristotle, who also has an educational scheme, but he knows better than to discuss it under the head of æsthetic. (Æsthetic is as ultimate a term as moral. It is questionable whether the Republic can stand for the subordination of æsthetic to moral, or *vice versa* for that matter, in the education of its citizens at one stage or another; whether the didacticism which college Seniors resent in the presentation of the arts ought not to be resented also by small boys in grammar schools.) But Plato could not lay his hands on the artists who would co-operate with him in this worthy purpose. Homer played him false. The modern Plato will say of course, "Hire the artist." Unfortunately the hireling artists are not generally the best artists, they do not turn out well; what they gain in ideality they lose in particularity and verisimilitude, and nature is not fairly imitated. You cannot make a contract with your artist, or if you do you cannot enforce it. If dedicated in the first place to the imitation of nature, then he will have to let morality take its chance in the exhibit.

In the name of their high and mighty causes, the world's moralists have always wanted to coerce the artists, and failing that to canonize or excommunicate them according to performance. Each age has its examples of this termagant Platonism. Today it is perhaps the admirable Neo-Humanists who most deserve, in view of their eminence, to be cited. They censor literature on the basis of its conformity with Aristotelian ethics, a course upon which Aristotle himself had not the temerity to venture. There was Mr. Babbitt. And now there is Mr. Shafer, in the Summer Number of *The American Review*, defining with his orthodoxy the function of literary scholarship, and commending what he strangely regards as a "new movement" that is actually practising it:

> Literature has never been, is not, and, for better or for worse, can never be simply a photographic reflection of life. As an art it unescapably interprets life, directly or by implication, in re-creating it. Hence there is always present—deeply and darkly imbedded it may be, but, still, actively present—in literature of whatsoever kind a hard core or backbone of philosophical ideas. And it is this central characteristic of literature which gives it importance and makes it a uniquely valuable means of liberal education. The revolutionary movement under discussion, moreover, is simply a determined effort to act in accordance with fact, to study and teach literature in close relation with philosophical ideas and their vicissitudes. Many students, to be sure, have long been concerned with the history of thought and with its critical presentation. What is new and, indeed, nothing less than

revolutionary is the attempt to bring philosophical ideas, in the broadest sense of the term, and literature together, for the light each may shed on the other.

I am not sure how new this last sort of thing is; nearly every systematic application of scholarship as we understand the term today is relatively new; but the study of literature with some sort of respect to its philosophical ideas is hoary with age. The scholars involved in it are the faithful old horses that turn the ancient mill.

On the other hand, one knows that Neo-Humanism is too various and living a movement to be confined within this practice. I recall reading long ago some passage from a Shelburne essay in which Mr. More cited feelingly a bit of "romantic" verse about nature, and made only a little remark, which was to this effect: "Here we have that strange beauty so dear to the modern spirit." His refusal to go farther seemed eloquent of the conviction that in a case like this no "hard core of philosophical ideas" was discoverable. He was confronted with a simple piece of imitation which was self-sufficient, and deprived missionary idealists of their professional function.

Aristotle did not talk about art as an imitation of nature trying surreptitiously to convey the metaphysical "Behind-nature"; that is, suggesting Big Ideas, or a Higher Reality, or a Concrete Universal or Absolute. It simply didn't. Nor did he regard art as entertaining that easier and not less noble project, the communication of moral universals. Nor, finally, did he think of it as a handmaiden to science (which he loved), busying itself in supplying case-illustrations for common universals of any sort. He was a fairer surveyor of art-works than some modern sociologists of my acquaintance who use contemporary literature as their case-book, and seem to think it was composed for this express purpose and their express benefit. Fairer than many professors of literature, who solicit the acquiescence of their colleagues in the study of letters on the ground that it teaches so much history, economics, biology, philosophy, and psychology. It is true that any particular, including the one imitated in the art-work, will illustrate a number of universal laws, but it exists in its own right and not for the sake of illustraion. An illustration is just an instance, but an art-object is an individual.

I am aware that it is commonly said, by Butcher for example, that Aristotle required the artistic imitation to emphasize the typical and to eliminate the local and characteristic; which would be, precisely, to pass into the mode of being an instance or illustration. I do not think this is so. The imitation had to look natural and not strange; that is about the substance of Aristotle on this point. If poetry is truer than history in his estimation, it is because of his understanding of history. History is either a compilation of marvels, as in Herodotus, whom Aristotle cites, or it is science pursuing a thread of ideas by an abstraction as perfect as possible; in neither sense an imitation of nature. Compare it with fiction; or compare the documentary sources of Shakespeare's *Histories* with the thing he at length learned to make of them when he freed the imitative or imaginative impulse from deference to what we call historical "authority." Aristotle asserts that the hero must not be too wonderful or we shall not find him like enough to ourselves to arouse the pity and the terror; that is, to feel the force of an imitation. His discussions of probability are by way of improvising a calculus of verisimilitude. The fact is that he assumed as too certain to be questioned the intention of the imitation to tell the truth. He was fully prepared to defend its truth even though it might be charged that it did not literally represent anything discoverable on earth; as when it represented a human action in which the gods participated. The last section of the *Poetics* contains much common sense on this point.

There are two ways of transcribing nature, and between them they exhaust the possibilities of formal cognition. One is by the graphs or formulas that record the universal relations, the "cores of constancy," in nature; and very useful instruments they are, constituting all that we include under science. The word physics means "naturalism," or the knowledge of nature; it is clear that the scientific transcript has appropriated for its own monopoly the great name, leaving it to be inferred perhaps that no other study is really about nature. The other transcript, however, is the one which makes imitations or full representations of nature, and these are the works of art.

The two forms are highly specialized; they have doubtless been so in any society civilized enough to leave its records behind. Thus the scientist knows how to interest himself strictly in the universals; he admits no individuals to his attention, except as the initiation of new studies or the verification of old ones. The artist interests himself entirely in individuals, or he should; if he does not really, he should declare himself a scientist or a moralist. But—I hasten to say this—if he is of a mature or observant mind his individuals are likely to be rich and suggestive; tempting the scientist, and the critic infirm of æsthetic purpose, to translate them into interesting generalities and in doing so to lose them as individuals.

Mimesis is as much a passion as science is; perhaps it would be more dignified to say, as normal and as human. It aims at a kind of cognition which is unknown to pure science and which grows increasingly difficult for us in practical life. It wants to recover its individuals, abandoned in science, in business, and in affairs. It has a right to them, since they are there. Individuals are ultimate, Aristotle conceded, though the interest he took in them was cursory; he had a temperamental deficiency, and many moralists, scientists, and philosophers share it with him.

Here is a book of physics, filled with characteristic scientific transcripts of nature. And here is a page packed systematically with symbolic denotations, some of them numerals, others letters, both Greek and English. It is a ballistic table, telling the path a bullet will take when fired from a rifle, through miles of air-resistance; under what skies, we wonder, over what conformations of landscape, towards the heart of a person having what personality? The transcript is perfectly silent about such details, about "setting"; it is not proposing to imitate nature. In arriving at it, as we gather from the story, the scientists used a great many particulars, but only under the aspect of "cases"; that is, with an eye not for their particularity but for their generality; putting them in fact into laboratories and stripping off as much particularity as human wit could devise. And now that the transcript is complete, the particulars are dismissed, and the mind rests in its lordly table of universals. Or perhaps there is another use for it; perhaps we are going to shoot a bullet. We give the bullet the direction and velocity that the table prescribes, and the calculation succeeds; "beautifully," I think the word is; the bullet goes home. But even in this crowning operation the bullet, the gun, and the enemy himself are without individuality for us. The bullet for example is any bullet in its class; as meek a little instance as ever experienced the stupendous exaltation of being subsumed under its class concept. In this case, as throughout our practice, the object we attend to is just as abstract as the rule by which we handle it. The particularity of nature is certainly not a property which we are forced to be at pains to respect.

But apparently we return periodically to nature

for precisely this purpose. Here is another transcript —an imitation of nature representing, let us say, to make the example as easy as possible, a landscape in water-colors. The thing recorded here has an infinite degree of particularity. If we care to attend to it, it is by a labor of love, for we cannot possibly use it. We trace its configuration, colors, planes, objects, till we are satisfied; that is, till we have received the sense of how infinite this particularity may be. It is probably a wholesome exercise for us, since it may help to keep us sane and "realistic" beneath the incessant bombardment of bragging public universals; it improves our understanding of nature. But we do not have to improvise a motive. We are drawn to the painting by an interest which, as Aristotle said, is common to mankind but not given to the beasts. We are sensible of the love behind all the labor that the patient artist has put into his work, and we respond with ours.

I use the term love not too fearfully. The motive for engaging upon the other kind of transcript is glory, according to the metaphysical idealists; duty, according to the moralists; power, according to the practical scientists; and, for the appetites, greed. It is a single series, and as opposite to love at one place as another.

One of the trick questions in æsthetic suggests itself here, with its proper answer in terms of Greek mimesis. Why would not a photograph of the landscape be superior to the painting? The idea is that the photograph would be both fuller and more accurate as a presentation. But it is not fuller, strictly speaking; to be particular at all is to be infinitely full of detail, and one infinite is as full as another. And it does not matter about the meticulous accuracy of representation; the painter's free version may be for the eye the more probable version and the more convincing, by the same reasoning by which Aristotle prefers poetry as an imitation to history. The great difference between the two versions lies elsewhere. The photograph is a mechanical imitation perhaps but not a psychological one. It was obtained by the adjustment of the camera and the pressing of the button, actions so characterless that they indicate no attitude necessarily, no love; but the painting reveals the arduous pains of the artist. We are excited by these pains proportionately; they give the painting its human value; and carrying this principle a little farther, we never discover in the work a single evidence of technique, discipline, deliberation, without having the value enhanced further. The pains measure the love.

Artists have left massive labors behind them; they are still at work. The imitative impulse is frequently disparaged, but I suppose in respectable circles there is no such arrogance as to deny it, or to propose to strip it from the various context of the human will. Aristotle did not have this kind of recklessness.

Nevertheless I am very much interested in a final question: what would be the connection between catharsis, the medical function of certain arts, and mimesis, the impulse behind the arts in general, including the most innocent ones? I am afraid there is an ominous connection.

Disapproving terror, pity, and enthusiasm, Aristotle authorized a specific horrendous art and a specific orgiastic music to purge off these emotions periodically and fit the spectator for responsible public life as citizen, scientist, worker, or whatever career was sober and desirable. But the artistic impulse was ubiquitous. It gave rise to arts of all sorts, big ones and little ones, here and there; based simply on the imitation of nature, and that did not seem so direful a thing; yet it meant the love of nature, and that reversed the ordinary relation that Aristotle desired between man and his environment.

He left the arts standing; he sanctioned them. But perhaps this course was subtler than it seems and not merely an acquiescence, not a compliment. Did not the arts, with their discharge of love in so many harmless conventional forms, act as cathartics to purify the souls of citizens? I believe so; I mean that probably this was the action that must have been imputed to them by Aristotle, if he had been challenged to define their action, and also that it must have been imputed with reason. For the worst thing about our situation as civilized beings—it grows worse with the progress of our civilization—is evidently that we vent our love of nature not in the usual actions of living but in the random and occasional moments when we indulge ourselves in the special arts; that the arts are intercalary and non-participating experiences in respect to the "serious" side of life; and that most of the time we are not human, so far as it is a mark of the human dignity to respect and know the particularity by which we are so constantly environed. We live, by inveterate habit now, abstractedly. If we were better men we might do with less of art, for we should take care to find æsthetic enjoyment in everything we were doing. But we should probably also have to do with less of science; that is, with an impure and less effective science.

The doctrine of catharsis denies nothing human, but it is far from being indifferent or non-partisan as between the modes of human activity. Its object is to intensify the æsthetic moment in order to minimize and localize it, and clear the way for the scientific moment.

Sentimental Exercise

IT HAS been demonstrated that the race is capable of heroisms and persistences—as capable upon occasion as other animals are. There are always leaders coming forward to enlist us on principle as against any milder standards; they view us, and themselves, as creatures devoted to policies just as aggressive and nearly as simple as those of the animals. They feel that it is a dispersal of our strength to practise the arts, which are worthless in any practical sense, or to have "personal" relations, which are sentimental and not based on strict principle. Publicly theirs is a common type of mentality, but in private life there is almost nobody who can stimulate his own action up to the strenuousness they require. On the contrary, there is a furtive understanding that they may be a little primitive in their view of human nature. One of their commonest aspects, for example, is as economists.

"Business is business," they say. We have business men reiterating it for us, querulously, and forever. They mean that business is an empire of thought very pure, effective if we will let it take its course, and jealous of softening foreign influences. It is based on the single principle of exchanging utilities, with the understanding that the only utilities that can be put up for exchange are those which have public or market value.

But it has been observed that values are declared sometimes which fall beyond the scale of business valuation, unless they fall below it. These are the sentimental values. For example: a rich man declines the market price for the village house where he originated, probably will not consider any price for it, nor does it matter how shabby the old place is, nor how impossible for his living in now. Another man cherishes just as irrationally an old horse or an old wife. It may be lucky for the old house, horse, or wife that it is exempted from the fair or market valuation. But business, which deals only in the uses of things, does not know in the least why exemption should be made. Business may not care very much, either, since there evidently are utilities enough left to trade on, and the unaccountable element introduced by sentiment does not interfere fatally with turnover.

Theoretically, sentiment is a painful exception to business sense; its existence should indicate to business-minded persons that their science may be perfect in itself, but that the public for whom it is intended does not respond to it; that psychologically its basis must be a little wrong. And not being safe for business, this public will not be safe for science, and for rational institutions generally. Probably in the last resort it is the sentimentality of the personnel that forever postpones the millennium of welfare and reason, often and lovingly as that has been described by lawgivers like Plato, Hegel, Comte, Marx, and many modern planners.

We need not expect help in this matter from business. But psychology, or perhaps I should say anthropology, the theory of man as a peculiar species of animal, should both know and care about a phenomenon so strange. What is the matter with men that it is not in them to be perfect economists and to submit themselves with full consent to business, or, for that matter, to science, statecraft, and all the forms of power? In the machinery of the human mind a screw is loose, so that action manifests a vagary; that may be the supposition. But one may suggest that humanity will hardly manage to tighten its own screws; the looseness may be built in. What, then, is sentiment?

It is common as a pattern of mental behavior; it is merely unaccounted for in our ordinary understanding of the mind. So far as my reading goes, the literature of psychology does not yet offer any real treatment of sentiment in this sense of the term. Very properly, the new science is now epistemologizing with all its might; that is, forming a theory of how we acquire our knowledges, and what their historical relations are to one another. But psychology has not yet caught up with the task of describing the gross and obvious patterns of knowledge, and appears to be too young to have attended to one so delicate and, in an age when knowledge is instructed that it must be "instrumental," so useless. I improvise a little outline treatment of sentiment, and it will have to be dangerously sketchy.

We may begin by considering the kind of object upon which sentiment fixes. I will offer a progressive definition of this object, designed to emphasize the feature which might be most startling to conventional psychologists. Sentiment certainly attaches often to the following object:

First, to an old or familiar object, with which we have had a great deal of traffic. Familiarity enforces acquaintance. If we had to encounter the object only a few times, we might very well fail to know it. Sentiment requires close acquaintance with the object.

Second, to a familiar object when it is gone, so that the sentiment is only for a remembered object, as idle a thing as that; better, perhaps, to a familiar object when it is antiquated, when in respect to utility it has been superseded by another object. Sentiment is very close to nostalgia. This inclines us to say that it is for a loved object, but that would be a kind of tautology. The love is the sentiment, and could not have got there before the sentiment did. As often as not, the sentiment comes in without intention on our part; it is spontaneous and involuntary. We started in to use the object, we conclude by loving it. Sometimes this unforeseen consequence is in defiance of the character under which we conceived ourselves, for we had proposed to be hard and businesslike. But there it is.

Third, to a familiar and vanished object, or a familiar and antiquated one, which is highly individual, or has a great deal of quality over and above that which constitutes its utility. The sentiment likes to dwell on those of its properties in which its utility never resided. (Item: the old oaken bucket, which is iron-bound, moss-covered, and so on.) Sentiment is non-utilitarian though it attaches to useful objects. Professional psychologists may be inclined to reject the thought of a man's attending by preference to the features of an object which are unuseful; can an animal then forget his biological good, or prefer less prosperity to more? But we do so, and I should think that we need not quite be charged with madness, though we have forgotten to be efficient. We are merely out for æsthetic experience. Sentiment is not useful, nor moral, nor even disciplinary; it is simply æsthetic.

And therefore, fourth, and finally, to a familiar, antiquated, individual object which requires of us only that it be known. Love, respect, tenderness, fixation upon the object, all these terms would define an attitude in subjective or emotional terms, but they mean nothing until we study what we are really trying to do with the object. We are only trying to know it as a complete or individual object; and, as a corollary undoubtedly, to protect it against our other and predatory kind of knowledge which would reduce it to its mere utility. Sentiment is æsthetic, æsthetic is cognitive, and the cognition is of the object as an individual. And this, I imagine, is all the mystery that will be discovered in sentiment.

We review the matter of the old house and the rich

man's foolish regard for it. When a boy, it may be supposed that he made the round of ordinary uses of his father's house, and was led at first into a smug proprietary attitude that would care to know the house only to the extent of how to use it. Perhaps he was precocious, and manifested at a tender age that unadulterated business sense which was destined to make him rich, and estimated the house properly as but a poor one, worth two or three thousand dollars. He went in and out of its doors, worked and rested and ate and slept in it, heated it and cooled it, lighted it and darkened it, had specific uses for its different spaces, and on the whole, had more transactions with it than with any other object of like dimensions in the world. Therefore he could not avoid a thorough acquaintance with it. Its walls were of wood or of brick, it had ten rooms or six, hardwood floors or carpets, plumbing fixtures or pails and washstands; it does not matter in the least; law cannot prescribe a kind for its detail, of which the peculiar character was that it exceeded or spilled over any classification to which it might have been submitted. The point is that it refused to exhibit its utilitarian features without exhibiting also its others. And now the house takes Christian revenge for all its indignities in this manner: when he thinks of it he recalls its qualitative superfluity, and acknowledges it as an energetic and independent object; it is more than the sum of all its uses, of which the value might be conveniently reckoned as equal to the price of any other real property in its class. It fixed its innocent or unuseful features upon his mind without his knowing or intending it. (I think psychology can describe that process.) They are there overpoweringly now; a remembered look it wore from some angle of vision exterior or interior; its relation to the trees or slopes of its terrain; a kind of surface its walls had here or there; some uncompromising oddities, as a floor board above the level of the others, or the special darkness of a hall, or the ridiculous shape of its banisters. Sharp specific items like these, because of their perfect inconsequence for utility, may define for him an untutored but authentic kind of æsthetic experience, and might become invidious if he tried to publish them as universal æsthetic patterns. Probably he will not do this, considering his present showy associations, but will keep his sentimental indulgences to himself; suspecting perhaps, however, that his associates will be having sentimental indulgences of their own, just as private and homely as his are. But under whatever features the house appears to him now, they will be features peculiar to that house and not to be expected in any other house that he might attempt to substitute. Utilities are replaceable and negotiable, and this fact is the life of trade; but complete or individual objects are not, and those with which we become familiar must not be sold.

The range of objects which invite this slow growth and final crystallization of a sentiment is wide. Mere things invite it, as we have seen; things big and variegated, to which we have often had to go for our practical needs. Collective institutions do—the school, the town, the church, the state—provided they are important practically, and we have routine dealings with them. And certainly persons do, and compose a set of objects available beyond all others. We consider it monstrous if one does not acquire a sentimental regard for one's brother, or mother, or close business associate; close principally in the sense that we frequently encounter the person and become acquainted with his personal quality. But one is not immoral, strictly speaking, in not having this regard; Kant would have thought that having it was a moral weakness. One is simply deficient æsthetically. The person who is its object should be indeed a person, or one inclined to assert his own personality. A person may yield more complacently to our wishes than any other object, and be construed as a purer utility, because he may improve his natural passivity as an object by his conscious effort to please us. But he may also be more difficult for us, reinforcing his natural resistance as an object by wilful opposition to being used. For perfectly obliging persons we may have an intellectual indifference, or at best a feeling of gratitude, which is not enough. Gratitude is probably a moral development, causing us to say: "I will be good to you because you have been good to me." It shames us into that degree of altruism. But it is consistent with a complete lack of interest in the private being of the object, and is not a cognitive interest.

Sentimental and æsthetic attitudes, the two being

nearly indistinguishable in their final analysis, go together to make an opposite to the utilitarian and scientific attitudes and, I think, to the moral ones. Professed utilitarians, positivists, and moralists—all persons who professionally ignore individuals and concern themselves with classes and laws—are in the position of trying to suppress a substantial group of experiences.

Therefore a remark, which might be of philosophical importance. The fact seems to be that this first group of attitudes, the sentimental and æsthetic, alone in our mental economy is systematically devoted to salvaging for knowledge one of the two prime aspects of the world: the full private content of its specimen parts or objects, which is a rich field of contingency. The other group will usually admit for theory that the world wears this aspect in some measure, but in practice devotes itself to burying the actual objects beneath certain respective and convenient species, as if the actual objects were indifferent. It would like to observe the world only in its other partial aspect, the "cosmic" one, as an intelligible system of kinds and laws, without that stubborn crowded privateness which every object will manifest if we care to look.

From this point of view, we should estimate the function and status of the scientists. Devoted scientists, those who in private life do not relax from their professional obligations, are deficient exemplars of humanity. I cannot help it if this seems to disparage them, for it is on the ground of a certain obtuseness which is in their habit of mind. It is the same obtuseness which animals characteristically display. In fact, it is easy to see that the pure animal appetites proceed by precisely that strict technique which is praised by idealistic philosophers and practised by good scientists: the discipline of withdrawing attention from the privacy of the object and fixing it upon the object's kind or class. The surplus of qualities that makes the object more than a member of its class must be suppressed equally by the effective animal and by the efficient scientist. A hungry man, for example, must perform an animal act, and it is interesting to watch him do it, and to observe that the obtuseness cannot be eliminated. The man wants food, and goes into his favorite restaurant to get it. The service in that restaurant may be dainty, and the music soft, while the man may be the most nice and cultivated person imaginable, yet the act still manifests its animal logic, which is the logic of science. Imagine this conversation between the man and his obliging waiter.

Waiter: "Good evening, sir. Here is your regular seat, sir. And what will it be this evening?"

Man: "I am very hungry. What would you recommend?"

Waiter: "Our steaks are very fine today. I would suggest a porterhouse."

Man: "Very well. A big tender one."

Waiter: "How will you have it, sir?"

Man: "Medium done."

Waiter: "With butter on it, sir?"

Man: "Yes, and serve it hot."

Waiter: "Any other directions, sir?"

Man: "No, of course not. What other directions are you talking about?"

Waiter (smiling and rubbing his hands): "I was wondering, sir, if you would care to identify the particular steak. Perhaps you may prefer to eat a steak which you have already become acquainted with, and conceived a sentimental fondness for. It might seem rather more delicate than just ordering up any steak, or a steak with which you have had no previous relations."

Man: "I have had no relations with your steaks, and no desire to make any except in so far as eating one is concerned. What are you talking about? You are a fool. Hurry up with my order."

Waiter: "Very good, sir. No offense meant, sir."

Quite precisely, this waiter is a fool; except for the bare chance that he may be a witty sentimentalist trying to shame a gentleman with a healthy animal appetite; perhaps a Doctor of Philosophy for whom the New Deal's re-employment service has found a job that is not congenial. The gentleman's selectivity as a fine animal is considerable. There are hundreds of dishes, but he selects a certain kind of dish, and there are many ways of preparing it, but he knows the way he wants. But, for that matter, no animal applies the rule of indifference completely when he seeks his satisfactions, or he would perish; he applies it within limits which depend on his natural constitution and which with respect to the infinity of the objective world are arbitrary. Philosophers understand that, and know that even with the most catholic tastes they cannot view the world at all except under an extreme bias which is constitutional to their peculiarly human nature. Of course, some animals are more fastidious than others; this gentleman, for example. But cutting the thing as fine as possible, his election is still within the kinds of food and not within the privacies of actual objects. It is absurd to suggest that hunger aims at a private object rather than an object as commodity, or kind. If the gentleman had an affection for a certain cow, or ox, which is entirely conceivable, he would not like to be reminded of his eating it. It is true that there is a restaurant in Denver which invites the customer wanting a fish for his dinner to go to the pool in the lobby and have the attendant catch in a net the fish of his choice. But this is not out of regard for the individuality of any fish. On the contrary, it is a mildly teasing procedure in which the customer is invited first to sense tentatively the sort of individuality which the fish might eventually assume for him if he went on to a real acquaintance with it, and then quickly to destroy the fish because it falls within a category of edibles. It is a cynical or anti-sentimental foray in which animal practice claims another victim, and this victim is made to symbolize ever so slightly the world of individual objects.

All natural or biological needs involve this obtuseness. The infant must not come into the world with a sentimental fixation upon the exclusive person of his mother, or infant mortality would be much higher than it is. What he demands is simply a series of commodities, like milk, warmth, care, within an infinitely wide range of negotiability or substitution. His individual attachments come later; historically they are "higher." As an animal he is automatically equipped with the scientific attitude, if it is right to define that as the gift of fixing exclusively upon class properties. I imagine that I, personally, was in no sense exceptional in being brought up with a glowing appreciation of the noble character of scientists; and that I was not exceptional, either, in being disturbed by an insidious disloyalty which presented itself in this form: how is it that the scientist, wonderfully precise at defining the kind of the object, which is its public character, never bothers himself, as the poet or painter or even the sensitive humble person does, with its whole or private character? Or why is science so brutal and blind? But the answer lies in our confessing frankly what science is undertaking to do. Animal need is always gross enough to get its satisfaction out of a certain minimal quality in the object; science, an instrumental knowledge serving animal need, has devoted itself to the study of this minimal character; and the minimal character, defined and extracted by science, becomes, precisely, a public character and a commodity.

An intelligent individual attachment is, therefore, a great luxury, permitted to human animals almost exclusively, because they are the only animals who can afford it with safety. Our trained scientists, marvellously advanced in technique beyond the lower animals, are valuable to us because their labors improve the production and distribution of necessary commodities and also, incidentally, enable us to indulge sentiment without having suicidal mania. But to the extent that they have to stick to their profession and devote themselves only to commodities, they are scapegoats. They are not infants or lower animals, but it is their fixed rule to pursue the general rather than the particular, and that is exactly the infantile or animal practice. To use an adult and human analogy, under this restriction they are like the sailor in port who pursues generic rather than individual woman.

Persons who are idealists by conviction, or on general principles, are simply monsters. (I mean the Platonic ones, the kind of idealists who worship universals, laws, Platonic ideas, reason, the "immaterial.") Unlike the scientists, they are of no use, yet they wilfully take upon themselves the disability of the scientists, and not only do they have no pleasure in individual objects but they even solicit the public to make the same sacrifice. Professionally they tend to be philosophers, preachers, and educators, and from these positions infect us with their vice and keep us, in the range of our interest, more like animals and less like human beings than we have a right to be.

I do not think the term vice is too strong. With the reservation that I have already indicated, that it must not affect our animal security, I take it that knowledge of individuals is a definite though not an animal good. Its pursuit is a development of interest that we come to if we are advanced human beings; that is, if we live in a society efficiently served by its scientists with respect to its animal needs, and if we indulge an interest that is normal and seems appropriate to our special advantages. Why should we indulge it? I think the final and irrefutable answer is simply that we want to. Certainly we have the organs for it, and in the sentiments and the arts we have the technique, and it does no harm. This knowledge adds a great complication to the theoretical constitution of the world, but what is metaphysics for? And to the theoretical constitution of the mind, but what is psychology for? It is likely to be resented by those theorists whose theory has no room for its implications. These are such as positivists (scientists who assert that there is no knowledge but scientific knowledge) and Platonic idealists. They would like to enforce an arbitrary simplification upon us, rather than to recognize a complication which exists. And that is repressive and anti-humanistic, or, in short, it is vicious. We may assume that it is vain.

The moralists are in rather a stronger position; they are like the scientists, definitely useful. The term moral is elusive, if we look at the literature of the subject. But whenever it receives a specific meaning, it turns out to have nothing particularly to do with the range of our cognitive interest, adding nothing to knowledge, and burdening only the will. The Golden Rule may be taken as a formulation of the moral impulse. If we want something more technical, there is Kant, who formulated the Supreme Law of Pure Practical Reason in these terms: "Act so that the maxims of your will may be in perfect harmony with a universal system of laws." Equally from Kant's extended discussion of his law and from the stiff details of his private moral life do we receive the impression that morality is simply the faculty, partly native and partly acquired, for treating our animal selves as indifferent instances of the human family, entitled to nothing better than the other instances are. Science produces commodities, and morality sees that they are fairly evenly distributed. The latter is very nearly as essential as the former to our security, and therefore to our being in a position to afford the æsthetic luxuries. Morality is heroic, but it does not widen or alter the form of our knowledge.

Returning to the sentiments. They will arise involuntarily if they have to, as if the exuberance of objective nature had refused to stay quiet and not to impress itself upon our consciousness. They will push their way into the dominating patterns of thought before we have suspected their existence, and even though we might have willed them away if we could. But it is poor strategy for their apologist to make too much of this side of the matter, and probably I have made that mistake. For not all persons are so surly as to resist them. Most well-bred persons deliberately set in to plant, water, and honor them, and are rewarded by having their minds converted into gardens. The civilized tradition instructs us in sentiments, and history records them in many charming pictures. They are the flowers of civilization, if that term will stand for what is fragrant and useless; and I suppose they do best when nourished by properties and privacies, and by rites or ceremonies which pay no dividends and must look stupid to utilitarians. I think this means that they bloom preferably out of the corners of bourgeois institutions; these have the merit of being loose and comfortable, not too abstract nor too efficient for the human nature which has to adapt itself to them.

It will probably be agreed that women have much more aptitude for the cultivation of sentiments than men do; and this would be because women have been exempted from the binding obligations of economic production and planning. A good housewife, unless she is enslaved by excessive drudgery, finds even in her tasks an interest that is always changing yet needs never fail; for she makes it a point—or allows her own nature unconsciously to make it—not to have merely useful or abstract relations with the things and persons of her ménage, but to seek in addition a delicious knowledge of them as individual objects. She likes to "treat" them in such a way as to subordinate their utility and bring out their individual quality. She arranges and decorates her house, she makes her meals simulate the formal rather than the economic occasions of society, and her interest in dress becomes the pursuit of lines, colors, textures that are mostly irrelevant to utility. Her moments, if I can imagine them, are not likely to have the poverty to which the processes of males are characteristically bound.

But sentiments are available to men also if they like, and usually they are inevitable. For business men there is always the chance, for example, that a friendship will intrude itself. Aristotle paid honor to friendship and discussed it at almost disproportionate length, under a leading conception that may seem peculiar: as the occasion of a great extension of knowledge. The parties are interested in each other; that is, each in the other's complex of personality. In conversation and companionship these complexes are explored. If the interest is not a cognitive one, I believe the phenomenon of friendship is unaccountable.

And there is, of course, love, for both sexes, in the romantic sense, an experience which bourgeois tradition supports with every possible recommendation. The parties have such an imperious animal use for each other that the romantic relation had better be encouraged. The so-called social proprieties, the rites of betrothal and marriage, and the rule of monogamy, are the formal safeguards. Under these auspices the beloved object is the object of a knowledge immeasurably wider than the awareness of his functional utilities. Here, as in all appetites that the cunning human animal seeks to gratify, only more so than usual, the strength of the natural emotion seems so disproportionate to the simplicity of the function as to suggest the desirability of finding a much more substantial object; namely, the personal and not the functional object. As the Aristotelians honor friendship, the Platonists and Neo-Platonists honor love, and Milton is in the orthodox tradition when he represents the care that Adam and Eve took to increase the range of their relation and to complicate biological love with much "rational discourse." Justifying their nuptial rites, when conducted on these principles, he exclaims:

> Here Love his golden shafts imploies, and lights
> His sovran Lamp, and waves his purple wings,
> Reigns here and revels;

which as a piece of description is nonsense to a pair of merely animal lovers.

But tradition justifies the formal arts as much as the sentiments; they are alternative forms of æsthetic knowledge. In actual fact, I think the sentiments furnish the race with a much larger volume of this experience than the arts do. This ought to be a sufficient excuse for an essay in æsthetics which scarcely mentions the arts. Another excuse is that it is peculiarly the sentiments, not the arts, that have been neglected in the theory. If they, too, pursue æsthetic effects, they have not commonly been reported in that sense by æstheticians, any more than by general psychologists. The two forms do not necessarily exclude each other, like rivals. Artists and lovers of art may be gifted at sentiment as well as not, and persons with developed sentiments may or may not have much understanding of the arts.

The differences are easy ones. We have a sentiment for an object which has been before us for a long time, but the artist, with his superior flexibility of mind, may represent in short order an object whose acquaintance he has freshly made. Our sentiment, or knowledge of the object, simply grows, and it may be involuntary; but in art the subject is quite aware of what knowledge he seeks, and obtains it by an intense effort of concentration. And the knowledge which may be inarticulate and only half-conscious in sentiment becomes explicit in the work of art. The creation of art, or the understanding of it by its public, requires a skill that the whole population is far from possessing. But sentiment, which must be fairly universal, may be perfect in attitude and intention only; it does only the best it can.

Art is capable of such a masterly grip upon its object—in the poem, in the painting—that its critics have an interesting term which they use sometimes to disparage certain inferior performances: these are "sentimental." They mean, I think, that the artist has the right sentiment for the object, but articulates the object no better than a man who has merely the sentiment. Unable to communicate the precise object, he would communicate at least his feeling for it, or his election of it as an object, and he is right in assuming that feelings are contagious among spontaneous persons. So he points reverently to it, and indicates the state of his own affections, and leaves us to explore the object mostly for ourselves.

The works of art are specially brilliant but detached fragments of knowledge. It is the sentiments which attend us daily, and keep us constantly, or at least recurrently, up to the decent level of our historic humanity.

The Tense of Poetry

THE text will have to come out of—Tennyson. But not from just either, indifferently, of the contrasted personalities that can be identified under that name; not from the exemplary laureate, of orotund and mildly official strains. Rather from the Tennyson who was temperamentally, like most of the profounder poets, melancholic; who did not entirely reconcile himself to the creature comforts of his century, was nostalgic almost to the point of bitterness, and puzzled about the source of his resentment. No philosophical psychologist, so far as I know—and no other kind of psychologist will do—has speculated seriously upon that oppression of spirit which is celebrated in the "Tears, Idle Tears."

Anticipating this more expert analysis, it occurs to me that we have here a first-class instance of the poet sensible of wrongs which time has inflicted upon him; but subtle wrongs, scarcely permitting of definition; not defined for the poet. Why the tears? "I know not what they mean." Flowing from what wound? "From the depths of some divine despair." The poet can tell, however, the sort of occasion upon which they arise:

> In looking on the happy Autumn-fields,
> And thinking of the days that are no more.

The fine spectacle produces a homesickness, not clearly directed. What days are referred to?

Now the scene which prompts the tears is as gentle, and presumably as pleasant, as any of the aspects which nature wears. But lest it appear that he grieves because he is reminded of some simple loss particularly associated with it, like the death of a sweetheart or a parent, or the alienation of the property, or even because it provokes him to some bourgeois and much-parodied sentiment about the passing of his youth, he gives other occasions provocative equally: the ship coming up over the horizon, the sound of the bird to the awaking ears at dawn. It really does not matter so much about the occasions, except for the consideration that they all seem remarkably innocent and charming; but what they produce is not joy so much as sadness.

Nostalgia is frequent with poets; it is the subject I wish to examine. But it occurs to them in two different ways, of which this is only one. It calls from them a tribute to the vague undated past; a sense that life somehow used to be happier, that life now is scarcely tolerable; that we have gone from bad to worse. And this results in reflective or "philosophical" poetry. Parallel with the present poem are such poems as Wordsworth's idealization of the dimly recalled excellence of the child-state. This poetry is more ruminative than creative, and not of the ultimate order of artistic objectivity.

The other nostalgia does not discuss itself, nor

brood over the whole vague past, but recovers out of the past the specific experience, and out of that makes the poem. Its performance is sharp, dramatic, brilliant Of this order are most poems, perhaps. Tennyson writes them. He is continually going back to the simpler world of the past, though it may be of the racial past rather than his own private one, and elaborating with love its occasions: in "Mariana," which is medieval, or in "Lotus Eaters" and "Ulysses," which are Greek.

A poem like Keats's "Grecian Urn" is of course a mixture; it offers a specific situation, but reflects upon it as the example of how art salvages the image of happiness out of the stream of time, and makes of it—not the happiness but the image—a monument and a reproach.

The poetic reflection and the poetic re-creation: we will keep them both. The first offers a document for æsthetic theory; it illuminates the second. Tennyson is saying in the poem about the tears: This is the sort of obsession which the poets have to carry; this is the attitude of the modern poet to his present; this is serious, it looks bad, make what you can of it.

2

Poets would not have to direct their attention to the past if they could find their poetry in the present; they would not revive the dead and gone if they did not find the living and actual too prosy.

Poetry is a kind of language, and therefore a kind

of experience. It distinguishes itself by an act of will from prose, which is also a language and an experience. Probably that is its whole intention. If there were no prose, there would not have to be a poetry; and the more ubiquitous the tyranny of the prose, the more necessary it is to undertake the poetry, and the harder.

The history of the race in this matter might seem to us, if we cared to reconstruct it, to run through three periods, as follows:

First a Golden Age, such as Ovid describes; or a Garden of Eden period, if we prefer to dwell on a fuller version which we have sometimes liked to claim as our special inheritance; a period in which there was only one language. Call it the age of neither prose nor poetry, or the age when prose and poetry were one. It was certainly a prehistoric period; it exists only as a legend, or as an atavistic memory if such a thing is possible. (It seems possible to the extent that we recapitulate in our private development the history of the race.) And referring back to the past, it cannot easily be referred to the future, as a prospect to which we are approaching again. The dualism in our lives, the vicissitude of prose and poetry, has set, and can scarcely go back into the undifferentiated unity of experience.

Second, the historical epochs, when prose—the language spoken by business, morality, science—has existed in steadily increasing efficiency or purity; and when—for this had to follow immediately—poetry has arisen by an effort to stand beside it, or against it. All the periods we are familiar with have had this double character.

But third, an occasional late or "modern" age, like the present one for our society, when poetry has had to torture itself, becoming difficult and strange, in order to be poetry at all; that is, when it has been all but impossible for it to establish its own identity as other than prose, and to offer the advantages which we require when we wish to resort to poetry. Prose marches right along, a perfect serial progress, finding each step easier than the last one. Poetry fights against an increasing resistance. The resistance is located, if we like, in the objects that refuse to submit themselves to poetical treatment because they have already been experienced prosily; the agents of prose, who are all over the earth, having successively invaded every field of objects that has occurred to them as worth claiming. Or it is located, if we prefer, in our own minds, which have acquired such a prose habit that those parts which are not active in prose are thoroughly suppressed, and can hardly break through and exercise themselves.

We alternate between prose and poetry, and neither one, for quite different reasons, is a sufficient and proper experience. But I suggest, in parenthesis, that we can support life if we must on this dualistic diet. It is not necessary to be panicky about it. It may be that we wrench ourselves with some violence from prose to poetry, and then slip back into the prose, both modes being less than satisfactory, yet both when put together managing to involve all our powers. It seems that we know little but dualisms, pluralisms, successions, the discharge *seriatim* of quite different functions, in these longitudes. Philosophically we are always crying out for the perfect integers of a monistic experience, the all-at-once, but though we can conceive them we have them very rarely if ever. Yet we survive.

3

It is probably impossible to enforce the distinction between prose and poetry, or science and poetry, upon persons who have not discovered it for themselves. But it is an ancient distinction. The legend of the Garden of Eden is concerned with it, telling, I think, how prose made its appearance in the world. (I suppose it tells something; this venerable piece of symbolic Oriental wisdom could not likely have been so childish as the ordinary Occidental interpretations of it.) The tree of knowledge from which man abstained originally, and in abstaining perpetuated his happy state, was the tree of prose; that is, of knowledge as technique and knowledge as power, of all those hard calculations by which he could have set in to act more effectively upon nature. But if he really abstained, it was for an earliest period only, and a short one—really a period that we must regard as inferential, and highly fanciful. Adam soon ate of the fruit, whereupon his history started, and became the only kind of history which the race has really known. Now God had not meant in his providence that Adam should saddle himself with the responsibility of the specific prose knowledges. God, assisted by His angels, was willing to know and manage the causes of things, a task too painful for human strength, and to operate the difficult universe according to the laws of maximum efficiency and perfect harmony. (I am informed that the universe is operated along these lines.) The role which He assigned to Adam was of an economic simplicity amounting to amateurism: to keep and dress the garden. It took no technique, involved only what today we should call unskilled labor, and that of a kind permitting what modern labor has almost universally renounced: enjoyment, or free sensibility. Probably this labor did not even invite distinction as contrasting especially with play, or leisure. But Adam repudiated this role and undertook the specialized and efficient functions. Regretfully, and it would seem a little ironically, God acquainted him with the direful consequences, and made to Himself a remark which it is hard to understand:

> 22. Behold, the man is become as one of us, to know good and evil; and now, lest he put forth his hand, and take also of the tree of life, and eat, and live forever:
>
> 23. Therefore the Lord God sent him forth from the Garden of Eden, to till the ground from whence he was taken.

The Lord God seems to be observing that man has involved himself in the toils of time, the consciousness of mortality, and nostalgia; that he will learn eventually to sigh with Tennyson,

> O Death in Life, the days that are no more!

"To know good and evil": Adam enters now upon the moralistic stage; which seems to his historian an evolution, a disintegration, a decadence from his nobler estate. Originally, one day unfolded filially and blissfully from a previous day, Adam taking them as they came, accepting the massive experiences they brought, with unlimited sensibility. But now begin criticism, choice, exclusion, and denial, all provoked by the insidious little worm named "ought"; now comes the drive of the efficiencies, producing instantly just those inhibitions which will culminate in the extreme self-tortures of Puritanism, or for that matter in the incredible labors of a Ford factory employee of the twentieth century A. D. Lugubrious outlook, for a Creator who had meant kindly.

At any rate, the idea was that man thereupon entered upon his famous upward career, which may be defined as that of a technician. His record has been one of wonderful progress in his prose, or in his acquisition of the techniques. It has also been one of an ever-sharpening dualism, or disintegration. He has had to be at one moment an efficient fellow (scientist, economist, and so on) and at the next moment, by a difficult and awkward effort at compensation, a poet. Usually, it may be supposed, he has been the prose man for three or four moments, the poet for one moment. We hear in certain branches of learning about the "lags," or unequal rates of development as between different features of an organic assemblage. Probably the stubbornest lag in human history has been the lag of poetry, trying to keep up with prose, and falling always a little farther behind.

4

It is unfortunate, but it must be conceded that the state of the original Adam is not the happiness that has been supposed; that the idea we have formed of it is an unsound inference. That flattering moment in the career of the race does not answer to logic. Adam, in the absence of technical thought-processes, was incapable of a distinguished æsthetic experience. No percept without a concept, sharp percepts mean sharp concepts, rich percepts mean a multiplicity of concepts; and lacking the latter he could not have had the former, and his integral or unitary experience could not have been like the thing exhibited in the work of art, but must have resembled the life of the uninformed child, or even that of the insensitive beasts. The brilliant effect we admire in a poem is the result of compounding many prose effects, and technical or specific ones. The business of poetry, in fact, is to take the technical prose effect, which is hard, and soften or dissolve it in a total experience.

But here is a paradox. The possibility of poetry depended on an event that carried also the possibility of its destruction. The technical knowledges give rise to poetry, and submit to it for a time, then they go on their way too fast for poetry to keep up with them. Sensibility implies efficiency, but the efficiency becomes an end in itself, and does not any more intend to be picked up and completed by sensibility. Though Lucretius may have felt assured that the contemporary science was capable of a poetic rendering, and though Wordsworth, confronted by the much more formidable science of his day, was not sufficiently apprehensive but hoped that the poetry would always, and automatically, arise which could follow it up and express it, we know definitely now that no such thing is possible. There are hundreds of common techniques which are entirely too technical for poetry to handle, and which will never surrender a scrap of their technicality in the interest of poetry. Efficiency has outdistanced sensibility.

Rebels, Utopians, in the recklessly efficient societies, appeal to an age of innocence as prior to all efficiency; but what they really mean is an age when sensibility and efficiency were equal, and married, and had the prescriptive respect of husband and wife for one another. They deceive themselves in thinking that happiness obtained best before the cruel husband appeared at all, or when he was but an infant; it could not have been marriage with the husband lacking, or between children whose sexual distinctiveness was not yet realized.

The loving reconstruction of the idyllic state is one of those feats of anachronism, by which we would recover all the privileges and cancel all the disadvantages of an extant culture, when they are equally the consequence of one historic movement. To put this more circumstantially, and in terms for the present occasion:[1] Adam could not have been anything so admirable as an ante-bellum Louisiana planter. He could not have smoked cigars, nor trimmed his beard, nor had money and accounts, nor, in the modern sense, travelled, nor sat on the piazza reading the newspaper, nor savored in one intelligent breath the magnolias on the lawn and the odors from his kitchen, nor comforted himself with allegiance to any cause or principle, church or state, nor raised cotton or known the uses of it, nor enjoyed any one of those pointed "interests" whose sum is what we generally mean by civilization. Likewise every modern malcontent must assure himself that, in whatever choice local fashion he may represent to himself the happiness of life as it might be, original man did not have it.

When the pursuit of the techniques presents itself to sensitive moderns as having gone much too far, and too much by itself, they resent it excessively, and without qualification cry against science, specialization, "industrialism," or whatever the term be under which the formidable abstract techniques present themselves; they declare they would sweep the damned thing clean away. This is a violent reaction, and if successful would destroy the thing we want as well

[1]This paper appeared in one of the first issues of *The Southern Review*, at Baton Rouge.

as the thing we hate. More temperate would be the policy of not sweeping anything away before we asked precisely wherein science had failed to proceed *pari passu* with sensibility, and in what recent actions had removed itself to where sensibility could not reach it. That question itself might not be quite intelligible, and therefore answerable, in all cases. To act upon it would not be suicidal, though it would be sufficiently heroic. The action would be dictated by regard for the total economy.

This latter action is exactly what the creative poets, in their harmless make-believe, perform every day. They abandon the barrens of science—the areas not accessible to sensibility—and turn backward; they go till they reach some point where the totalitarian mind is still capable of assimilating its sciences. But the former action, the cutting off of science at its roots, is what the poets in their reflective moments like to brood upon.

5

Opposed to the intuition of the poets, who locate happiness in the past, and whose poetry recovers it out of the past if it can, is the view that it lies in the future, in front of a steady line of march which is called evolution. This view, if we consider the common drift of the testimony upon the issue, is heresy.

A heretic poet appears occasionally. Tennyson, whose sense of the thing as a spontaneous poet is intuitive and certain, is intimidated by the argument of scientists who know nothing about the psychology of happiness, and allows himself to "look forward." But Shelley is much more aggressive. A rationalist (see *The Necessity of Atheism*), personally versed in the scientific technique, a false or at least a biased theorist about the meaning of poetry, yet tortured like the other romantic poets by the tyranny of an age of prose, his career is not self-consistent. He never conceded that the health of poetry and the independent career of science were antithetical, and he could look to the future for the return of the Golden Age. His program, with a little patting down and fixing, is like a premature piece of Marxianism, as follows. Production, under the law of maximum efficiency; what a desolate area of prose! Distribution, under the law of love; now we applaud. Consumption, under the law of beauty; which is very fine if we can believe in it. The combination pictures very well the Shelley about whom everybody eventually has to ask himself the question: Would he really have matured if he had lived to attain the years of wisdom? But his poetry is, frequently, poetry, and it is in spite of his philosophy. His discomforts, as actually attached to the car of progress, are as authentic as anybody's, and express themselves in many "lines written in dejection," like the following:

> I could lie down like a tired child
> And weep away this life of care.

The Furies did not overlook this confident young man.

Wordsworth has less power of specific poetry, but a much better sense of its meaning. In his famous Preface he is repeatedly on the verge of laying down the principle that poetry looks necessarily to the past. For example, he says poetry is essentially an emotion *recollected*, it is not itself the original emotion; and in defiance of his contention about the power of poetry to assimilate any act of science, he argues on behalf of *humble and rustic life*, as its field, a policy which must bear the odium of being a regression, and to the smart among his contemporary readers did bear it.

Whatever certain poets may think, we cannot well rule out of court the nostalgia which is so commonly associated with poetry. Under its influence we may talk and think a little wildly about the "scenes of my childhood," and when called upon to be particular, we may fix it absurdly upon a lot of respective old oaken buckets. Such items are at least beyond reproach in the quality of their innocence; they stand probably for the whole fringe of our former outraged consciousness, or rather even for the major wealth of its content, which our technical procedures brushed too hastily aside. It is attended, one might argue, by the sense of sin, but probably sin not so much personal as racial, inherited, original. It may even be that nostalgia is nothing less than the concrete form of our time-sense. The basis of that sense becomes in this event a biological experience: the outrage performed upon one function of the mind, the æsthetic, by the progress of the other function, the efficient. This may be the natural history behind the formidable metaphysical concept of time; the concept might in this way define itself for us essentially, or internally, and not have to wait upon our external or material deprivations before it formed within our heads. I imagine such an account, if really eligible, would not be surprising to modern psychologists, who are very daring.

The biological intuition, concerning what has happened to us in the course of our progress, is necessarily correct if it is true that the evolutionary process is always from the generic to the specific, from the undifferentiated function to the definition of parts and the division of labor. In view of this common biological understanding I am unable to see how monistic philosophers, religionists, scientists if they bother about such things, and sometimes poets, can assume that we are moving toward, not away from, the birth of an integral mind in which our split personalities will be healed. There is nothing forward-looking about a nostalgia.

6

But all this has to do with the philosophical thesis, a very broad thing, which the poets entertain, and the lovers of poetry, with various degrees of explicitude. We ask what the specific poems, the ones that we cherish as perfect creations, are doing. I should say that they are dramatizing the past.

Prose has dominated the marketplace, the senate, the camp, the executive offices, the laboratories, the learned professions, and nearly all the public occasions. It is the language of the actual. Poetry has had to resort to—the stage. The stage may or may not be symbolic of all the artistic activities, but certainly it symbolizes poetry. The stage is not real life but make-believe; which is another way of saying that it handles the past, and in particular those clearly marked alternative paths which we came to in the past but did not take. On the stage are only actors; they transact business which is only "business," or simulated action, and they read their lines from a book. Now we may go about during the day and observe how men of action transact the business of life, or as men of action ourselves we probably know quite well how it is done: we know that we do not transact it right. So on the stage the actors are trying to show us, and we are crowding the hall trying to discover, from watching them, just how we would have transacted certain businesses if we had been integers, and not actual historic men; that is, alternations of business man and unhappy resentful æsthetic man by turns. Even if the business is murder, we should transact it in the manner of Othello, with fury, pity, horror, love, and circumstance, and not, let us say, in the professional and infra-human manner of Chapman or Dillinger. The stage shows how to enjoy business while transacting it; and to enjoy means technically, I believe, to transact with the whole of our being, and to make the transaction lack nothing of being a completely expressive experience.

A courtier in a play is represented as remarking that all the world is a stage; it suited his character to say this, for he was a person of no account in the world of affairs. A poet-king similarly announced that life is but a walking shadow, a poor player strutting his stage; the announcement came at a moment when the poetry was gaining on the kingship, and about to put it out of business. The reality of life suddenly vacated its usual aspect of efficient action and became poetry—the diffused and inclusive experience, nothing less. But the poet-king was a character in a play, in a poem; the actual ones are not generally like that. If they are, it may be apprehended that they will not long maintain their crowns. In practice the law of efficiency prevails, the poetry is pushed unceremoniously into the closet; to be rescued with sufficient difficulty later, when it can do no harm, because the occasion is safely past.

Poems are little dramas, exhibiting actions in complete settings rather than pure or efficient actions. We shall return presently to the dramatic characteristics of poetry.

Our arts, certainly our poems, should fill us with pride because they furnish our perfect experiences. But they fill us also with mortification because they are not actual experiences. If we regard them in a certain mood, say when the heat of action is upon us, they look like the exercises of children, showing what might have been. Participating in the show which is poetry, we expel the taint of original sin and restore to our minds freedom and integrity. Very good. But we are forced to note presently, when we go out of the theatre, that it was only make-believe, and, as we go down the same street by which we came, that we are again the heirs of history, and fallen men.

The tense of poetry is the past. More accurately, it is the pluperfect—the apodosis of a contrary-to-fact condition. The fullness of sensibility which attends the action in poetry is "true," which means that it is "recovered," which means that it had a sort of existence in the actual past; but that was a furtive one, from which attention was withheld, so that it registered only upon the faithful and disregarded camera of memory. In the poetry which goes back and seeks it, it is crowned with its dignity.

7

The efficient self pursues its way, which is economical with respect to the attainment of its specific goals, and wasteful with respect to the wealth of the successive situations through which it passes; a Sherman marching through a Georgia and destroying what he cannot use. But when it goes into camp for a day the æsthetic self, which has had very little part in directing so urgent a march, steals back upon the route, and here or there finds a place to stop, to make its peace with the violated region, and to enjoy the country.

This is figurative; and the figure may not work to the last detail. The point is that poetry retraces a certain line of progress and builds its own triumphant monuments somewhere in the superseded past. A question or two arises for the critic. First, in what spirit does this handsome gratification take place?

Poetry knows both pleasure and pain. The pleasure amounts to mirth, to an almost pure irresponsible joy, in some poems. The poet has forgotten the fatal tense and is almost completely under the spell of the illusion; just as there are writers of historical narrative who drop into the "historical present" and hypnotize themselves into such a lively impression of the events that they do not remember that these happened long ago and are no longer really accessible to experience. This is, on the whole, the "natural" or unreflective kind of poetry. It is not common in the "modern" periods, when poets realize poetry only by strenuous effort, and cannot be unaware of the technique of illusion by which, at one and the same time, we remark both that it is sustained and that its reality is vitiated. Melancholy and bitterness inform this kind of poetry; though it might be argued that when it is most successful the joy is intenser because we sense it as especially precarious.

The pain and the pleasure are intangibles; they may limit each other, or perhaps they may co-exist marvellously; their determination requires a better calculus than the psychologists have been able to provide.

An easier question is this one: At what point on the return is poetry to stop? The answer is, certainly, that it stops where it pleases, always provided that it pleases to stop where there is really a stopping-place.

Poets go back a long way, in excessive revulsion against the prose techniques, or they refuse to go very far, if stubbornly determined to bridge, and not merely to forget, the dichotomy that holds the mind apart. A succession of poetries might perhaps be arranged, not necessarily according to the chronology of composition, which would recapitulate all the substantial stages in the development of the individual mind; or for that matter of civilization. There are species of poetry addressed to adults which are so childish as to lay themselves open to suspicion by the morbid pathologists of being instances of infantilism. There is a predisposition on the part of poets to employ the "little" word; it seems a natural alternative to the technical jargon of the high-powered prose processes, but evidently poetry does not require it in some given overwhelming proportion to the polysyllabic constituents.

Poetry also chooses according to its taste among the broad historical or evolutionary stages. Accordingly it goes pastoral (Theocritus and Spenser); goes humble and rustic (Wordsworth) and goes humorous and rustic (Frost). It still fancies occasional Ptolemaic effects in an age of Copernicanism and, worse still, relativity. In a period when manners decayed, and the relations between the sexes were marked by grossness, the poets with finer sensibilities addressed to their imaginary ladies sequences of sonnets which recovered the highly ingenuous language of the courts of love: Elizabethan Petrarchism. When the Christian mysteries are dissipated under Protestant naturalism, English-speaking poets return to the age of miracles as Greeks, or as mediæval Romans; and when these recourses are unavailing, they try occult symbolism; sometimes it is the real or historic thing (the Masonic-Rosicrucian-Cabalist article: practised by A. E., Yeats, Eliot, if I am not mistaken), sometimes it is a private system (Blake), and sometimes perhaps it is a fraud and a pretense. (I confess I have suspected the late E. A. Robinson's inconclusive intimations in this direction of being faked; but then the plight of a religious poet in an age of reason is desperate; the honest Wordsworth himself could not find an objective expression.)

We survey these and other returns common to poets with misgivings. Is this as close as poetry can come to expressing the actual contemporary mind, which bristles with its prose techniques? Can poetry save nothing of the modern learning? I imagine that no very positive reassurance is possible.

The poetry which makes the manliest effort to be contemporary, and to retreat as little as possible upon the road that has been travelled, is like that of the so-called metaphysical school of the seventeenth century. It is being tried today by poets who are the real outposts of the poetic movement. I refer of course to the daring with which such poets attempt to furnish the comprehensive area of consciousness without rejecting all the pure prose terms, so that scraps of technical learning appear there along with the simple sensibles and do not seem foreign; as if we were at home at last with our modern accomplishments. A poetic experience of this kind is exhilarating. If the future of poetry is immense, this is the bold policy which it may have to pursue.

But I do not mean to seem too convinced about the immensity.

8

Drama is a good symbol for poetry, but it is really something closer than a symbol. Poetry is not literally drama; at least it does not have to be, and usually it is not specific drama, being a form of expression far freer and subtler. But historically and logically it looks like a derivative of drama. It maintains faithfully certain dramatic features. The poet does not speak in his own but in an assumed character, and not in the actual but in an assumed situation, and the first thing we do as readers of poetry is to determine precisely what character and what situation are assumed. In this examination lies the possibility of critical understanding and at the same time of the illusion and the enjoyment.

If a poem is not a drama proper, it may be said to be a dramatic monologue. This is the literary type, in an accurate yet flexible sense; whose pattern or outline can be made out in objective poems; and Browning only literalized and made readier for the platform of the concert hall the thing that had always been the poem's lawful form. For poetry must have discovered early that it was not necessarily an enterprise for a company, with a stage to fit out, and parts to work up, and the image of actual life to labor out in much detail and with much paraphernalia. A single performer could manage with an impersonation, or with what we call today a reading. This was enough to release him from his actual or prose self and to induce poetic experience.

There is not time to test this thesis laboriously. For a very easy case we recall that the Elizabethan poets often said to themselves: Let us play at shepherds. Hence the individual pastorals. The pastoral poet became a shepherd, sporting with a shepherdess, playing on his pipe, talking about fame and fate, plucking the flowers and moralizing the landscape; incidentally telling his sheep. Thus the Passionate Shepherd to his Love:

> Come live with me and be my love,
> And we will all the pleasures prove.

With regard to this my friend, Mr. George Gullette, notes: "Nobody who read this was simple enough to suppose from it that Marlowe, the author, was intent on seducing the British maidens." Marlowe was only impersonating a shepherd, and doing it neatly; had to do it, because he really failed in love, and failed in business, in that sense in which we have all failed at our economic and animal roles, even where we have been most successful—for the reason that we construed them prosily, or under the aspect of efficiency.

But there are many other parts besides the shepherd's which poets have assumed. Sometimes they are very subtle, yet they register distinctly a unitary personality; if they do not, there are always critics acute enough to expose their departures from what is appropriate to the "tone," or the "situation."

9

Expanding the idea of the dramatic monologue, we may in conclusion briefly examine the poetic technique. Retiring from his prose character, assuming a part not his own (but not so alien to his past that he cannot enter into it with detailed understanding), the poet commits himself to a poetic experience. Under what rules does he work? It should not seem too remarkable that the poet flying from the techniques appears to embrace one of his own making, and a hard one. The poet requires a technique for escaping techniques.

For poetry is an artifice, practised with an adult cunning. It is the failing of most æsthetic philosophies that their consideration is almost entirely of æsthetic experience in general, not of the enormously sophisticated work of art. Croce, for example, does not seem to suspect that the pre-logical experience of the child differs from the mature and sometimes desperate adventures of the artist; he says nothing about the genesis of art, nor its epistemological status as a construct. Yet, though we may envy the child his æsthetic experience, it is too plain that we seek for ourselves one of which he could have no conception, and that this is the one which ought to make the really interesting chapters of a treatise on æsthetics. It is as if the æstheticians had never experienced the urgencies nor understood the tricks of artists, and, seeing with how easy and theoretical an account of the matter they are satisfied, as if they had failed to note some obvious implications in the product; so that the dominion of this realm of speculation promises to pass from the philosophers to the mere psychologists precisely as some of these latter have said. The former talk about æsthetic experience, which is abstract; the latter examine the works of art.

I run the risk of making the formula too simple, but I suggest that the technique of writing poetry falls under two prescripts.

First, the poet puts on the mask. It places him before his public—and in his own mind for that matter—as an anonymous person and not as himself. The mask covers his face sufficiently to conceal his actual identity, and intimates that he is not to reveal it otherwise; if he should reveal it, it would cause the irruption into the poetic drama of external action, or prose. Now the mask is not actually a piece of cloth, but its equivalent for the purpose: it is the metre. For metre is an artificial language. One does not transact actual business in it, one does not appear before the Chamber of Commerce uttering metres. The poet within us is released by the adoption of a tongue whose principle is novel, and wholly irrelevant to the virtues of prose discourse. We require the foreign language. There is a paradox which holds good up to a point, I think, within the experience of any poet: the more accurate the metres, the freer and more incalculable the discourse. It is as if, once the poet has undertaken the obligation to make metres, he is relieved of the obligation to make practical sense. The two obligations are in theory, though fortunately not quite in fact, incompatible. Poetry does lack something of making perfect "sense," if we take that term in its purest prose meaning as involving those strict and homely sisters, Unity, Coherence, and Emphasis. The metre is the guarantee of an eternal "play," or looseness, in its substance. One of the features of prosody is rhyme, but Milton elected to sacrifice it, and the reason alleged was that rhyme made poets express things otherwise, "and for the most part worse," than they would else have expressed them.

It is questionable whether Milton himself felt the difficulty of rhyme in this manner. Linguistic skill may reach such proficiency that the metre ceases to be a serious impediment to logical expression. There are poets in any "modern" period who are not emancipated from prose by its employment, but remain prosy in spite of their metres. But this is contrary to natural expectation. It was calculated, we judge, that metre would bring about the abdication of prose and, if we are allowed but one flat historical generalization, we must say that the calculation was successful.

10

On the other hand, it is easy to overestimate the gaiety, the abandon, of metred expression. Prose is the supremely single and exclusive experience, possible only by an abridgment of personality. But poetry does not jump to the other extreme and seek the chaos of complete diffusion as its goal. As the expression of personality it needs direction and meaning. Therefore it submits to the other of its technical requirements.

The second prescript is this: the poet puts on the costume. It is a "period" costume perhaps; a rather conventional one, or else one that bears on the private history of the impersonator, or probably both at once; at any rate one that is distinct and identifiable, and implies a "business" to suit. The advantage of the mask is negative, inhibiting the prose function and releasing the æsthetic function, but the advantage of the costume is positive, giving form to the æsthetic activity. For the costume is selective. It binds the play of sensibility to the playing of a character-part, and unifies it by dramatic propriety.

The work of art is immensely important to its artist; it is inevitable, being his expression. Art would not strike us as being worth talking about unless we could premise the discussion on the sincerity of artists. And here the prescript of costume applies. The poem must have logic, meaning, sense; that is, character; but not the immediate character of the poet. He does not interrupt the poem to tell us about himself, though we might be interested in his difficulties; that would have the same effect as if he had interrupted his metres to insert some prose. He becomes the figure in the costume strictly. Naturally it is desirable that he should have elected a figure in costume congenial with himself, and of his own level of advancement; also that he should have the gift of minutely sympathetic imagination. Then the poem becomes formidable, because it expresses him.

So the poet's attention to mask and costume becomes a possible formula, and gives us one version of the poetic process: others may be entirely tenable. It seems to describe the sufficient technique by which poetry furnishes the perfect form of experience; and reminds us that it is a dramatic rather than a real experience.

Contemporaneous Not Contemporary[1]

ALEXEI TOLSTOI: *Darkness and Dawn.* This book, describing the revolution in Russia from its original groundswell through the mass outbreak during the World War and down to the Armistice, must be almost as masterly a performance as anything in the tradition of Russian fiction. It has perhaps an even larger breadth of action than anything, not even excepting *War and Peace.* Its author is related in blood both to Leo Tolstoi and to Turgeniev. So far as I am concerned, it answers satisfactorily the question whether literature will have a continuance under Soviet censorship. It shows the bitter effort and comes in sight of the final triumph of the Reds, but its artistic detachment is high above partisanship, in which respect it offers a lesson to the literary attachés of the proletariat farther west. It is unjust to say that it is the story of the revolution; it is strictly the story of several men and women enmeshed in it. The heroine and principal character is in the cause, though not consistently, and her husband is an officer in the Red army. But her sister's husband, just as noble a man, is an officer in the White army, and the course of the campaign is described as much from one point of view as the other. Every respect is

[1]A study of two novelists lifted from an omnibus review of the season's novels several years ago in *The Southern Review.*

paid to the heroic conduct of Denikin's army, in which nearly every private soldier was a former officer at the German front, and many stand for decided liberalization of the old régime. The philosophical issue between the parties is never settled dialectically though there is plenty of talk, as in all Russian novels. The author's feeling, or at least the one which he communicates to the reader, is that the Reds triumph because it is simply Russia's destiny, because the genius of Russia is simple and communal, but only after a struggle so vast and confused that no single participant was able to tell how things were going or why. Structurally, the novel is a masterpiece in the Russian manner, and that makes a fascinating study. There is even less of explanatory remark, less of the visible author as moralist and historian, than in most Russian novels, much less than in *War and Peace*. The materials are words, actions, pictures, and feelings of the simpler sort, thousands upon thousands of them. But how they march! A Russian novel is a military campaign in which an innumerable multitude of units are clashing without apparent direction, yet slowly assume their significant order. The heroine will manage and unify a fragment of them; she has a husband who will captain another fragment; but she also has a former lover, a sister, a brother-in-law, a father, who will accept commissions, and if it is necessary these know still other persons who will serve. But the atomic simplicity of the units is marvellous, exclusively a Russian phenomenon. Here is a picture out of a love narrative, and love, incidentally, needs no other kind of narrative for Russian novelists than just such successsions of simple items:

> The sun warmed her knees, and the wind touched her cheeks and shoulders and neck as if with rounded fingers; the flag flapping at the bow, the sailor sitting on a coil of rope—everything white, everything bathed in sunshine—it all, with herself and Ivan Ilyitch, floated slowly among the clouds, between the low, smooth banks.

Compare it with a fairly analogous scene from Western fiction:

> They were looking across the lake at the dark theatre of pinewoods on the farther shore, which man had hardly marked, and at the superior and dazzling theatre of white peaks, which man had not marked at all. She was not ordinarily an enthusiast of the Swiss landscape, for it seemed to her that if snow mountains were beautiful, then vanilla ices and meringues also must be conceded beauty. But she was exalted by the thin and glittering air; its quality suggested that water might become intoxicating not only when certain substances are added to it, but when others are taken away from it. All recollected climates seemed by comparison stained and cloddish.

This passage is from the novel which will be next under our discussion; its story and its people will differ from those of Tolstoi as much as the quality of this scene from his, and that is a difference as between two worlds. Studying this latter picture we may be inclined to mourn or to rejoice because the serpent has entered Eden, but at any rate we feel that nothing in our world is naïve and fresh, and that there cannot again be simple experience. And probably it is true. If we look for the depths of Russian feeling, again it takes a simple and childlike form:

> He walked on tiptoe past her cabin and to his own, and, when he had thrown himself down on his back in the berth and closed his eyes, he felt that he was shaken to his innermost soul, that he was filled with sounds and odors and the warmth of the sun and with a sharp incomprehensible sadness which pervaded it all.

The sharp but incomprehensible sadness; there is something mystical about it. The Russians are resolute primitives in their kind of fiction, as if they knew the native sources of their strength and had erected a taboo against the analytic practices of their Western brothers. Here is a phrase from the fiction of the West.

> It was impossible to carry on any truly contrapuntal conversation with him, in which theory and practice, or his particular experience and the general experience of all other beings, could be harmonized.

It would be ruinous to insert this into a Russian novel; it is of another mental age. It involves a development of syntax, of dialectical distinction, of that systematic association and dissociation of images which we call thought. Explicit thought, hardly admitted into Russian fiction and not altogether recommended, I imagine, for common Russian life, is probably relegated to the specialists in the sciences who are to develop its practical benefits. It would seem to follow from all this that Russian fiction is, as all literatures must at some time have been, in its anonymous stage. It has no author in the sense that it has none of that sense of personality which we receive from a style. And what is a style? The mind grows out of its childhood precisely by being inducted into the world of thought and becoming at home there. Simplicities cannot live in this world, where every item must receive its commentary. But each individual must have his own preferred kind of commentary, and that indeed is his individuality, for short of thought all experience is felt, if felt at all, as simply strange and mystical. The individual is a sort of chemist, compounding the simples into substances which, if he has the gift, are both rich and characteristic. The character of his commentary is his style; it is the public witness to his personality. The Russians as yet covet neither this personality nor this style which is its symbol. When fiction, the new and world-wide kind of literary architecture, appeared a century or two ago, it caught the Russian writers in the possession of a set of basic materials different from our own; it was as if they would have to build with uncut stones, when we had reduced ours to dust and then made with it synthetic brick and concrete of an infinity of colors and textures. But the figure is too disparaging to our novelists. There is more of the spirit's travail behind our Western product, the mark of a longer human appropriation is distinct in it, and its rewards are proportionate. The sighs of envy which we hear exhaling when certain readers look at the Russian novel puts them into a class with those effete persons who have thought they cannot live without ballads and a folk-poetry even though Shakespeare and Milton have already come and gone. After Shakespeare and Milton there cannot be ballads and folk-poetry again. We should not seriously want them.

Rebecca West: *The Thinking Reed.* I should say that Miss West is one of the most accomplished of writers because her book is perfect in a form so rare that hundreds of efforts must fail in order that one may be successful. A novel may want to be many things, but what it must be is a piece of architectural composition. The requirements are so severe that the novelist may come to the comfortable conclusion that he does well enough if he can put the easiest and most available objective materials together. Such comfort is not for Miss West, who disdains the usual staple of objective materials, and cannot use them till she has transformed them by passing them through the furnace (or the dance?) of her imagination. She has sentenced herself to write a fiction with her most personal style, and that is a different thing from writing little sketches with it, or formless meditations, or screeds like Milton's gorgeous ones, or even sermons like Jeremy Taylor's or, above all, poems. In poetry the style is everything, the architecture may be anything or nothing, and to poetry we shall always have to go in order to find those passages which focus the most of the living personality in an instant. Style is the thing which the Russians have not wanted but which Western writers have developed so lovingly; the symbol of personality which is precious to our battered civilization and worth all its fury and expense. *The Thinking Reed* is Miss West's Portrait of a Lady. By a coincidence the lady is named Isabelle, and her mind, like that of the other heroine, is still virginal though she is a widow when she goes to Europe to seek spiritual adventures, which obviously must come under the head of marital ones. The technique of the story is regular in the Jamesian sense that it all comes from Isabelle as the special reporter, in the third person, and of course she has precisely the æsthetic endowment of her author, which is nearly the ultimate among current writers. Between James and Miss West the relation is clearly one of succession, though the moral Puritanism which was already receding in the gentleman has had a further relaxation now. Before her second marriage Isabelle has an unhallowed romance with a man who, quite frankly,

> . . . had a hold on her for the simple reason that, when he and she were linked by passion, they formed a pattern which was not only æsthetically pleasing but was approved, and indeed almost enjoined, by everything in civilization that was not priggish.

Priggishness, hypocrisy, unkindness, shabbiness, are the enemies of happiness in Isabelle's world. Quite naturally, its condition is love; only in a great love is there escape from the vicious degeneracy of the wealthy in French and English society. But it would be a small and jealous love which would refuse its votaries participation in any other good thing, and there are many good things which only money can bring. Isabelle wants the fullness of life, and very nearly achieves it. Miss West, her author, is moved but not intimidated by the desperate philosophies fighting in these days for possession of the soul. She authorizes her principals to take what they can get, and what they can get is experience sharpened to æsthetic delight, like the effect of a cause, by what, if one may know from what one reads in the newspapers, may be the last splendors of the bourgeois decadence. But I solemnify the tone of her book, which resists the temptation to be shrill and tragic so well that once or twice it is slightly Rabelaisian and nearly comic, and we are concerned for its shining dignity. Taste, the æsthetic attitude, is nourished by what it feeds on, it does not like to run the risk of being more sumptuous than its expectations will justify. To the making of Miss West's style, which is her trained and public personality, all the best writers have probably contributed, except the anarchs like Joyce and Mrs. Woolf. It is as if George Moore came back to life in this passage:

> In the spring he would lay the foundation of his plans for public things and she would have her children, in the summer they would admire to see how their work fared in the heat of the day, in the autumn there would be harvest, and since the days grow shorter and they would have so much to talk over, no doubt winter also would not hang on their hands.

Henry James is everywhere. And perhaps the shade of poor Frances Newman is in this passage:

> But there was no help for that, since a woman cannot tell a man whom she is about to marry how pleased and amazed she is to find herself daily coming nearer to loving him, though in the circumstances he could not possibly hear better news. This discomfited her by its suggestion that the world in which human beings lived was not the same as the world of which they spoke and thought.

She is more exuberant than James, and much more opulent than Newman.

Shakespeare at Sonnets

ONE may be well disposed to the New Deal, and not relish the attitude of giving comfort to the enemy by criticizing Mr. Roosevelt publicly, yet in a qualified company do it freely. The same thing applies in the matter of the poet Shakespeare. It is out of respect to the intelligence of the editors and readers of a serious literary publication that I will not hold back from throwing a few stones at Shakespeare, aiming them as accurately as I can at the vulnerable parts. I have no fear that any group of intellectual critics may succeed beyond their intentions in demolishing Shakespeare, so that he will suffer extinction and be read no more, and I am well aware that if this should happen the public attendance upon poetry in our language would be reduced one-half. For Shakespeare is an institution as well established as the industrial revolution, or the Protestant churches. In the midst of the bombardment he will smile, and smile, and be a villain.

In this paper I must limit attention to the Sonnets, and within this field to a few features only. In a way the Sonnets should prove the most interesting of all this poet's works—unless the reader's interest in the poetry is tangled hopelessly with his interest in drama, the form which dominates most of Shakespeare's verse. For here I must propose a certain distinction, and it will be arbitrary in the sense that I will not argue it. Let us distinguish drama as one literary form, and lyric or pure poetry as another. In poetic drama, a hybrid, it is the dramatic form which rules. The poetry is the auxiliar. At any moment it is relative to the action, and to that extent determinate, not free. In the plays Shakespeare furnishes a multitude of characters with always-appropriate speeches—with speeches big and royal, tender and pitying, conspiratorial, even philosophizing speeches and soliloquies, indeed speeches of almost any sort, and thoroughly poeticized—but probably none of them will quite do as a round and separate poem. None is really so intended.

The standard of poetic range and complication which is practical for a successful producing playwright cannot be so high as that adhered to by some formal poet who cares nothing about the affections of the people, and knows that his art for a long time, certainly since Caxton set up for business, has been of a mental age far beyond its original oral condition. I will come to my point at once. It is not likely that John Donne could have written Shakespeare's plays, but on the other hand it seems impossible that Shakespeare could have got into the plays the equivalent of Donne's lyrics.

The virtue of formal lyrics, or "minor poems," is one that no other literary type can manifest: they are the only complete and self-determined poetry. There the poetic object is elected by a free choice from all objects in the world, and this object, deliberately elected and carefully worked up by the adult poet, becomes his microcosm. With a serious poet each minor poem may be the symbol of a major decision. It is as ranging and comprehensive an action as the mind has ever tried.

Shakespeare left monument enough behind him, but no face of it is of that precise significance which is attested by a large and assorted volume of minor poems. The truth is that Shakespeare, as compared with writers like Sidney and Spenser, had rare luck as a literary man, and I do not mean to say this out of any regard to whether he was or was not a superior man naturally. It would be impossible to tell how much our poet was determined by the fact that he was not an aristocrat, did not go to the university and develop his technical skill all at once, got into the rather low profession of acting, grew up with the drama, and never had to undergo the torment of that terrible problem: the problem of poetic strategy; or what to do with an intensive literary training. Yet Shakespeare did indulge in one diversion from his natural and happy career as a dramatist. He composed a laborious sonnet sequence. And in the degree that the sonnets are not tied down to "story," to the simple dramatizing of the stages in a human relation, they give us a Shakespeare on the same terms as those on which we are used to having our other poets.

2

I begin with a most obvious feature: generally they are ill constructed.

They use the common English metrical pattern, and the metrical work is always admirable, but the logical pattern more often than not fails to fit it. If it be said that you do not need to have a correspondence between a poet's metrical pattern and his logical one, I am forced to observe that Shakespeare thought there was a propriety in it; often he must have gone to the pains of securing it, since it is there and, considering the extreme difficulty of the logical structure in the English sonnet, could not have got in by a happy accident. The metrical pattern of any sonnet is directive. If the English sonnet exhibits the rhyme-scheme ABAB CDCD EFEF GG, it imposes upon the poet the following requirement: that he write three co-ordinate quatrains and then a couplet which will relate to the series collectively.

About a third of the sonnets of Shakespeare are fairly unexceptionable in having just such a logical structure. About half of them might be said to be tolerably workmanlike in this respect; and about half of them are seriously defective.

Already the poet Spenser had calculated very well what sort of thing could be done successfully in this logical pattern. It was something like the following (*Amoretti*, LVI):

> Fayre be ye sure, but cruell and unkind,
> As is a Tygre, that with greedinesse
> Hunts after bloud; when he by chance doth find
> A feeble beast, doth foully him oppresse.
>
> Fayre be ye sure, but proud and pitilesse,
> As is a storm, that all things doth prostrate;
> Finding a tree alone all comfortlesse,
> Beats on it strongly, it to ruinate.
>
> Fayre be ye sure, but hard and obstinate,
> As is a rocke amidst the raging floods;
> Gaynst which, a ship, of succour desolate,
> Doth suffer wreck both of her selfe and goods.
>
> That ship, that tree, and that same beast, am I,
> Whom ye do wreck, do ruine, and destroy.

Now Spenser's metrical scheme has a special and unnecessary complication, it exhibits rhyme-linkage; the second quatrain begins by echoing the last rhyme of the first quatrain, and the third by echoing the last rhyme of the second. It makes no difference logically. The three quatrains are equal yet sharply distinct. Possibly the linking was Spenser's way of showing off his virtuosity at rhyming, and possibly also he used it as a mnemonic device, to say, The new quatrain must be just like the old one, a logical coordinate, but wait till we come to the couplet, which will not be linked and must not be co-ordinate. At any rate, his quatrains nearly always are true co-ordinates. In his architectural design he is superior, I believe, to any other writer of the four-part or English sonnet.

And this means that he carefully attended to the sort of object which might permit this three-and-one division. In the given example each quatrain is a simile which he applies to the lady, and the couplet is a summary comment which is brief, but adequate because the similes are simple and of the same kind. It is not every matter, or logical object, which allows this; and, particularly, the couplet does not give enough room for the comment unless the burden of the quatrains has been severely restricted. If the poet is too full of urgent thoughts, he had better use the two-part or Italian form, which is very much more flexible. The English form, with the more elaborate and repetitive pattern, implies the simpler substance; in this it would be like other complicated forms, such as the ballade or sestina.

But structurally good also is the following Shakespearean sonnet, the one numbered LXXXVII:

Farewell! thou art too dear for my possessing,
And like enough thou know'st thy estimate;
The charter of thy worth gives thee releasing;
My bonds in thee are all determinate.

For how do I hold thee but by thy granting?
And for that riches where is my deserving?
The cause of this fair gift in me is wanting,
And so my patent back again is swerving.

Thyself thou gav'st, thy own worth then not knowing,
Or me, to whom thou gav'st it, else mistaking;
So thy great gift, upon misprision growing,
Comes home again, on better judgment making.

Thus have I had thee, as a dream doth flatter,
In sleep a king, but waking no such matter.

This sonnet is daring and clever. It is legalistic, therefore closely limited in its range, yet the three quatrains all manage to say the same thing differently, and the couplet translates the legal figure back into the terms of a lover's passion.

It is only a large minority of Shakespeare's sonnets in which we can find this perfect adaptation of the logic to the metre. In the others we can find the standard metrical organization, and then some arbitrary logical organization which clashes with it. At least twice we find only fourteen-line poems, with no logical organization at all except that they have little couplet conclusions: in LXVI, "Tir'd with all these, for restful death I cry," and in CXXIX, "The expense of spirit in a waste of shame." Occasionally, as in LXIII, "Against my love shall be, as I am now," the sonnet divides frankly into octave and sextet, so far as the logic goes, though it does not follow that an honest printer has set it up just so. Many modern sonnet-writers, such as my friend, Mr. David Morton, are careful to have their sonnets set up as two-part structures though their rhyme-scheme is four-part. I am afraid some critics will always be wondering whether the poets are unequal, or simply insensitive, to the logical demands made by the English form. I scarcely think that Shakespeare's practice sanctified a procedure.

Possibly the commonest irregularity of logical arrangement with Shakespeare is in sonnets of the following type (LXIV):

> When I have seen by Time's fell hand defac'd
> The rich proud cost of outworn buried age;
> When sometime lofty towers I see down-raz'd,
> And brass eternal slave to mortal rage;
>
> When I have seen the hungry ocean gain
> Advantage on the kingdom of the shore,
> And the firm soil win of the watery main,
> Increasing store with loss and loss with store;
>
> When I have seen such interchange of state,
> Or state itself confounded to decay,
> Ruin hath taught me thus to ruminate,
> That Time will come and take my love away.
>
> This thought is as a death, which cannot choose,
> But weep to have that which it fears to lose.

Here the three quatrains look co-ordinate, but only the first two really are so. The third begins with the same form as the others, but presently shows that it is only summary of their content, and then actually begins to introduce the matter which will be the concern of the couplet. We must believe that Shakespeare found the couplet too small to hold its matter, so that at about line ten he had to begin anticipating it. But, as I said, this sonnet represents a pattern fairly common with him, and it is possible to argue that he developed it consciously as a neat variant on the ordinary English structure; just as Milton developed a variant from the Italian structure, by concluding the logical octet a little before or a little after the rhyme-ending of the eighth line.

Probably Shakespeare's usual structural difficulty consists about equally in having to pad out his quatrains, if three good co-ordinates do not offer themselves, and in having to squeeze the couplet too flat, or else extend its argument upward into the proper territory of the quatrains. But when both these things happen at once, the obvious remark is that the poet should have reverted to the Italian sonnet.

Structurally, Shakespeare is a careless workman. But probably, with respect to our attention to structure, we are careless readers.

3

Poetry is an expressive art, we say, and perhaps presently we are explaining that what it expresses is its poet; a dangerous locution, because the public value of the poem would seem to lie theoretically in the competence with which it expresses its object. There is no reason why it should not offer an absolute knowledge of this object, so far as the adjective is ever applicable to a human knowledge, including a scientific knowledge, and a knowledge however "objective." Nevertheless one knowledge will differ from another knowledge in glory, that is, in the purity of intention, and sometimes it is scarcely a knowledge at all; it is rather a self-expression. There is probably a poetry of the feelings just as much as there is a poetry of knowledge; for we may hardly deny to a word its common usage, and poetry is an experience so various as to be entertained by everybody. But the poetry of the feelings is not the one that the critic is compelled to prefer, especially if he can say that it taints us with subjectivism, sentimentality, and self-indulgence. This is the poetry, I think, which we sometimes dispose of a little distastefully as "romantic." It does not pursue its object with much zeal, and it is so common that it involves in a general disrepute all poets, the innocent as well as the guilty, by comparison with those importunate pursuers, the scientists—who will not exactly be expected to fail to make the most of the comparison.

This sort of poetry, I am afraid, is as natural to Shakespeare as language is, and he is a great master in it. In XXXIII we read:

> Full many a glorious morning have I seen
> Flatter the mountain-tops with sovereign eye,
> Kissing with golden face the meadows green,
> Gilding pale streams with heavenly alchemy.

It is pure Shakespeare, it sounds like nobody else; and in it the failure of objectivity, or perhaps "realism" we might prefer to call it, is plain about as soon as we look closely. What the poet intends is simply to have something in the way of a fine-morning quatrain, with an all-ruling fair-weather sun to be the symbol of his false friend, as the sonnet goes on to disclose. But this sun is weakly imagined; rather, it may be said to be only felt, a loose cluster of images as obscure as they are pleasant, furnished by the half-conscious memories attending the pretty words. (In strict logic: I suppose this sun's eye flatters the mountain-tops in that his look makes them shine; but at once he is kissing the meadows, which is unseemly for a face that contains a sovereign eye; then in the character of an alchemist he is transmuting streams. A mixed and self-defeating figure, and a romantic effect unusually loose; but it does not seem to matter.)

So this is poetry; a poetry that has in mind the subjective satisfactions of the poet, and of reputed millions of readers after him. The cognitive impulse of the participating millions has to be of low grade, yet there is an object, and it is rich and suggestive even while it is vague and cloudy. This is what we might call an associationist poetry. The pretty words have pleasing if indefinite associations; and they are fairly harmonious, that is, the associations tend rather to cohere than to repel each other. And if they do not cohere into a logical or definitive object, at any rate —this is the subtlety of the romantic style—they are arranged externally with great care into a characteristic musical phrase, or at least a metrical one, which is really (by comparison) objective and absolute. Metric saves this kind of poetry, and its function could not be shown to better advantage than here; a meretricious function, as it lends its objectivity to an act in which the subject does not really propose to lose himself in the object. In other words, it persuades us, unless we are professionally critical, that this is a poetry of wonderful precision, when logically it is a poetry of wonderful imprecision, and the only precision it has is metrical, therefore adventitious. It is not without significance that the age gave to this poet his adjective: sweet. It would be hard to estimate the extent of the influence which Shakespeare's way of writing poetry has exerted upon subsequent English poetry. But Exhibit A would be the actual poems, and Exhibit B, scarcely less significant, would be the critical dictum upon which almost innumerable writers seem to be in perfect agreement, that science if it likes may try to know its object, but that the business of poetry is to express its author's feelings. The Restoration and Eighteenth Century in their poetry resisted Shakespeare's example of sweetness, but the Nineteenth Century did not, and when we are grieving because modern poetry has learned how to furnish such exquisite indulgences to the feelings and yet at the same time so little food for the intellect, there is no reason why we should not remember who is its most illustrious ancestor.

The image is often conventional, or "literary,"

which means that it is not really shaped by a genuine observation. In LIII:

> Describe Adonis, and the counterfeit
> Is poorly imitated after you;
> On Helen's cheek all art of beauty set,
> And you in Grecian tires are painted new.

Asseverations like this are the right of a literary lover, but they do more credit to his piety than to his wit. (The mediæval lover had a code which obliged him to say, My lady is more beautiful than yours, though I have not seen yours.) The urgency is that of a subject to express his own feelings, not that of an object so individual as to demand expression. But the phrasing is grave and musical; there is great care behind it to get words with the right general associations, and to make the melody; phrase, in this subjective sense, and regarded as the trick of the poet as workman, receives commonly the particularity that might have gone into the object.

Mr. Santayana says something like this when he remarks, with his usual wisdom, that Shakespeare's poetry is an art like landscaping; for it is pervasive, and tones down every object exposed to it, and is not like architecture, which articulates its objects right to the last constituent stone. Carrying out our figure, Shakespeare's poetry would not be so much the wall, or the temple, as the ivy that clings to it sentimentally, and sometimes may very well even obscure it.

Violence of syntax and of idiom is supposed to express strength of feeling. In the sonnets are many violences. For instance, in XXV,

> The painful warrior famoused for fight,

and in LXIV,

> The rich proud cost of outworn buried age.

In the first of these Shakespeare makes a verb of an adjective, but his coinage could not give it a currency, for it is not that kind of adjective. He also makes a qualitative noun of *fight*, which is less exceptionable, though its present currency seems to lie within the American sporting jargon. Both these forced meanings follow surprisingly upon *painful*, which is exact and even Miltonic. The other bristles with logical difficulties. They attach to the meaning of *cost*, and of the adjective series *rich* and *proud*, and of *outworn* and *buried*. Malone worried over the line and proposed *rich-proud*, but it still strongly resists paraphrase. These phrases will illustrate what is common in romantic poetry: a very great "obscurity," unknown to some "intellectualist" poetry which popularly rates as difficult.

I quote also, and I think not vindictively, from XII:

> When I do count the clock that tells the time,
> And see the brave day sunk in hideous night,
> When I behold the violet past prime,
> And sable curls, all silver'd o'er with white. . . .

The third line of this quatrain interests me as a critic. Shakespeare ordinarily plays safe by electing good substantial conventional objects to carry his feelings, but here his judgment should have come tc his aid. The violet, in its exalted context, looks to me like a poet's *ridiculus mus*, for no instance of floral mortality could well be more insignificant. This little mouse had the merit of being named with three syllables, and a two-minute imaginary tour in the garden does not seem to disclose another one of like syllabic dimensions who would do any better. Shakespeare did not bother; he trusted in the music, and the power of the pleasant associations, to make the line impervious to logical criticism. He trusted also, and not without reason, for the point will generally be conceded by critics who are grateful for any excellence in their difficult art, in the comfortable faith that a poetical passage is unlike a chain in that its true strength is that of its strongest part.

On the other hand, there are certainly sonnets of Shakespeare's in this romantic vein which are without absurdities, structural defects, and great violences, and which are also compact, that is, without excessive dispersion in the matter of the figures; and they are doubtless the best sonnets of the kind there could possibly be. It would be presumptuous to deny this general type of poetry, or Shakespeare's occasional mastery of it.

Those perfect sonnets are not many. It is not a wild generalization, when we look at the sonnets, to say that Shakespeare was not habitually a perfectionist;

he was not as Ben Jonson, or Marvell, or Milton, and he was not as Pope.

4

The sonnets are mixed in effect. Not only the sequence as a whole but the individual sonnet is uneven in execution. But what to the critic is still more interesting than the up and the down in one style is the alternation of two very different styles: the one we have been considering, and the one which we are accustomed to define (following Doctor Johnson) as metaphysical. What is the metaphysical poetry doing there? Apparently at about the time of *Hamlet*, and perhaps recognizably in the plays but much more deliberately and on a more extended scale in the sonnets, Shakespeare goes metaphysical. Not consistently, of course.

So far as I know, Shakespeare has not ordinarily been credited with being one of the metaphysicals, nor have specimen sonnets been included in lists or anthologies of metaphysical poems. But many sonnets certainly belong there; early examples of that style. If it was not then widely practised, had no name, and could hardly yet have been recognized as a distinct style, then I would suppose that the sonnets as a performance represent Shakespeare seeking such effects as John Donne, a public if still unpublished wonder, by some curious method was achieving. But there was also, on a smaller scale, the example of a genuine pioneer in this field in the person of Sidney, if Shakespeare cared to look there; see his *Astrophel and Stella,* XCIV, "Grief, find the words, for thou hast made my brain."

Certainly Shakespeare's LXXXVII, "Farewell! thou art too dear for my possessing," already quoted as an instance of good structure, is in the style. For its substance is furnished by developing the human relation (that of the renouncing lover) through a figure of speech; a legal one, in which an unequal bond is cancelled for cause. Three times, in as many quatrains, the lover makes an exploration within the field of the figure. The occasions are fairly distinct, though I should think their specifications are hardly respective enough to have satisfied Donne. But the thing which surprises us is to find no evidence anywhere that Shakespeare's imagination is equal to the peculiar and systematic exercises which Donne imposed habitually upon his. None, and it should not really surprise us, if we remember that Donne's skill is of the highest technical expertness in English poetry, and that Shakespeare had no university discipline, and developed poetically along lines of least resistance.

He is upon occasions metaphysical enough, but not so metaphysical as Donne; nor as later poets, Donne's followers, who were just as bold in intention as their master, though not usually so happy in act.

The impulse to metaphysical poetry, I shall assume, consists in committing the feelings in the case—those of unrequited love for example—to their determination within the elected figure. But Shakespeare was rarely willing to abandon his feelings to this fate, which is another way of saying that he would not quite risk the consequences of his own imagination. He censored these consequences, to give them sweetness, to give them even dignity; he would go a little way with one figure, usually a reputable one, then anticipate the consequences, or the best of them, and take up another figure.

The simplest way to define Shakespeare's metaphysical accomplishment would be by comparison with Donne's, which is standard. I have often tried to find the parallel cases where the two poets developed the same figure of speech. But I have always been forced to conclude that these poets do not even in outline or skeleton treat quite the same things; Shakespeare's things being professionally conventional, and Donne's being generally original. The nearest I can come to this sort of illustration is by comparing Sonnet LV with that Valediction of Donne's which has the subtitle: *of the booke.* It is a "strong" sonnet, not quite intelligent enough to be metaphysical It begins,

> Not marble, nor the gilded monuments
> Of princes shall outlive this powerful rime,

yet what it develops is not the circumstantial immortality of the rime, and of the beloved inhabiting it, but the mortality of the common marbles and monuments, an old story with Shakespeare, and as to the immortality makes this single effort:

> 'Gainst death and all-oblivious enmity
> Shall you pace forth.

The only specific thing here is something about a gait.

The immortality of the rime, and of the beloved preserved in it (like a beautiful fly stuck in amber? let poets tell) is as classical, or typical, as anything in European sonnetry; but its specific development is not. It remained for Donne, and hardly anybody or nobody else, really on its own merits to develop it, or an easy variation from it, and that not in a sonnet. In the Valediction he bids his lady, when he is going on an absence from her, to study his manuscripts, "those Myriades of letters," and writes the annals of their love for the sake of posterity. I quote the third stanza, with a little editing of the punctuation:

> This Booke, as long-liv'd as the elements,
> Or as the world's forme, this all-graved tome
> In cypher writ, or new made Idiome
> (We for love's clergie only are instruments),—
> When this booke is made thus,
> Should again the ravenous
> Vandals and Gauls inundate us,
> Learning were safe; in this our universe
> Schooles might learn Sciences, Spheares Musick,
> Angels Verse.

One understands that he really means what he says: a book. In the three stanzas following he shows respectively what the Divines, the Lawyers, and the Statesmen will learn from this book, and in a final stanza returns to relate to a lover's absence the labor of compiling it. Donne would have performed well with an English sonnet-structure, where he might have gone on three separate little adventures into his image; there are three here, though the stanza is bigger, and perhaps therefore easier, than quatrain. (Structurally, there is no firmer architect of lyric anywhere in English than Donne.) The trick consists, apparently, in guiding the imagination to the right places and then letting it go. To make this controlled yet exuberant use of the imagination is an intellectual feat; though it would not follow that there is no other recipe which will confer upon verse its intellectual distinction.

Metaphysical poetry has received in our time a new analytic attention, and for example from Professor Grierson. (Less formally if not less influentially from Mr. T. S. Eliot.) The revival of interest in this poetry evidently suits the taste of our post-romantic generation. And Professor Grierson says in many places that what Donne does is to combine intellect and passion. But no poet would find that a practicable formula; and we may well shiver with apprehension lest theory, or the æsthetic of poetry, waver and relax and perish under such a definition. The primary business of theorists is to direct their analyses of poetry to what is objective in it, or cognitive, and they will always be safe in assuming if they like that behind any external body of knowledge there will have been feeling enough, possibly amounting to passion, to have attended the subject through his whole exercise. Indeed, the feeling must have been entirely proportionate to the exercise. It is right to attribute the feelings to Donne's lover, in the poem, but our assurance is inferential; the intellectual effects appear as the fruits of the feelings. Ferdinand's feelings for Miranda, said Prospero to himself, are measurable better by the wood he will chop for her than by the passion, or even the iambic melody, of his protestations.

But may I talk a little about feelings? I have often wanted to. It is conceivable that Ferdinand might have expressed his in a garland of metaphysical poems, and that Prospero might have been fully competent to judge of the comparative values in this art, and therefore that the poems might have served alone as a sufficient index, obviating the wood-pile. They would have been just as objective an evidence. For what are feelings? I am sure I do not know, but I will suppose for the present they are calls to action, and always want to realize their destiny, which is to turn into actions and vanish. I will suppose also, and this is from experience, that we find ourselves sometimes possessed of powerful feelings and yet cannot quite tell what actions they want of us; or find ourselves even learning to enjoy the pangs of feelings, in the conceited consciousness they are our very own, and therefore reluctant to resolve them in action, and taking a perverse pleasure in stirring them up, like a harrowing of hell; for we are marvellously indeterminate in our inner economy. That is what comes fundamentally, I think, from our egoism, a strange and peculiarly human faculty. For I do not think animals distinguish their feelings at one end of a scale from their actions at the other end, since Nature as plain biologist would hardly seem to require it. But we distinguish; clearly we are able to stop at the feeling-end, or to perform half-way actions that will partly relieve the feelings and partly permit them still to luxuriate, but less painfully.

Lovers (and other persons too) often have feelings which cannot take, and do not seek, their natural outlet in physical actions. The feelings may be too complex anyhow, and too persistent, to be satisfied with simple actions, they overrun the mark; or perhaps the lovers have to go upon an absence, and the feelings get dammed up. Then they find appropriate actions through imagination, in intellectual constructions. These lovers at their best are poets. These poets at their best perform complete actions, very likely by means of metaphysical poems. So, on the one hand, there is an associationist poetry, a half-way action providing many charming resting-places for the feelings to agitate themselves; and, on the other hand, there is a metaphysical poetry, which elects its line of action and goes straight through to the completion of the cycle and extinction of the feelings.

This gives us associationist poetry *versus*, I think, behavioristic. For our discussion seems to have turned psychological. If romantic poets are not fully aware of what they are doing, metaphysical poets are self-conscious and deliberate, and in fact they are very like technical psychologists. They start with feelings, they objectify these imaginatively into external actions. They think that poetry, just as behavioristic psychologists think that psychology, can make nothing out of feelings as they stand.

5

And now a little moralization.

A metaphysical poem is an intellectual labor, and all the intellect may be active in it, but it is under the presidency of imagination. And here comes a difficulty. Feelings are not satisfied by a ridiculous and impossible action, for they themselves are painfully real. But what is imagination? A faculty of excessive versatility: equally ready to take the photograph of objective reality, or to reproduce it from memory, or to create it originally in a painting; and if the last, the detail is perceptual but not actually perceived. This is the great trouble. The deterrent to our reception of metaphysical effects is distrust; we do not believe in the validity of the imaginative organ. It is for us a powerfully inherited distrust, going back to the tyranny of that modernism, technically to be defined as scientific positivism, which killed the religious credulity of Europe, beginning in the Renaissance; it was going strongly by Shakespeare's time, and was quite sufficient to damn the foolish magic which Spenser, by mistaken strategy, had lifted from mediæval poetry and stuffed into his *Faerie Queene*. We cannot escape it. A nice exhibit of our scruple is to be found later in Coleridge's rejection of fancy as the irresponsible bastard variety of the image-forming faculty, though necessarily he discovered insuperable difficulties in drawing the exact line round it. And altogether proper must we think anybody's insistence that imagination must be representative, or realistic, in order that poetry may speak the truth. It seems too early in our history, or else intelligence is simply too weak, to arrive at any but dogmatic judgments respecting a nest of exquisite problems with which sensitive moderns are too well acquainted: how far a "metaphysical" particularity which goes beyond actual observation is valid; how far the body of modern science, symbol of what is valid and eternal, is itself built upon this sort of particularity; whether any particularity is still eligible in religion, which deals with supernaturals that always escape observation; and, at the same time, whether natural bodies do not imply supernatural ones, and whether there can be supernatural ones which propose to have no particularity at all. We can only observe that the moment looks favorable to an improvement in the public status of imaginative works.

But Professor Grierson makes an acute observation when he notes the almost solid Catholic front (Anglo-Catholic and Roman) upon which we are fairly astonished to find the seventeenth-century metaphysical poets arrayed. (This test might eliminate Shakespeare, if we applied it too strictly, for he does not group with them in a public or official sense.) It is hardly a mere coincidence. Catholicism is not afraid of particularizing the God, evidently believing that you cannot have "God in general," you must have

Him in particular if at all. But Protestantism is afraid. It is subject to a fatal scruple of conscience. On its behalf it should be said that for modern men Protestantism is probably a necessity; it represents the scepticism which is incidental to sincere epistemological studies, and at a certain point of scientific advancement is inevitable. But this scepticism once started finds no end, and promises to conclude by destroying what is most peculiarly human in our habit of mind; indeed, it seems to proceed on a psychological assumption suitable to the animal societies, that superfluous feelings are not significant, and that it is simple, and desirable, to suppress them.

Doctor Johnson had a dry Protestant temper, and also something of the Catholic inheritance which he may have thought of as an old-fashioned decency. Oscillating fairly between these two prejudices, he was a just if never profound critic. He admired while he deprecated and repudiated the metaphysical poets. But in 1747 he prepared for Garrick's reading a Prologue upon the opening of Drury Lane Theatre, and began it as follows:

> When Learning's triumph o'er her barbarous foes
> First reared the stage, immortal Shakespeare rose;
> Each change of many-colored life he drew,
> Exhausted worlds, and then imagined new;
> Existence saw him spurn her bounded reign,
> And panting Time toiled after him in vain.
> His pow'rful strokes presiding Truth impressed,
> And unresisted Passion stormed the breast.

A defender of metaphysical poetry might suggest that in these eight lines the poet cites about that number of separate figures, and takes the profit of them, when there could be no profit to be taken except on the understanding that they were as mines, that might be or had been worked by real metaphysical imaginations. This poet offers no bodily manifestations of Learning triumphing o'er her foes, and then rearing the stage, which she could never have accomplished without being involved with shapes, agents, and events that were capable of images; or of Shakespeare rising, exhausting old worlds, imagining new ones, spurning the bounds of Existence; or of Time panting in his pursuit; or of Truth presiding over something, and impressing Shakespeare's strokes; or of Passion in some military manner storming the breast. It is necessary after all to raise the question of intellectual integrity against Doctor Johnson, as against many a Protestant at one time or another. If he rejects the metaphysicals he should reject also their fruits. These verses come out of the handsome enlightenment which lives substantially but without knowing on the scraps of a past from which it thinks it is emancipated.

6

But Shakespeare honestly realizes the metaphysical image, and I shall cite, with some remark, the sonnets in which he seems to me to have the most conspicuous success.

I begin with XXX, "When to the sessions of sweet

silent thought"; it is smart work, but only half the sharpness belongs to the strict object; the rest is accidental or mechanical, because it is oral or verbal; it is word-play, and word-play, including punning, belongs to the loose poetry of association. Technically perfect and altogether admirable in its careful modulation is LVII, "Being your slave, what should I do but tend"; and so faithfully does it stick to the object, which is the behavior suitable to the slave kept waiting, that not till the couplet is there any direct expression of the feelings of the actual outraged lover.

Sonnet LX, "Like as the waves make toward the pebbled shore," is ambitious and imperfect. The first quatrain says that our minutes are always toiling forward, like waves. The second quatrain introduces a different and pretentious image of this tendency, and shows its fatal consequence:

> Nativity, once in the main of light,
> Crawls to maturity, wherewith being crown'd,
> Crooked eclipses 'gainst his glory fight,
> And Time that gave doth now his gift confound.

The lines will be impressive to that kind of receptivity whose critical defences are helpless against great words in musical phrases. Nativity means the new-born infant, but maturity seems only an object in his path, or at the goal of his path, evidently a crown which he puts on. Thereupon the astrological influences turn against nativity, and Time enters the story to destroy his own gift; this must be the crown that nativity has picked up. We are confused about all these entities.

In the third quatrain Shakespeare declines to a trite topic, the destructiveness of Time, and represents him successively as transfixing the flourish set on youth (however he may do that), delving the parallels in beauty's brow (as a small demon with a digging instrument?), feeding on the rareties of nature's truth (as gluttonous monster), and mowing everything with his scythe (as grim reaper). A field of imagery in which the explorer has performed too prodigiously, and lost his chart.

And now LXXIII, with its opening quatrain:

> That time of year thou mayst in me behold
> When yellow leaves, or none, or few, do hang
> Upon those boughs which shake against the cold,
> Bare ruin'd choirs, where late the sweet birds sang.

The structure is good, the three quatrains offering distinct yet equivalent figures for the time of life of the unsuccessful and to-be-pitied lover. But the first quatrain is the boldest, and the effect of the whole is slightly anti-climactic. Within this quatrain I think I detect a thing which often characterizes Shakespeare's work within the metaphysical style: he is unwilling to renounce the benefit of his earlier style, which consisted in the breadth of the associations; that is, he will not quite risk the power of a single figure but compounds the figures. I refer to the two images about the boughs. It is one thing to have the boughs shaking against the cold, and in that capacity they carry very well the fact of the old rejected lover; it is another thing to represent them as ruined choirs where the birds no longer sing. The latter is a just representation of the lover too, and indeed a subtler and richer one, but the two images cannot, in logical rigor, co-exist. Therefore I deprecate *shake against the cold*. And I believe everybody will deprecate *sweet*. This term is not an objective image at all, but a term to be located at the subjective pole of the experience; it expects to satisfy a feeling by naming it (that it, by just having it) and is a pure sentimentalism.

No. LXXXVII, "Farewell! thou art too dear for my possessing," which we have already seen and remarked, needs only the further comment that it is rare and charming among sonnets for the almost complete prevalence of the feminine rhyme.

I cite XCIV, "They that have power to hurt and will do none"; it has proved obscure to commentators, but I think it is clear if taken in context, as an imaginary argument against the friend's relation with the woman, or with any woman, exactly opposite to the argument of the sonnets which open the sequence. And XCVII, "How like a winter hath my absence been," where the logical structure has some nicety though the detail is rather large of scale.

I am interested in CVII, which begins,

> Not mine own fears, nor the prophetic soul
> Of the wide world dreaming on things to come.

The argument is that the auguries of disaster and death to his love need not be trusted; it concludes disappointingly in an old vein, that at any rate this love will endure in the poet's rhyme. I am particularly bothered by the image of the world's prophetic soul; as who is not? The world-soul is a technical concept, I suppose, in the sense that it was of use to Paracelsus and to other theosophists, who knew what they wanted to make of it. It indicates a very fine image for some metaphysical poet who will handle it technically; for Donne or another university poet. It is not fit for amateurs. The question is whether Shakespeare's theological touch here is not amateurish; elsewhere it sometimes is, as in Hamlet's famous soliloquy beginning, "To be or not to be." It is my impression that our poet is faking, or shall we say improvising; the *wide,* denoting extension, seems to destroy the world's aspect as soul, the *dreaming* is too pretty a form for the prophetic action.

There is evenness in CIX, "O! never say that I was false of heart." In CXXI, " 'Tis better to be vile than vile esteem'd," the language of the opening quatrain sounds close and technical enough for a passage of Donne's, but the argument is rather obscure; the later quatrains seem to shift the argument. No. CXXV, "Were 't aught to me I bore the canopy," is admirable though not unitary enough to be very metaphysical. And finally there is CXLVI, "Poor Soul, the centre of my sinful earth," the most Platonic or "spiritual" sonnet in the entire sequence, a noble revulsion in the progress of the poet's feelings, and the poet might well have employed it to conclude the unhappy history, leaving quite off the eight miscellaneous and indeterminate ones that follow. Perhaps he would have done so if he and not the printer had directed the publication.

7

I conclude with a note, which is in answer to an editorial query, and may serve as anticipating what will probably be a dissatisfaction on the part of some readers over my estimate of Shakespeare as a metaphysical poet.

Is not Shakespeare a very bold and successful contriver of metaphysical effects in his later plays? For the sonnets come before the final period of playwrighting, and it is our common impression that this poet's powers developed steadily to their final climax.

It has been remarked above that drama is no place to look for complete little poems; that metaphysical lyrics in particular, like Donne's, would be destructive of any drama into which they might be admitted. Shakespeare's characters have to speak to the point, that is, to an immediate situation within the action of the play. But sometimes a character will get into general difficulties, and have profound if not quite directed feelings of despair; or into a state of happiness, and feel a diffuse joy; and such a character may be allowed to soliloquize (a very suspicious action dramatically, which shows Shakespeare trying to burst the bonds of drama in favor of a freer poetry); and why should not the result be a sizable passage of true metaphysical poetry?

The odds on its being so are here at their greatest. But I should think the passage will be too intellectual to give the oral effect necessary for an audience; for that matter, cannot be spontaneous enough even to suit a reader's sense of dramatic propriety. I look through a few of the soliloquies and seem to find my point confirmed. Macbeth's speech upon hearing of the Queen's death (in V, v) is cited for my benefit, but here is the speech:

> To-morrow, and to-morrow, and to-morrow,
> Creeps in this petty pace from day to day,
> To the last syllable of recorded time;
> And all our yesterdays have lighted fools
> The way to dusty death. Out, out, brief candle!
> Life's but a walking shadow, a poor player
> That struts and frets his hour upon the stage,
> And then is heard no more; it is a tale
> Told by an idiot, full of sound and fury,
> Signifying nothing.

It is a very fine speech. But instead of presenting a figure systematically it presents a procession or flight of figures. The tomorrows creep along till they have crept far enough, and bring up against—what? A syllable; remarkable barrier. After the tomorrows, in the whirling sub-logical mind of this harried speaker, the yesterdays, by the suggestion which prompts antithesis; and, at a venture, he remarks that what they did was to light fools to their death. (I do not know why dusty death; it is an odd but winning detail.) But speaking now of lights, out with this one, a mere candle! Lights also imply shadows, and suggest that life is a walking shadow. Then the lights lead to the torches of the theatre, and the walking shadow becomes a strutting player, who after an hour will be heard no more. Finally, since one thing leads to another, we may as well make life into the thing the player says, the story, whose sound and fury have no meaning. The connections between part and part in this speech are psychological, and looser than logical, though psychological will always include logical, and indeed act as their matrix. And the point is that mere psychological connections are very good for dramatic but not for metaphysical effects. Dramatically, this speech may be both natural and powerful; so I am told. Metaphysically, it is nothing.

Once more: Shakespeare could put a character into a situation that called for a desperate speech, and give him one. But he could not seat this character at the table to compose a finished poem, and then let him stand up and deliver it.

If this is the way of the drama at its most favorable moments, there is still less chance of its achieving metaphysical effects in the usual give and take of dialogue. I think of the brilliant figures crowding a late work like *Antony and Cleopatra*, and note, at random, the passage where Antony is having his account with Cleopatra after the defeat at Actium (III, ix):

> Now I must
> To the young man send humble treaties, dodge
> And palter in the shifts of lowness. . . .

Antony is a figurative man, and full of feelings. The sending of humble treaties is not enough to express them, therefore he elects to dodge, and also to palter, and he will be in shifts of—of what? Lowness will do. And this vigorous jumping from one thing to another registers Antony very well, and may claim its theoretical justification under dramatic method. But in the coherent poetry of Donne and the metaphysicals there is nothing like it; no more than there is anything there like the peculiar jumpiness and straining of a modern such as, let us say, Mr. Joseph Auslander.

It is not likely that the plays of Shakespeare, even the later ones, can furnish better metaphysical effects than the sonnets do, which deliberately intend them, and in intending them do not have to worry about the peremptory and prior claims of drama.

Art and Mr. Santayana

Among philosophical personalities the most urbane and humanistic since Socrates may well be Mr. Santayana. I imagine he is what Emerson might have been if Emerson had had a philosophical instead of a theological background; in other words, if his Harvard had been the Harvard of today or yesterday. As an Emerson disturbs the theologians, a Santayana disturbs the philosophers—an admirable function. Each speaks luminously, and that dismays his professional colleagues and drives them to speak primly; and each pours out an incessant gnomic wisdom, so that the colleagues look a little innocent or empty. The likeness goes further: each possesses the technical accomplishment of verse. But here the report is not so favorable. Emerson was too much the theologian to be quite released by poetry, and Mr. Santayana is imprisoned with all his graces in the net of his intellectualism. They do not command the freedom of poets.

And here the parallel stops, for Emerson did not undertake to compete with Hawthorne in another art, but Mr. Santayana has written a big novel, at the moment when his wisdom is ripest. Unfortunately the wisdom, the great shining blocks of it, is a little adventitious for the special purpose of fiction, which on its side happened at the same moment to have reached a stage of enormously subtle proficiency. *The Last Puritan* has distinguished merits, but this is not the novel which will cause the author's secular competitors to cancel their projects and rush off to Academies and Stoas in order to acquire technical philosophy before they write again. It is still they who determine for us what fiction is to be. The flexibility of Mr. Santayana's mind, which is extreme when judged by the standards of philosophical writing, is hardly sufficient for verse and fiction. The philosopher consumes the artist; a very old story. And just as his practice does not quite indicate an understanding of the art-work, neither, I think, does his published theory.

The published theory is scarcely to be found in any one locus, for Mr. Santayana's writings are lavish and various. A good single volume for a quick look at the later and characteristic doctrines is the choice collection of essays, *Obiter Scripta*—an indispensable book for all amateur or general readers with the slightest pretension to knowledge. But I think we had better go farther back, to the time when the characteristic doctrines were not yet established, in order to see how and why the Santayana æsthetic had to take its form. As a Harvard professor Mr. Santayana admired Greek philosophers and abhorred German idealists. If one should offer the opinion that the five volumes published in 1905 under the general title, *The Life of Reason,* are excellent, without effecting much displacement in the existing body of theory, it would be a misinformation unless one added: But they have an extraordinary literary finish, and the vitality of a discourse that is fertilized by metaphor.

We come to Volume IV of this series, *Reason in Art;* and what is the view taken of the meaning of the arts? It is quite commonplace: they are actions which are useful and expressive at the same time. These two requirements are commented on and illustrated, and we are given to understand that they govern both industrial art, which must not be merely useful, and fine art, which must not be merely expressive. Many a pretty application of this formula can be made by a literary philosopher.

But expressiveness and utility: if the phrase sounds determinate to the uncritical, nevertheless it must be one of the best examples of the worst tradition of philosophical rigmarole. The currency of formulations like it is a disgrace to philosophy, and in particular has doomed æsthetic to remain its most undeveloped branch. This can be said without especially disparaging Mr. Santayana, who has long since thrown the foolish formula away.

Utility may stand, for at least it says something. The utility of a work is objective, and measurable in terms of the satisfactions which man as a biological species exacts of a resistant environment. Economics has appropriated this term perhaps, but the goods with which economics deals are no other than those perfectly arbitrary ones defined by the peculiar human organism. Utility will even stand, I think, with Mr. Santayana's qualifications, as one of the requirements of fine art. We are in the habit of saying that a piece of art must be important, or must have an interest, but the import and the interest are biological too. Mr. Santayana has conceded that it need not be a direct or possessive interest; Kant enforced this point, and we repeat it when we say that the interest is felt in an imaginary rather than an actual situation. The fine arts are all symbolic, and rest on a conscious fiction, or illusion; it is the illusion of reality; "true to life" as we say, or "a preparation for living" as Mr. Santayana says. Schopenhauer showed that even music must symbolize life, and otherwise could not move us as it does; Mr. Santayana shows it too, and is more explicit than Schopenhauer.

Expressiveness, on the contrary, is a term exquisitely calculated to conceal thought, if there is really thinking on these premises; or, what is more likely, to evade thought. Of what is art expressive? Mr. Santayana is thoroughly uncomfortable with the term, and in using it seems as often as not to be a species of demonologist, and to think that art expresses certain impish, irrational, and unproductive impulses, too trifling for him to track down and name, not ruled by common sense nor aiming at the worth-while biological values, insisting democratically on their right to expression, and humored without doing much harm in anomalous exercises called works of art. It is as if he said, Art is a kind of scientific performance enacted with a great deal of foolishness; but, not telling us what foolishness is, permitted us to believe the worst.

By this strategy he runs the risk of instructing his readers to make a savage comment on his own pretty prose and melodious sonnets, as follows:

> We admire the utility of Mr. S.'s philosophical discourses, but it is obstructed and indignified by his weakness for rhetoric, and we think we shall return after all to those philosophers who attend strictly to business. As for his verse, which seems to have niched for itself a secure if modest corner in the monument of literature, we have looked that up and found the place where he tells us about a too-aspiring metaphysician:
>
> Ah, the thin air is cold above the moon!
> I stood and saw you fall, befooled in death,
> As, in your numbéd spirit's fatal swoon,
> You cried you were a god, or were to be;
> I hear with feeble moan your boastful breath
> Bubble from depths of the Icarian sea.
>
> This metaphysician is certainly in a plight, but it is absurd to say he has flown higher than the moon and fallen into the sea, and what is ever gained by absurdities, or by false accents and musical accompaniments? If this represents a side of Mr. S.'s nature which had to be expressed, he should have had the goodness to be ashamed of it and to express it in private; most grown men are, and do.

For by the doctrine of expressiveness, in the hands of persons not its enthusiasts, art is disreputable.

But suppose the doctrinaire says that art is expressive not of a contemptible residue of little impulses, disloyal to the practical successes of the organism, but of personality itself, which is imposing, which in fact is the whole organism? The position of art is not much improved. What an odd collocation of terms! Art as utility is dealing with perfectly objective ends, and at the same time as expression is trying to please a perfectly subjective personality. And what is personality? It can only mean: whatever in the organism is responsible for whatever in the work of art is not utility. Personality is mentioned because the doctrinaire is not analytical enough to make out the form that expression takes but can remark sagely that something, probably something big, with about five syllables, is expressing itself. If the utilitarians can point out the objective utility of art, which is indistinguishable from that of science, the personalists might try to point out the objective differentiation which removes art from science. The utility and the residue are equally in the objective record, which is the art-work itself.

Objectively, the works of art make a great show in the detritus of the civilizations; they all but rival the aggregate exhibit of the sciences. The testimony which they furnish is certainly adequate. Yet so little have philosophers done to distinguish the art from the science that intelligent teachers of literature are still addressing astonished pupils in this manner:

> Our poem brings to us, then, young gentlemen, a nugget of wisdom, a principle that makes for righteousness and the welfare of humankind. See that you cherish it. But it is only by an abstraction that I have paraphrased it in prose and taken it out of context. The prose statement is the practical

or scientific meaning. But the object really before us is the work of art, whole and untranslatable. It is richer than its scientific abstract. In what way richer we cannot exactly say, but if we are spiritually sensitive we can feel it. At best we may say that the artist has fused the bare meaning in his genius and in his personality, and made it glowing and expressive, till it has suffered this sea-change. Such is the magic and the mystery of art.

In the meantime the sceptical scientific population, perpetually on the increase, is rudely remarking that it does not believe in magic, and asking of the apologists of poetry to show what the poet has added to the scientific record except irrelevance and disorder. The apologists presently are obliged in honesty to confess that the scientific or prose value of the poem is often trite and therefore slight, as if in satisfaction of a merely formal requirement, and that the unique or characteristic value of all the poetry everywhere, a sum heroic in magnitude, must depend on other but to them invisible considerations. With which confession in their pockets, it may be predicted that the sceptics with renewed confidence and in even greater numbers will be asking whether there is demonstrably anything in the whole world of human actions except scientific ones, dictated by the animal needs of the organism; and whether any distinction can ever be made between actions except in the respect that they may have different degrees of rigor, or consistency, and therefore may be the more or the less perfect; the so-called sciences more, and the unhappy arts a great deal less.

2

Mr. Santayana evolved and grew, like a good biological organism, and produced doctrines which are original, within the limits which must confine originality at a late stage of philosophy. I shall refer to them so far as they seem to have consequences for æsthetic theory.

He cannot have been happy with his word expressive, and the like words, for the kind of commentary which I have improvised is too easy to have escaped him. He had an objective problem and was falling back upon a vague subjective solution: a bad business for any philosopher, and worse for one who had made it his specialty to point to the healthy metaphysical state of Greeks and to deride subjectivism. In 1923 appeared *Scepticism and Animal Faith*, a body blow at the idealists. Animal faith is the new and ingenious weapon. William James had talked about pragmatic truth and the will to believe, so that one might say to an idealist who believed in mind more than in matter that these things were perfectly optional. But Mr. Santayana says no, that belief is compulsive, in mind and in matter alike, being part of the animal function which has to act upon environment. Scepticism is not the mark of the living animal; and unbelief in matter, if it could be genuine, would be far on the road to inaction and death. Idealism, that perverse attitude, could have suggested itself hardly anywhere else than among the romantics of the Northern races. (Idealism as if by the principle of equal and opposite reactions has produced behaviorism, its latest and most precise counterpart, which believes in matter but not in mind; a punishment visited upon the world for the crimes of the Nordic idealists.)

I suppose the new doctrine has no application to æsthetic unless indirectly: it dramatizes more sharply the question whether art is really distinct from science. Is art only another work of animal faith? The form and purpose of its animality are not disclosed. And the truth is that the lover of art, who will "feel" a good deal that he cannot know explicitly, would expect to find its residuary properties quite different from those which interest animals. The Christians need not be brought into the argument, but the Greeks, including even Aristotle, held that man is in part an animal but also in part a god. If in his sciences he has insight into objective nature so far as it is serviceable to an animal, perhaps in his arts he may have a more innocent and indeed a divine insight into nature as it is. But waiving theology entirely, I am sure that many art-lovers have a secret notion which goes like this: Art distinguishes man from the other animals in kind, since they have none of it, while science distinguishes him only in power or efficiency, which means degree. Mr. Santayana had almost behaved too handsomely by animality.

He atoned for it handsomely in the two-volume *Realms of Being*, his chief philosophical work, of which *The Realm of Essence* appeared in 1927 and *The Realm of Matter* in 1930. Very properly for this Platonist, essences engaged him first; they are his version of the Platonic ideas.

A refined and even attenuated version, for Plato's have some animal odor on them as compared with the Santayana essences, upon which no animal would think of trying to support life. Yet Plato's ideas, like all the varieties of essence to which his sons have ever become attached, fall short of having the fullness of natural or material existences. Plato punished his animality through being fastidious, in a manner not necessarily aristocratic and indeed rather mean for a Greek: the manner of an animal who has become painfully self-conscious, and who has conceived a powerful preference for his rational or "higher" activities and a distaste for the fortuitous pleasures of sense. This is the ascetic or Puritan pattern of fastidiousness. It is not the only one, for Plato might have decided to embrace what he could not cure and to cultivate even the diffusive senses under the standard which is called taste. Its acquisition is laborious enough to have satisfied the schoolmaster in him. (In England the Cavaliers did not go to school less than the Roundheads but more.) But it would not have produced any Platonic ideas. The world of sense, like real property, may be "improved" in a number of ways, but taste would like to bring it under arts, fashions, rites, and manners, which emphasize those residuary splendors that are of no animal importance. Not electing this sort of discipline, Plato went in for ideas, and created them after the likeness of his preferences: as natural substances dried out, purified, and made fit for disaffected but very rational animals. They claim to be the archetypal forms of all created things, but we know nothing about that; and they claim "really" to constitute the present natural world, but that only means that they might have done so if contingency and confusion had not got into nature. So Plato qualified them as only "real" or "essential" constituents of the world, and we need not waste time objecting; it is a locution against which it would be a great deal of trouble to legislate. But I think I know the briefest and best description of the Platonic ideas: they are *ideals;* moral and religious ones. They have a degree of practicability. They are effective in so far as they can persuade men actually to occupy their minds with rational essences rather than with the whole of the contingent world; and is there not an incorrigible and irreducible Platonic faction in every civilized Western population? It is easy to work with nature as animals must, and then to pretend that we are working with essences, which are so neat and clean.

Mr. Santayana's kind of essence abandons even the rational core of body; yet abandoning so much it is a more honest ghost than the Platonic idea. A body is a locus of properties numerically infinite, while the properties of an essence are numerically finite. But we might arrange essences in a series as including more or fewer properties, and Mr. Santayana's would stand at the end; the poorest excuse for body imaginable, but possibly for that very reason, in their void of animal utility, the noblest essences. They make no pretense to existence, and are not in the least norms or ideals. They are nothing but the pure qualities, each one unique and incomparable. Their realm comprises all the qualities in the world, but it is a grammatical or paper realm. They are the atoms of nature in a quaint qualitative sense, for they are single, when it is well understood that nature, even in its smallest and most empty-looking piece, must offer itself as a vast collocation of qualities. And how have they acquired a realm? I suppose it is very simple. Whenever one comes upon a new quality one takes a picture of it and puts it into a drawer. Perhaps one may return one day and look at the pictures. It would be a harmless pastime, though probably a dull one, not like animal pleasure, not like moral pleasure; and not, one would think, like æsthetic pleasure.

But if the realm of essence is quaint, like a child's collection of colored blocks, it is not so with the realm of matter. Essences are just harmless adjectives, but the forms of matter, the things, are nouns, and in action they are frightful things for an animal to have to deal with, because their activities are unpredictable, and evil more often than good; and they are sadly or comically unsuitable for a scientist, because they cannot be held to strict accountability like the nouns in dictionaries but are possessed of an obscene and malignant fertility for spawning fresh adjectives as long as he has the courage to observe them. Mr. Santayana's account of this realm is a great literary achievement, and should be recommended equally to soft-hearted sentimentalists and hard-headed positivists. The account is more exciting than Milton's picture of Chaos, because nothing should have been expected of Chaos except the chaotic, but in nature we hope to find perfect animal fulfilments and rational processes; for, though we may often have been cheated, we have animal faith.

The animal lives in the realm of matter, which is the natural world, and occupies himself with wresting and worrying his living out of it; and if Mr. Santayana's realm of essence were called to his attention he would find it rather beneath his notice or, as its author might say, above it; but actually he will hardly know nor care if there is such a realm. I come back to the original question, and now it will be in the new terms which Mr. Santayana has furnished: With which is the specific vision of the artist concerned, with essence or with matter?

Mr. Santayana has dallied with essences as if they were to be the fruits of his well-spent life. His long road has led him to this sharp categorical division as if precisely in order that he may justify artists at last; for I cannot find any other occasion for it. But at this stage his admirer, though hoping that he will place the feet of the artists on very firm ground, must feel many ignoble apprehensions lest they suffer the fate of his ambitious metaphysician if it should turn out that he has only essences to give them.

He has only essences. That appears from the papers relating to art which are dated from 1925 on, so far as I can judge from those in the *Obiter Scripta*, which are several. In 1925 he is emphasizing ". . . the fact that beauty, as I feel it, transports us altogether into the realm of essence, and that no pleasure, interest, or admiration becomes a sense of beauty unless it does so. Every image, however, if animal faith is suspended in its presence, is an essence seen under the form of eternity."

I may as well remark at once crudely, for it will be already clear that I do not subscribe to this view, that it seems to require us, if we would be artists or follow them, to get out of the world where essences inhere in the living substances, and into the drawer where the little flat images are kept. It does little good to say that in this drawer is a treasure which neither moths can corrupt nor thieves break through and steal, inasmuch as everything here is under the form of eternity. Essences are eternal enough; a similar way of thinking has led Mr. Whitehead to name them eternal objects. To eternize an object is to save it by withdrawing it from circulation; from circulation in the battering and incessant transaction of nature, which is life; but it is a peculiar method of salvation, amounting to death. Mr. Santayana has had a peculiar history as a philosopher. He has censured the idealists for not believing their own natural images, but that is exactly the policy he now recommends to them if they would have æsthetic experience; they are to fly to a realm too thin to pretend to support belief. If we should hold him to his verbal commitments, which might be too harsh a procedure, we should have to say that this is one of the most profound of scepticisms, and that Mr. Santayana himself is a Puritan, and in the last extremity.

A remark about essence as the scientists construe it; for we should keep all these essences straight. Of course they never permit it to receive the modest indefinite article, and this implies that they are under the bondage of animal faith when they handle it. To be scientific is to pursue an exclusive interest effectively, and so the scientists abstract from natural forms what they take to be a nucleus or core of properties, and set this aside as "the essence" of a whole series of forms. They do not put it into an attic drawer but rather into the office files. For these essences are Platonic ideas somewhat vulgarized; that is, more shrewdly selective, and believed in not as broad ideals but as sure things, or specific working formulas. Yet the sum of the scientific interests covers the whole range of animality, and if we should define the world in terms of scientific ideality it might easily wear the look of a perfect Christmas party, where all the drinks and sweets were delicious without painful consequences and all the toys obedient to the mechanics' pleasure; so much it might lack of the austerity of the Platonic vision. At any rate, scientists define "the essential" pattern of an object that interests them, and "the essential" conditions for its production. Both the scientific essences and the Santayana ones are obtained by abstraction, but theirs are for hard animal use, and his are for innocent contemplation; non-animal contemplation, I think we must say.

3

In 1929, Mr. Santayana reports a windfall. Proust, fullest and richest if most laborious of all the novelists, has published an æsthetic doctrine scarcely distinguishable from his. It occurs in the last volume of Proust's great work, the one in which he most broods, I think, upon his preoccupation with the past and the meaning of æsthetic joy. Mr. Santayana writes briefly upon it. I quote from his footnote and with his omissions a passage taken out of Blossom's translation:

> The being that was called to life again in me by uniting the present impression with something in the past draws its sustenance only from the essence of things, in that alone does it find its nourishment and delight. . . . Let a sound already heard or an odor caught in bygone years be sensed anew, simultaneously in the present and the past, real without being of the present moment, ideal but not abstract, and immediately the permanent essence of things, usually concealed, is set free and our true self . . . awakes, takes on fresh life as it receives the celestial nourishment brought to it. . . . This contemplation, though part of eternity, was transitory. And yet I felt that the pleasure it had bestowed on me at rare intervals of my life was the only one that was fecund and real. Is not the indication of the unreliability of the others suf-

ficiently evident either in their inability to satisfy us . . . or in the despondency that follows whatever satisfactions they may give? . . . And so I was decided to concentrate myself to this study of the essence of things, to establish its true nature. . . . And if I recapitulated the disappointments in my life, so far as it had been lived, which led me to believe that its real essence must lie somewhere else than in action . . . I came to realize clearly that disappointment in a journey and disappointment in a love affair were not different in themselves but merely the different aspects they assumed in varying situations by our inability to find our real selves in physical enjoyment or material activity.

Commenting on this passage, Mr. Santayana thinks it shows an awkwardness in grasping the essences, which does not affect the value of its testimony:

No wonder that a sensibility so exquisite and so voluminous as that of Proust, filled with endless images and their distant reverberations, could be rescued from distraction only by finding certain repetitions or rhymes in this experience. He was a tireless husbandman of memory, gathering perhaps more poppies than corn; and the very fragility and worthlessness of the weeds collected may have led him to appreciate their presence only when lost, and their harsh scent only when recovered. Thus he required two phenomena to reveal to him one essence, as if essences needed to appear a second time in order to appear at all. A mind less volatile and less retentive, but more concentrated and loyal, might easily have discerned the eternal essence in any single momentary fact. It might also have felt the scale of values imposed on things by human nature, and might have been carried towards some by an innate love and away from others by a quick repulsion: something which in Proust is remarkably rare. Yet this very inhumanity and innocent openness, this inclination to be led on by endlessly rambling perception, makes his testimony to the reality of essences all the more remarkable. We could not have asked for a more competent or a more unexpected witness to the fact that life as it flows is so much time wasted, and that nothing can ever be recovered or truly possessed save under the form of eternity which is also, as he tells us, the form of art.

From the last sentence of Mr. Santayana's passage we receive the sense of a philosopher seizing on the treasure which is not a treasure, because it comes to him under the hollow form of eternity. And from the last sentence of Proust's passage we receive what? The sense that the artist finds his characteristic pleasure, though it is invidious to say that he finds his "real self," not in animal activity but somewhere else. That is one part of Proust's testimony. The other part is more difficult to translate into intelligible terms: the part which has to do with the special importance of memory in Proust's æsthetic practice. Memory is so unrelated to the doctrine of essence that it is not strange that Proust hardly knows what to do with it, nor that Mr. Santayana in effect has to cancel what he does. I do not know who is so adventurous as to dispute Proust's transcript of actual experience, but it is not to be expected that Proust will have the gift for theorizing it; and if Mr. Santayana has the gift it is hardly to be expected that he will theorize it either, being committed already to fixed theories.

Proust has a repertory of simple images which he employs to invoke the past, and with their assistance he lives and finds his delight in the past. His fiction is about the things past, and it is autobiographical. A psychologist should study these key-images to see of what sort they are; it might lead to an understanding of nostalgia, which is the clear emotional overtone of, I think, more than half of lyric poetry, and perhaps of an even larger fraction of music. Proust mentions here a sound and an odor. A sound is heard which transports him into the past, and he testifies that it is by the help of the past that he fixes upon this sound as an essence and enjoys it. But that seems meaningless; and more important to an understanding of the experience might be the fact, which I think could be established, that it was no such sound as, say, the dinner bell; it was not a sound which might lead the animal in him into an act of retrospective imagination in order to lick its chops. (It might have been such a sound, but not in the kind of experience to which Proust refers.) An odor is caught, but it is that of a flower perhaps, not that of animal sweat, or food. Nearly any distinct and "unimportant" sound or odor would do; these senses are specially innocent, in that their images are generally not attended to in the fury of the animal processes. And once these images start the thing, other images come pouring out of the past, the past takes form again. The past which they invoke would seem to be, pending the psychologist's report, *precisely that past which the man as animal did not attend to.* Memory retained it while he was not attending to it, and memory is available. The automatic memory seems disposed to preserve an innumerable troop of meek and homeless items that the animal consciousness has rejected; but are they not just the items that are waiting to be attended to? It is in art, or in the informal indulgence of memory, that we come back and attend to them. For Proust or for us there are always images accompanying present experience which are just as innocent as those were, but it is as hard to attend to them now as it was then, since we are still, presumably, good animals.

The consequence is that what must seem like a disproportionate fraction of art is a fairly literal reading of the memory, and autobiographical; the artist already has a record of the world more complete than he can transcribe, and need not take the trouble to invent a fiction. For that matter, the fiction when it is invented has to be pieced out of the odd scraps furnished by the memory. It is by employing the device of systematic memory, which recovers a past relieved of its animal urgency, or the device of fiction, which is too hypothetical to engage the inhibitory animal, that the civilized races, who are the mechanized and the highly scienced, obtain their most solid æsthetic experience. Art serves them better than nature. And if we often seem to detect in the makeshift aspect of art the trace of something sly, roundabout, and for theoretical admiration unfortunate, when we have come from watching the bold front, the almost cynical directness, with which the confident animal moves upon his objectives, that is only another way of saying that art in action is artificial, or indirect. It has to be. It has learned its technique in a hard school.

But I cannot think it credible that Proust's joy should consist, as he and Mr. Santayana believed, in obtaining the simple sound, or odor, and then collapsing into eternity, which is trance, emptied of further consciousness, beside it. The state does not seem likely enough to be even pathological. Freudians have wonderful imaginations, and use them ingeniously to account for a strange phenomenon: the fascination and terror which an apparently simple image may exercise over the morbid; and their answer is that through the mechanism of memory it sets in motion a vast, secret, and terrifying train of imagery, so that the total agent is not simple at all. But for Proust we are told that the image is really simple, and unaccompanied; that this is its whole virtue. If it then can be the cause of so profound an experience as art, we are out of the range of the human economy so far as we have had any understanding of that.

4

If Mr. Santayana as a free personality in a dull professional world reminds us of Emerson, in the light of his systematic philosophy he is a diffused modern version of Schopenhauer. Both are very well aware of the customary unmannerly ferocity of man as an animal, with Schopenhauer of course grieving more than tolerant Mr. Santayana about that; the animal directing and corrupting the most remote-looking and publicly esteemed pursuits, like tribal morality, which passes for disinterested action, or science, which passes for the pursuit of pure knowledge; yet kennelled, or put to sleep, or transcended, in at least one free and charming activity, which is æsthetic experience. In art, according to Schopenhauer, we at last have knowledge without desire. It remains only to determine just what this knowledge is about, and there again the two philosophers pronounce similarly. Knowledge of the Platonic ideas, said Schopenhauer, but explained them very mistily; and knowledge of the pure essences, says Mr. Santayana, but they look inadequate.

It cannot be impertinent to refer Mr. Santayana, and those who may have followed or preceded him into the ethereal climate of essences, to that remarkable work of metaphysical description, *The Realm of Matter*. The images of art are too crowded, contingent, and energetic to be of much use to scientific animals. But the reason is that they belong to the realm of matter as scientific abstracts do not, and not to the realm of essence as scientific abstracts do. In them the scientific or useful essence finds itself accompanied by an infinite residue, and for scientists this residue is exactly what they have charged: irrelevance and foolishness, which cannot suit the limited aims of animals. But all wealth of circumstance and event is within the realm of matter; Mr. Santayana has precisely distinguished the realms and then has not looked at the right one. From it countless works of art have been equipped with their substance, yet it is undiminished and ready for fresh works. What these works intend is, simply, the widest and most unprejudiced knowledge of nature that is possible. There may not be gods to whom knowledge of this sort is the constant form of their activity, for who knows? But there is man, who is not merely animal, and whose animal preoccupations ought never to have become so binding as to exclude a constant exercise of this free knowledge. Now, in his inevitable decadence, he has fallen apart, and the pursuit of it has become one of the specialized and technical functions of his divided mind.[1]

[1]Mr. Santayana's new book, *The Realm of Truth*, is out; I have not had time to read it through. It concerns the relation between the essences, so pure and delightful (as he finds them) for the mind, and the disorderly realm of matter. There is truth, I suppose, when the matter fits into the mind's pattern of essences. But this is rarely, and imperfectly. Mr. Santayana is more Platonic and unworldly than ever. Poetry would be for him, like truth, the hopeless affirmation of the essences. Poetry does not feel like that to me; and poets, I cannot but think, are prodigious materialists; even Plato thought so. (Mar. 4, 1938.)

Criticism, Inc.

It is strange, but nobody seems to have told us what exactly is the proper business of criticism. There are many critics who might tell us, but for the most part they are amateurs. So have the critics nearly always been amateurs; including the best ones. They have not been trained to criticism so much as they have simply undertaken a job for which no specific qualifications were required. It is far too likely that what they call criticism when they produce it is not the real thing.

There are three sorts of trained performers who would appear to have some of the competence that the critic needs. The first is the artist himself. He should know good art when he sees it; but his understanding is intuitive rather than dialectical—he cannot very well explain his theory of the thing. It is true that literary artists, with their command of language, are better critics of their own art than are other artists; probably the best critics of poetry we can now have are the poets. But one can well imagine that any artist's commentary on the art-work is valuable in the degree that he sticks to its technical effects, which he knows minutely, and about which he can certainly talk if he will.

The second is the philosopher, who should know all about the function of the fine arts. But the philosopher is apt to see a lot of wood and no trees, for his theory is very general and his acquaintance with the particular works of art is not persistent and intimate, especially his acquaintance with their technical effects. Or at least I suppose so, for philosophers have not proved that they can write close criticism by writing it; and I have the feeling that even their handsome generalizations are open to suspicion as being grounded more on other generalizations, those which form their prior philosophical stock, than on acute study of particulars.

The third is the university teacher of literature, who is styled professor, and who should be the very professional we need to take charge of the critical activity. He is hardly inferior as critic to the philosopher, and perhaps not on the whole to the poet, but he is a greater disappointment because we have the right to expect more of him. Professors of literature are learned but not critical men. The professional morale of this part of the university staff is evidently low. It is as if, with conscious or unconscious cunning, they had appropriated every avenue of escape from their responsibility which was decent and official; so that it is easy for one of them without public reproach to spend a lifetime in compiling the data of literature and yet rarely or never commit himself to a literary judgment.

Nevertheless it is from the professors of literature, in this country the professors of English for the most part, that I should hope eventually for the erection of intelligent standards of criticism. It is their business.

Criticism must become more scientific, or precise and systematic, and this means that it must be developed by the collective and sustained effort of learned persons—which means that its proper seat is in the universities.

Scientific: but I do not think we need be afraid that criticism, trying to be a sort of science, will inevitably fail and give up in despair, or else fail without realizing it and enjoy some hollow and pretentious career. It will never be a very exact science, or even a nearly exact one. But neither will psychology, if that term continues to refer to psychic rather than physical phenomena; nor will sociology, as Pareto, quite contrary to his intention, appears to have furnished us with evidence for believing; nor even will economics. It does not matter whether we call them sciences or just systematic studies; the total effort of each to be effective must be consolidated and kept going. The studies which I have mentioned have immeasurably improved in understanding since they were taken over by the universities, and the same career looks possible for criticism.

Rather than occasional criticism by amateurs, I should think the whole enterprise might be seriously taken in hand by professionals. Perhaps I use a distasteful figure, but I have the idea that what we need is Criticism, Inc., or Criticism, Ltd.

The principal resistance to such an idea will come

from the present incumbents of the professorial chairs. But its adoption must come from them too. The idea of course is not a private one of my own. If it should be adopted before long, the credit would probably belong to Professor Ronald S. Crane, of the University of Chicago, more than to any other man. He is the first of the great professors to have advocated it as a major policy for departments of English. It is possible that he will have made some important academic history.

2

Professor Crane published recently a paper of great note in academic circles, on the reform of the courses in English. It appeared in *The English Journal*, under the title: "History Versus Criticism in the University Study of Literature." He argues there that historical scholarship has been overplayed heavily in English studies, in disregard of the law of diminishing returns, and that the emphasis must now be shifted to the critical.

To me this means, simply: the students of the future must be permitted to study literature, and not merely about literature. But I think this is what the good students have always wanted to do. The wonder is that they have allowed themselves so long to be denied. But they have not always been amiable about it, and the whole affair presents much comic history.

At the University of Chicago, I believe that Professor Crane, with some others, is putting the revolution into effect in his own teaching, though for the time being perhaps with a limited programme, mainly the application of Aristotle's critical views. (My information is not at all exact.) The university is an opulent one, not too old to experience waves of reformational zeal, uninhibited as yet by bad traditions. Its department of English has sponsored plenty of old-line scholarship, but this is not the first time it has gone in for criticism. If the department should now systematically and intelligently build up a general school of literary criticism, I believe it would score a triumph that would be, by academic standards, spectacular. I mean that the alive and brilliant young English scholars all over the country would be saying they wanted to go there to do their work. That would place a new distinction upon the university, and it would eventually and profoundly modify the practices of many other institutions. It would be worth even more than Professor Crane's careful presentation of the theory.

This is not the first time that English professors have tilted against the historians, or "scholars," in the dull sense which that word has acquired. They did not score heavily, at those other times. Probably they were themselves not too well versed in the historical studies, so that it could be said with honest concern that they scarcely had the credentials to judge of such matters. At the same time they may have been too unproductive critically to offer a glowing alternative.

The most important recent diversion from the orthodox course of literary studies was that undertaken by the New Humanists. I regret to think that it was not the kind of diversion which I am advocating; nor the kind approved by Professor Crane, who comments briefly against it. Unquestionably the Humanists did divert, and the refreshment was grateful to anybody who felt resentful for having his literary predilections ignored under the schedule of historical learning. But in the long run the diversion proved to be nearly as unliterary as the round of studies from which it took off at a tangent. No picnic ideas were behind it.

The New Humanists were, and are, moralists; more accurately, historians and advocates of a certain moral system. Criticism is the attempt to define and enjoy the æsthetic or characteristic values of literature, but I suppose the Humanists would shudder at "æsthetic" as hard as ordinary historical scholars do. Did an official Humanist ever make any official play with the term? I do not remember it. The term "art" is slightly more ambiguous, and they have availed themselves of that; with centuries of loose usage behind it, art connotes, for those who like, high seriousness, and high seriousness connotes moral self-consciousness, and an inner check, and finally either Plato or Aristotle.

Mr. Babbitt consistently played on the terms classical and romantic. They mean any of several things each, so that unquestionably Mr. Babbitt could make war on romanticism for purely moral reasons; and his preoccupation was ethical, not æsthetic. It is perfectly legitimate for the moralist to attack romantic literature if he can make out his case; for example, on the ground that it deals with emotions rather than principles, or the ground that its author discloses himself as flabby, intemperate, escapist, unphilosophical, or simply adolescent. The moral objection is probably valid; a romantic period testifies to a large-scale failure of adaptation, and defense of that failure to adapt, to the social and political environment; unless, if the Humanists will consent, it sometimes testifies to the failure of society and state to sympathize with the needs of the individual. But this is certainly not the charge that Mr. T. S. Eliot, a literary critic, brings against romanticism. His, if I am not mistaken, is æsthetic, though he may not ever care to define it very sharply. In other words, the literary critic also has something to say about romanticism, and it might come to something like this: that romantic literature is imperfect in objectivity, or "æsthetic distance," and that out of this imperfection comes its weakness of structure; that the romantic poet does not quite realize the æsthetic attitude, and is not the pure artist. Or it might come to something else. It would be quite premature to say that when a moralist is obliged to disapprove a work the literary critic must disapprove it too.

Following the excitement produced by the Humanist diversion, there is now one due to the Leftists, or Proletarians, who are also diversionists. Their diversion is likewise moral. It is just as proper for them to ferret out class-consciousness in literature, and to make literature serve the cause of loving-comradeship, as it is for the Humanists to censure romanticism and to use the topic, and the literary exhibit, as the occasion of reviving the Aristotelian moral canon. I mean that these are procedures of the same sort. Debate could never occur between a Humanist and a Leftist on æsthetic grounds, for they are equally intent on ethical values. But the debate on ethical grounds would be very spirited, and it might create such a stir in a department conducting English studies that the conventional scholars there would find themselves slipping, and their pupils deriving from literature new and seductive excitements which would entice them away from their scheduled English exercises.

On the whole, however, the moralists, distinguished as they may be, are like those who have quarrelled with the ordinary historical studies on purer or more æsthetic grounds: they have not occupied in English studies the positions of professional importance. In a department of English, as in any other going business, the proprietary interest becomes vested, and in old and reputable departments the vestees have uniformly been gentlemen who have gone through the historical mill. Their laborious Ph.D.'s and historical publications are their patents. Naturally, quite spontaneously, they would tend to perpetuate a system in which the power and the glory belonged to them. But English scholars in this country can rarely have better credentials than those which Professor Crane has earned in his extensive field, the eighteenth century. It is this which makes his disaffection significant.

It is really atrocious policy for a department to abdicate its own self-respecting identity. The department of English is charged with the understanding and the communication of literature, an art, yet it has usually forgotten to inquire into the peculiar constitution and structure of its product. English might almost as well announce that it does not regard itself as entirely autonomous, but as a branch of the department of history, with the option of declaring itself occasionally a branch of the department of ethics. It is true that the historical and the ethical studies will cluster round objects which for some reason are called artistic objects. But the thing itself the professors do not have to contemplate; and only last spring the head of English studies in a graduate school fabulously equipped made the following impromptu disclaimer to a victim who felt aggrieved at having his own studies forced in the usual direction: "This is a place for exact scholarship, and you want to do criticism. Well, we don't allow criticism here, because that is something which anybody can do."

But one should never speak impromptu in one's professional capacity. This speech may have betrayed a fluttery private apprehension which should not have been made public: that you can never be critical and be exact at the same time, that history is firmer ground than æsthetics, and that, to tell the truth, criticism is a painful job for the sort of mind that wants to be very sure about things. Not in that temper did Aristotle labor towards a critique in at least one branch of letters; nor in that temper are strong young minds everywhere trying to sharpen their critical apparatus into precision tools, in this decade as never before.

It is not anybody who can do criticism. And for an example, the more eminent (as historical scholar) the professor of English, the less apt he is to be able to write decent criticism, unless it is about another professor's work of historical scholarship, in which case it is not literary criticism. The professor may not be without æsthetic judgments respecting an old work, especially if it is "in his period," since it must often have been judged by authorities whom he respects. Confronted with a new work, I am afraid it is very rare that he finds anything particular to say. Contemporary criticism is not at all in the hands of those who direct the English studies. Contemporary literature, which is almost obliged to receive critical study if it receives any at all, since it is hardly capable of the usual historical commentary, is barely officialized as a proper field for serious study.

Here is contemporary literature, waiting for its criticism; where are the professors of literature?

They are watering their own gardens; elucidating the literary histories of their respective periods. So are their favorite pupils. The persons who save the occasion, and rescue contemporary literature from the humiliation of having to go without a criticism, are the men who had to leave the university before their time because they felt themselves being warped into mere historians; or those who finished the courses and took their punishment but were tough, and did not let it engross them and spoil them. They are home-made critics. Naturally they are not too wise, these amateurs who furnish our reviews and critical studies, But when they distinguish themselves, the universities which they attended can hardly claim more than a trifling share of the honor.

It is not so in economics, chemistry, sociology, theology, and architecture. In these branches it is taken for granted that criticism of the performance is the prerogative of the men who have had formal training in its theory and technique. The historical method is useful, and may be applied readily to any human performance whatever. But the exercise does not become an obsession with the university men working in the other branches; only the literary scholars wish to convert themselves into pure historians. This has gone far to nullify the usefulness of a departmental personnel larger, possibly, than any other, and of the lavish endowment behind it.

3

Presumably the departments of English exist in order to communicate the understanding of the literary art. That will include both criticism and also whatever may be meant by "appreciation." This latter term seems to stand for the kind of understanding that is had intuitively, without benefit of instruction, by merely being constrained to spend time in the presence of the literary product. It is true that some of the best work now being done in departments is by the men who do little more than read well aloud, enforcing a private act of appreciation upon the students. One remembers how good a service that may be, thinking perhaps of Professor Copeland of Harvard, or Dean Cross at Greeley Teachers College. And there are men who try to get at the same thing in another way, which they would claim is surer: by requiring a great deal of memory work, in order to enforce familiarity with fine poetry. These might defend their strategy by saying that at any rate the work they required was not as vain as the historical rigmarole which the scholars made their pupils recite, if the objective was really literary understanding and not external information. But it would be a misuse of terms to employ the word instruction for the offices either of the professors who read aloud or of those who require the memory work. The professors so engaged are properly curators, and the museum of which they have the care is furnished with the cherished literary masterpieces, just as another museum might be filled with paintings. They conduct their squads from one work to another, making appropriate pauses or reverent gestures, but their own obvious regard for the masterpieces is somewhat contagious, and contemplation is induced. Naturally they are grateful to the efficient staff of colleagues in the background who have framed the masterpieces, hung them in the proper schools and in the chronological order, and prepared the booklet of information about the artists and the occasions. The colleagues in their turn probably feel quite happy over this division of labor, thinking that they have done the really productive work, and that it is appropriate now if less able men should undertake a little salesmanship.

Behind appreciation, which is private, and criticism, which is public and negotiable, and represents the last stage of English studies, is historical scholarship. It is indispensable. But it is instrumental and cannot be the end itself. In this respect historical studies have the same standing as linguistic studies: language and history are aids.

On behalf of the historical studies. Without them what could we make of Chaucer, for instance? I cite the familiar locus of the "hard" scholarship, the center of any program of advanced studies in English which intends to initiate the student heroically, and once for all, into the historical discipline. Chaucer writes allegories for historians to decipher, he looks out upon institutions and customs unfamiliar to us. Behind him are many writers in various tongues from whom he borrows both forms and materials. His thought bears constant reference to classical and mediæval philosophies and sciences which have passed from our effective knowledge. An immense labor of historical adaptation is necessary before our minds are ready to make the æsthetic approach to Chaucer.

Or to any author out of our own age. The mind with which we enter into an old work is not the mind with which we make our living, or enter into a contemporary work. It is under sharp restraints, and it is quite differently furnished. Out of our actual contemporary mind we have to cancel a great deal that has come there under modern conditions but was not in the earlier mind at all. This is a technique on the negative side, a technique of suspension; difficult for practical persons, literal scientists, and aggressive moderns who take pride in the "truth" or the "progress" which enlightened man, so well represented in their own instance, has won. Then, on the positive side, we must supply the mind with the precise beliefs and ways of thought it had in that former age, with the specific content in which history instructs us; this is a technique of make-believe. The whole act of historical adaptation, through such techniques, is a marvellous feat of flexibility. Certainly it is a thing hard enough to justify university instruction. But it is not sufficient for an English program.

The achievement of modern historical scholarship

in the field of English literature has been, in the aggregate, prodigious; it should be very proud. A good impression of the volume of historical learning now available for the students of English may be quickly had from inspecting a few chapters of the Cambridge History, with the bibliographies. Or, better, from inspecting one of a large number of works which have come in since the Cambridge History: the handbooks, which tell all about the authors, such as Chaucer, Shakespeare, Milton, and carry voluminous bibliographies; or the period books, which tell a good deal about whole periods of literature.

There is one sense in which it may be justly said that we can never have too much scholarship. We cannot have too much of it if the critical intelligence functions, and has the authority to direct it. There is hardly a critical problem which does not require some arduous exercises in fact-finding, but each problem is quite specific about the kind of facts it wants. Mountains of facts may have been found already, but often they have been found for no purpose at all except the purpose of piling up into a big exhibit, to offer intoxicating delights to the academic population.

To those who are æsthetically minded among students, the rewards of many a historical labor will have to be disproportionately slight. The official Chaucer course is probably over ninety-five per cent historical and linguistic, and less than five per cent æsthetic or critical. A thing of beauty is a joy forever. But it is not improved because the student has had to tie his tongue before it. It is an artistic object, with a heroic human labor behind it, and on these terms it calls for public discussion. The dialectical possibilities are limitless, and when we begin to realize them we are engaged in criticism.

4

What is criticism? Easier to ask, What is criticism not? It is an act now notoriously arbitrary and undefined. We feel certain that the critical act is not one of those which the professors of literature habitually perform, and cause their students to perform. And it is our melancholy impression that it is not often cleanly performed in those loose compositions, by writers of perfectly indeterminate qualifications, that appear in print as reviews of books.

Professor Crane excludes from criticism works of historical scholarship and of Neo-Humanism, but more exclusions are possible than that. I should wish to exclude:

1. Personal registrations, which are declarations of the effect of the art-work upon the critic as reader. The first law to be prescribed to criticism, if we may assume such authority, is that it shall be objective, shall cite the nature of the object rather than its effects upon the subject. Therefore it is hardly criticism to assert that the proper literary work is one that we can read twice; or one that causes in us some remarkable physiological effect, such as oblivion of the outer world, the flowing of tears, visceral or

laryngeal sensations, and such like; or one that induces perfect illusion, or brings us into a spiritual ecstasy; or even one that produces a catharsis of our emotions. Aristotle concerned himself with this last in making up his definition of tragedy—though he did not fail to make some acute analyses of the objective features of the work also. I have read that some modern Broadway producers of comedy require a reliable person to seat himself in a trial audience and count the laughs; their method of testing is not so subtle as Aristotle's, but both are concerned with the effects. Such concern seems to reflect the view that art comes into being because the artist, or the employer behind him, has designs upon the public, whether high moral designs or box-office ones. It is an odious view in either case, because it denies the autonomy of the artist as one who interests himself in the artistic object in his own right, and likewise the autonomy of the work itself as existing for its own sake. (We may define a chemical as something which can effect a certain cure, but that is not its meaning to the chemist; and we may define toys, if we are weary parents, as things which keep our children quiet, but that is not what they are to engineers.) Furthermore, we must regard as uncritical the use of an extensive vocabulary which ascribes to the object properties really discovered in the subject, as: *moving, exciting, entertaining, pitiful; great,* if I am not mistaken, and *admirable,* on a slightly different ground; and, in strictness, *beautiful* itself.

2. Synopsis and paraphrase. The high-school classes and the women's clubs delight in these procedures, which are easiest of all the systematic exercises possible in the discussion of literary objects. I do not mean that the critic never uses them in his analysis of fiction and poetry, but he does not consider plot or story as identical with the real content. Plot is an abstract from content.

3. Historical studies. These have a very wide range, and include studies of the general literary background; author's biography, of course with special reference to autobiographical evidences in the work itself; bibliographical items; the citation of literary originals and analogues, and therefore what, in general, is called comparative literature. Nothing can be more stimulating to critical analysis than comparative literature. But it may be conducted only superficially, if the comparisons are perfunctory and mechanical, or if the scholar is content with merely making the parallel citations.

4. Linguistic studies. Under this head come those studies which define the meaning of unusual words and idioms, including the foreign and archaic ones, and identify the allusions. The total benefit of linguistics for criticism would be the assurance that the latter was based on perfect logical understanding of the content, or "interpretation." Acquaintance with all the languages and literatures in the world would not necessarily produce a critic, though it might save one from damaging errors.

5. Moral studies. The moral standard applied is the one appropriate to the reviewer; it may be the Christian ethic, or the Aristotelian one, or the new proletarian gospel. But the moral content is not the whole content, which should never be relinquished.

6. Any other special studies which deal with some abstract or prose content taken out of the work. Nearly all departments of knowledge may conceivably find their own materials in literature, and take them out. Studies have been made of Chaucer's command of mediæval sciences, of Spenser's view of the Irish question, of Shakespeare's understanding of the law, of Milton's geography, of Hardy's place-names. The critic may well inform himself of these materials as possessed by the artist, but his business as critic is to discuss the literary assimilation of them.

5

With or without such useful exercises as these, probably assuming that the intelligent reader has made them for himself, comes the critical act itself.

Mr. Austin Warren, whose writings I admire, is evidently devoted to the academic development of the critical project. Yet he must be a fair representative of what a good deal of academic opinion would be when he sees no reason why criticism should set up its own house, and try to dissociate itself from historical and other scholarly studies; why not let all sorts of studies, including the critical ones, flourish together in the same act of sustained attention, or the same scheduled "course"? But so they are supposed to do at present; and I would only ask him whether he considers that criticism prospers under this arrangement. It has always had the chance to go ahead in the hands of the professors of literature, and it has not gone ahead. A change of policy suggests itself. Strategy requires now, I should think, that criticism receive its own charter of rights and function independently. If he fears for its foundations in scholarship, the scholars will always be on hand to reprove it when it tries to function on an unsound scholarship.

I do not suppose the reviewing of books can be reformed in the sense of being turned into pure criticism. The motives of the reviewers are as much mixed as the performance, and indeed they condition the mixed performance. The reviewer has a job of presentation and interpretation as well as criticism. The most we can ask of him is that he know when the criticism begins, and that he make it as clean and definitive as his business permits. To what authority may he turn?

I know of no authority. For the present each critic must be his own authority. But I know of one large class of studies which is certainly critical, and necessary, and I can suggest another sort of study for the critic's consideration if he is really ambitious.

Studies in the technique of the art belong to criticism certainly. They cannot belong anywhere else, because the technique is not peculiar to any prose materials discoverable in the work of art, nor to anything else but the unique form of that art. A very large volume of studies is indicated by this classification. They would be technical studies of poetry, for instance, the art I am specifically discussing, if they treated its metric; its inversions, solecisms, lapses from the prose norm of language, and from close prose logic; its tropes; its fictions, or inventions, by which it secures "æsthetic distance" and removes itself from history; or any other devices, on the general understanding that any systematic usage which does not hold good for prose is a poetic device.

A device with a purpose: the superior critic is not content with the compilation of the separate devices; they suggest to him a much more general question. The critic speculates on why poetry, through its devices, is at such pains to dissociate itself from prose at all, and what it is trying to represent that cannot be represented by prose.

I intrude here with an idea of my own, which may serve as a starting point of discussion. Poetry distinguishes itself from prose on the technical side by the devices which are, precisely, its means of escaping from prose. Something is continually being killed by prose which the poet wants to preserve. But this must be put philosophically. (Philosophy sounds hard, but it deals with natural and fundamental forms of experience.)

The critic should regard the poem as nothing short of a desperate ontological or metaphysical manœuvre.

The poet himself, in the agony of composition, has something like this sense of his labors. The poet perpetuates in his poem an order of existence which in actual life is constantly crumbling beneath his touch. His poem celebrates the object which is real, individual, and qualitatively infinite. He knows that his practical interests will reduce this living object to a mere utility, and that his sciences will disintegrate it for their convenience into their respective abstracts. The poet wishes to defend his object's existence against its enemies, and the critic wishes to know what he is doing, and how. The critic should find in the poem a total poetic or individual object which tends to be universalized, but is not permitted to suffer this fate. His identification of the poetic object is in terms of the universal or commonplace object to which it tends, and of the tissue, or totality of connotation, which holds it secure. How does he make out the universal object? It is the prose object, which any forthright prosy reader can discover to him by an immediate paraphrase; it is a kind of story, character, thing, scene, or moral principle. And where is the tissue that keeps it from coming out of the poetic object? That is, for the laws of the prose logic, its superfluity; and I think I would even say, its irrelevance.

A poet is said to be distinguishable in terms of his style. It is a comprehensive word, and probably means: the general character of his irrelevances, or tissues. All his technical devices contribute to it, elaborating or individualizing the universal, the core-object; likewise all his material detail. For each poem even, ideally, there is distinguishable a logical object or universal, but at the same time a tissue of irrelevance from which it does not really emerge. The critic has to take the poem apart, or analyze it, for the sake of uncovering these features. With all the finesse possible, it is rude and patchy business by comparison with the living integrity of the poem. But without it there could hardly be much understanding of the value of poetry, or of the natural history behind any adult poem.

The language I have used may sound too formidable, but I seem to find that a profound criticism generally works by some such considerations. However the critic may spell them, the two terms are in his mind: the prose core to which he can violently reduce the total object, and the differentia, residue, or tissue, which keeps the object poetical or entire. The character of the poem resides for the good critic in its way of exhibiting the residuary quality. The character of the poet is defined by the kind of prose object to which his interest evidently attaches, plus his way of involving it firmly in the residuary tissue. And doubtless, incidentally, the wise critic can often read behind the poet's public character his private history as a man with a weakness for lapsing into some special form of prosy or scientific bondage.

Similar considerations hold, I think, for the critique of fiction, or of the non-literary arts. I remark this for the benefit of philosophers who believe, with propriety, that the arts are fundamentally one. But I would prefer to leave the documentation to those who are better qualified.

Postscript

In this Postscript I must acknowledge a bad lapse of judgment in two of the foregoing essays. One was "A Cathedralist Looks at Murder," where I set myself against the stylistics of Mr. Eliot's poetic drama. The other was "Shakespeare at Sonnets," in which I must have seemed bent upon diminishing even the greatest of poets. But Eliot's reputation is still secure, and the totality of Shakespeare's achievement is still reckoned as a monument.

My review of *Murder in the Cathedral* (1935) was composed in a fury; that is to say, in a matter of a few hours, at a time when I was deeply immersed in my admiration for Milton's *Samson Agonistes*. I approved the firm pentameters of the speakers, and the more lyrical deliverances of the Chorus; that play is the best of all the English adaptations to the Greek style of tragedy. But it was published in 1671. Such an overwhelming devotion to an imposing but dated author might suggest a certain caution in the critic, especially if he is on call for reviewing books of contemporary verse. He has immobilized his critical faculties. I was freed only when I read my essay in the printed and irrevocable text of this book.

Once I got myself into a painful and memorable situation. Perhaps about 1941, after the *Kenyon Review* had started publication, I wrote to ask Eliot to send us a poem, or an essay. He replied promptly and politely that he had nothing at the moment, but added a wry postscript to remark that evidently he liked my verse better than I liked his. That was a blow that hurt. I knew that he meant no great compliment to my verse, for he knew as well as I that I was not of his stature. I had to make apology, but I could not simply write a little note to say that I thought he was a grand poet. I must write a very best essay, commending some notable verse of his without stinting. But I dallied. Finally I did write at length about his "Gerontion," when I knew it was too late. The poet had gone. I was paying tribute to his memory, and was only one of a host of witnesses honoring his name in the big book which Allen Tate recently edited.

But I cannot rest on that essay. I must settle my account with the *Murder* play, and it will not be too hard. But even that scarcely seems to cover the payment of interest on my long default; I wish to write first on a broader and earlier topic. I am interested in the relation which his tiny book of *Poems* (1920) bears to *The Waste Land* (1922), and even to the *Ash-Wednesday* of 1930. It will be largely a prosodic study; my rebellion against Eliot had been largely on that score. But it will have two dimensions, in both of which Eliot was serving his apprenticeship. First comes the prosody. We know that a right prosody requires a great deal of labor if it means to make a music of the words. Of course there must be lines and phrases; the words must not only be right semantically for their phrases, but frequently they must chime with each other in their respective vowels or consonants for tone-color; and if all goes well the poet will have hit on words which are both apt and splendid, and fill the reader with wonder. And as for the other dimension: we know that Eliot was like many another young man who had lost his faith and was trying to recover it. That is the point of the argument which determines the text in the first place.

In *Poems* we tread upon high lyric ground. But the first poem is "Gerontion," which happens to be last in the order of composition. We will talk of it last. I do not know whether Pound persuaded Eliot to put it first, or whether both said at the same time, "Put your best foot forward." Then there are four poems in French (a language in which Eliot was quite adequate), and they include the original of the Phlebas poem which Eliot made into the single lyric which constitutes the fourth movement of *The Waste Land*, when he had translated his French hexameters into English pentameters. Let us waive this group, and assume that up to the conclusion of *Poems* there was nothing but seven lyrics in even succession; most of them are little masterpieces. All are in the Long Meter ballad stanza where the eight-stress ballad line occurs twice, but each line is cut into two exact halves, so that the result is a quatrain in which the second and fourth lines rhyme. Such an absolute little stanza cannot bear too many repetitions, and these pieces are properly short, ranging from eight to eleven quatrains. If the argument of any of these pieces were long and close, we would inevitably come to the point where we could not endure the subborn little stanzas, chopping up the text into so many bundles of kindling. Coleridge in his *Ancient Mariner* did well with his galloping ballad stanzas, till he knew that he must vary them by inserting extra lines, as he did in each of his seven parts.

We "Fugitives" at Vanderbilt in the early twenties knew these pieces well, and recited them to each other. I believe our favorite was "Sweeney Among the Nightingales"; the incomparable tough guy. Here Sweeney is dining in the restaurant, and being beset by two competent females who with the help of attendants are about to "roll" him. But Sweeney

> . . . Declines the gambit, shows fatigue,
> Leaves the room and reappears
> Outside the window, leaning in,
> Branches of wistaria
> Circumscribe a golden grin;
>
> The host with someone indistinct
> Converses at the door apart,
> The nightingales are singing near
> The Convent of the Sacred Heart,
>
> And sang within the bloody wood
> When Agamemnon cried aloud
> And let their liquid siftings fall
> To stain the stiff dishonored shroud.

The last six lines we may count as constituting a "still moment," which is to say, a holy moment, intruding at the end of a passage whose tone otherwise is completely satiric and acid. Eliot has not yet found this term for it, but we shall study that history later. All the poems of *Poems* display some such moment.

The most fabulous poem concerns "The Hippopotamus," though otherwise it is not quite one of the choicest. The 'potamus is having a bad time of it every way, while the Church manages to get whatever it wants. But the 'potamus dies:

> I saw the 'potamus take wing
> Ascending from the damp savannas,
> And quiring angels round him sing
> The praise of God, in loud hosannas.
>
> Blood of the Lamb shall wash him clean
> And him shall heavenly arms enfold,
> Among the saints he shall be seen
> Performing on a harp of gold.
>
> He shall be washed as white as snow,
> By all the martyr'd virgins kist,
> While the True Church remains below
> Wrapt in the old miasmal mist.

We have to concede that this is an extravaganza of holiness. But at any rate Eliot has got in his thrust against the ways of the modern Church, which he does not trust. Perhaps he is halfway in his progress from secularism back to the faith.

The one prosodic irregularity occurs in "A Cooking Egg." Suddenly a solitary line is interposed between the last two stanzas. The next to last one ends:

> The red-eyed scavengers are creeping
> From Kentish Town to Golder's Green;

but immediately the spirit of the poet rebels:

> Where are the eagles and the trumpets?

He answers himself in the contemptuous first line of the final stanza:

> Buried beneath some snow-deep Alps.
> Over buttered scones and crumpets
>   Weeping, weeping multitudes
> Droop in a hundred A.B.C.'s.

The second line is gracious enough to rhyme with the lone line; and the stanza breaks into confusion at the end by not having a final rhyme. There will be worse confusions than that in *The Waste Land.*

Finally—as we are supposing—comes the last and infinitely the best poem in the collection; it is "Gerontion" itself. But it is not easy to think of another poet who would dare to exhibit seven sizable lyrics such as we have seen; prosodically uniform and tiny and successive, yet individually brilliant and individual in accomplishing their themes. Would it be Donne, the "metaphysical" poet to whom Eliot relates himself? Donne insisted upon a fresh form for each of his lyrics, none like the others; and his

Satyres, though uniform in their prosodies and admirably close in style, are long drawn out. And Marvell? His best poems are perfect but they are few; he would never have proposed to make such a wanton show of strength as Eliot might have dared him to do. Nor would Herrick. And as for Shakespeare: his style was that of the convention, the "establishment," of the period; he could have done anything, but he never completely abandoned his base. I think Eliot must have been intent upon seeing how original his poems might be, and how unforgettable, in their simple Old Style; and just at the moment when he was about to show his "Gerontion," brand-new, for which he had invented a New Style, in what I have regarded as surely the most finished miniature symphony in our literature. Here was an empirical thinker, testing his prosodies. He invented his rhythms diligently and well. They accord with the idiom of our language, and with the broken music which modern musicians cherish. It is as if by one stroke Eliot had established a new poetry.

We go from there to *The Waste Land* itself. Its prosody is of many sorts, including Old Style and New. He does not resent the old meters. Otherwise he could not have said that the new poetry must never quite break away from the old; that is how he speaks in "Tradition and the Individual Talent." I believe I can afford, now, to say that new poets who are ignorant of the grand themes and the music of the High Style must commit themselves to commonplaces; and will rise to something better only if they have prodigious vocabulary and imagination enough to use it. *The Waste Land* is probably the most famous poem of this century in our language. It is a five-part symphony too, like "Gerontion," but as much greater as it is longer. It has magnificent orchestration, and the most astonishing miscellany of dramatic but disconnected parts. Within the five movements I count at least thirty individual passages; but they offer themselves pretty well under the titles of the five movements. The passages are generally sad and touching, and sometimes sordid. The overall theme is waste; the human spirit itself is wasting in the natural but symbolic desert which an unregenerate people deserves. Yet there are a few providential moments which by way of contrast present us with "still moments." (I keep harping on that locution because Eliot will rely upon it more and more, till in the *Four Quartets* it becomes his spiritual staple, and numbers many occurrences.) In Movement I, "The Burial of the Dead," the friend has been with his "hyacinth girl" in the park:

> —Yet when we came back, late, from the hyacinth garden,
> Your arms full, and your hair wet, I could not
> Speak, and my eyes failed, I was neither
> Living nor dead, and I knew nothing,
> Looking into the heart of light, the silence.

A little hope is offered in the Fifth Movement, "What the Thunder Said"; and Eliot knew from the first how to make an ending conclusive. For the most part this movement has no punctuation, though the clarity of the lines is not particularly disturbed. And what does the thunder say at last? Eliot offers a free version of the three precepts of the Upanishad Brahma: Give, Sympathize, Control. But such a discipline cannot yet take hold. We are warned in the final passage by the impossible huge knot of literary fragments from many sources and in at least three languages. Eliot is not yet freed from *The Waste Land*. It is even worse, perhaps, than it was in two absurd little groups of phrases in Movement III, "The Fire Sermon." The fire of course is sex. And we have hardly started before we come to this:

> Twit twit twit
> Jug jug jug jug jug jug
> So rudely forc'd.
> Tereu

And at the end of that movement to this:

> To Carthage then I came
>
> Burning burning burning burning
> O Lord Thou pluckest me out
> O Lord thou pluckest
>
> burning

The poet has done well and faithfully with the argument, but this "moment" is hardly a still one. The reference "To Carthage" is a scrap from Saint Augustine's *Confessions,* and the "burning" is both scriptural and Augustinian; the "O Lord" line is scriptural, but the repeat is only halfway, as if the speaker did not believe it; and the final "burning" has not even the honor of a capital. Those untidy mixtures are not frequent.

But with these observations I have come to a special feature of *The Waste Land* which is almost peculiarly Eliot's practice, and which distressed me for a long time. I mean, of course, the obscure references to quite specific items or texts within the "tradition," as it existed in many ages and languages. I think Eliot, with the approval of Pound who was himself a referentialist, must have reckoned that the common reader would make a fair sense anyhow out of the passages in which they were embedded. I didn't believe it, till I saw how many readers did get the sense, and skimmed easily over the references. I saw even better, right under my nose, how many young people liked the poem all the better by checking up the references. These were the ones inspired towards a fixed and lofty learning and/or towards the furtherance of their own poetic ambitions. I confess that when I was teaching Eliot I relied shamelessly on the work of professional scholars. These reacted to the hidden references as if they were some fine wine or other which they could not forego, because it answered to their tastes and to their reputations. Eliot's gift to the old scholars and to the young was generous, and largely accepted. And now I cannot hold my old prejudice on that point any longer.

We come now to *Ash-Wednesday* (1930). This symphony of six movements occupies seven-plus pages, whereas the diminutive "Gerontion" did not quite need three pages, and *The Waste Land* managed with barely thirteen. And if we look forward to *Four Quartets,* Eliot's crowning achievement, these too are symphonies and use altogether twenty-nine pages.

In the meantime Eliot has had his conversion and entered the Anglican Communion. But though he has triumphed, the process was difficult; he speaks at first as a neophyte who still strives, not yet too confident but still extremely humble, and only later utters prayers and partakes of the dispensations of a Providence which is beneficent. It is a lovely composition. But here I must quote twice from a young master, a student of prosody beyond his years and very sure in his judgments. The text is from *Essay on Rime* (1945), a little book of some seventy pages, and the author is Karl Shapiro. Every critic should know his book. I am quoting from his passage on Eliot:

> Eliot began with count of eye, but early
> (We hear of his destroying couplets) turned
> To more immediate music. One corrective
> He introduced, the even step of French,
> Opened a window on the Parisian schools
> Which at the same time looked upon the English
> For an exchange of form; an old artesian

Spring began to flow between these tongues,
Replenishing both. Yet this was incidental
To the main tide of metric. Poets abroad
Were all establishing prose cadences
In rime, some we have seen with ruinous
Effect, and Eliot and a skillful few
With revolutionary success. The clean
Conversational voice of the American
Once and for all outlawed the late Victorian
Lilt.

The prosodist is himself a charming poet. And next,

When it appears, the study of the music
Of *Ash-Wednesday* should compel the minds of all
Poets; for in a hundred years no poem
Has sung itself so exquisitely well.

I will pass over *Ash-Wednesday* briefly. But I have to note one passage which is very lovely, yet discomfited me sorely:

At the first turning of the third stair
Was a slotted window bellied like the fig's fruit
And beyond the hawthorn blossom and a pasture scene
The broadbacked figure drest in blue and green
Enchanted the maytime with an antique flute.
Blown hair is sweet, brown hair over the mouth blown,
Lilac and brown hair;
Distraction, music of the flute, stops and steps of
the mind over the third stair,
Fading, fading; strength beyond hope and despair
Climbing the third stair.

This scene is a fragment from Movement III where he remembers his ascent of the Ten Stairs of Purgation as recommended by Saint John of the Cross; and it is the scene of one of the finest possible "still moments," yet has to be rejected. Now I had kept a close watch over Eliot's "still moments," and for me it was sufficient if one of them presented a natural moment having an aesthetic conformation; and in my amateur's philosophy I had said to myself that such a moment seemed to bring us into the presence of the unknown God who gave us the sense of beauty and caused beauty to appear in his creation, establishing at least a moment of communion. Beauty ranked even above morality, and was our highest natural faculty. If I half felt these impressions, I was convinced by the aesthetic of Kant, which I took, and take, to be on the highest human authority. For Wordsworth in his early years, the natural revelations served as the cardinal point of faith. But here Eliot has found one moment to be supreme: when we commune in prayer with the God. It is evident many times that Eliot either prompts the reader by the mere mention of the particular natural moment, or works the moment out. But here Eliot has found one moment more to his taste when he advises the reader to pray in the darkness, and alone. In that preference there was a saintliness in Eliot, but he did not aspire to be a saint, nor spurn on this account the common experience of beauty; indeed there are only two or three occasions where he asserted the supremacy of the moment of prayer. How should I feud with him over the net benefits of the still moments?

This is the right time to try a little history of the phrase, "the still moment." There are several passages about it in *Ash-Wednesday*. The speaker refers sometimes to stillness; as for example, "Teach us to be still"; and utters a resonant couplet when he says,

> Against the Word the unstilled world still whirled
> About the centre of the silent Word.

The "still" is scriptural, as for example in Psalm 46. 10, "Be still and know that I am God." But for the full extension of the motto we have to look to *Coriolan*, where Eliot portrays his warrior-hero, riding imperial through the multitude, who pay him the closest attention:

> . . . the hands, quiet over the horse's neck,
> And the eyes watchful, waiting, perceiving, indifferent.

At the point of indifference to the multitude he has moved from "watchful" into his own still moment of absolute privacy:

> O hidden under the dove's wing, hidden in the turtle's
> breast,
> Under the palmtree at noon, under the running water
> At the still point of the turning world. O hidden.

The "moment," principally perhaps for the sake of the rhythm, becomes a "point." But the addition is "of the turning world." There we must surely be of the persuasion of old Heraclitus, the "first metaphysicist" in human lineage, as some have described him, who was one of the favorite philosophers to whom Eliot attended. But how does the ever-turning world consist with a still point of arrest? It is as if time and space had lost their usual interrelation. In the *Four Quartets* Eliot speaks also of "the intersection of the timeless with time." I fancy that he was not attracted to Bergson, who improved upon the current philosophers with a new wisdom which Eliot may have ignored because it was not applied importantly to aesthetic or religious experience. Yet Bergson was ready to confirm the defenders of art and theology if they consulted him. Bergson distinguished "time" from "duration." Time is measured as it must be for purely practical and physical appointments; but duration is time endured, or lived, when the occasion arises, with no sense of time till some appreciable physical change rules this possibility out for the spiritual man. I suppose philosophers generally confirm Bergson for his scientific proof of the human psyche, or spirit; he demonstrated experimentally that there were many occasions when distinct and remembered moments of consciousness in the psyche did not leave any tracks whatever within the physiology of the brain. And as for Eliot's other phrase, "the intersection of the timeless moment with time," I read somewhere not long ago, perhaps in the writing of an existentialist or theologian, that there comes recurrently the lift of the soul in the vertical direction, where the God is generally assumed to have his residence. At any rate, we are wondrously made, and Eliot's emphasis on the moment out of time seems to me altogether right. We may have been burdening ourselves with unnecessary mystification.

As of the last thirty years, if I should be reminded of some rule of propriety which forbade the intrusion of large blocks of prose into what must be regarded on the whole as a poetic drama, I would give it no attention. It would require us to cancel out the vast amount of prose in Shakespeare's plays, to their great impoverishment. Even more destructive would it be to *Murder in the Cathedral*, where the prose is suited precisely to its important speakers in the crucial action of the play. This is my belated apology to the author.

Murder in the Cathedral is a play of absolute contrasts. The saints are on one side and the sinners on the other; and the sinners have their way. But afterwards we are given good reason for believing that the deed was directed by a beneficent Providence. I wonder if that is not a good rule in human affairs generally. Heraclitus said that good and evil are equal and opposite, in order that the world may continue turning on its appointed course.

Murder in the Cathedral is the second of Eliot's six plays, and to my taste the most theatrical of them all; except of course for the two-part play of *Sweeney Agonistes*, in eleven and a half pages. Readers had better repair to it if they would like to see the thrilling end of poor Sweeney, presented in the jazziest style of its period. On stage, the play was a great success. It belongs in the canon of Eliot's six plays as surely as the big and leisurely ones.

But *Murder in the Cathedral* has its own flamboyance too, despite the conventions. Like *Sweeney* it has two parts, plus an interlude in the middle. It is an historical play as surely as the "Histories" of Shakespeare, though we are just as far from being given the full complexity of history behind the scenes. But Eliot dates the parts expressly: The Archbishop arrives on December 2, 1170; preaches his last sermon on Christmas morning, 1170; is killed on December 29, 1170. Eliot is more liberal than Shakespeare, who never tells dates.

The colleges nowadays contain many younger men and women who cannot have seen the play on stage, but are studying modern literature much harder than history, and now I enter a little interpolation meant for them. Three points need to be cleared. *First,* What is that "France" whither and whence so many people have been flitting across the English Channel at its narrowest point? The speakers are saying "France" when they should say "the Continent"; and it is not Eliot's fault. On the Continent is that Angevine Dominion which the Normans have wrested from France, now as large as the France proper. *Second,* Who is this Henry II who rules England, sometimes in England and sometimes from the Continent? He is the fifth of the six "foreign" kings who began with William the Conqueror and will end with Richard the Lion Heart. The foreign kings will be finished when King John comes to the throne, for he and his successors will have been born in England. Henry was seated on the throne by the Catholic Church, 1154, though he was no Christian and despised the Church. But he is a born statesman, laying down just laws for England and stripping the barons and the Church of their special courts and privileges. In 1166 he has initiated the law of Trial by Twelve Jurors, a practice which has been perpetuated in English-speaking countries to this day. *Third,* And who is this Becket of Canterbury? He is a man of imposing stature, with a record of soldiery, older than Henry, whom Henry at the beginning of his reign appointed as his Chancellor to see that the royal orders were obeyed; and diligent in that office. But in 1162 Henry required the monks of Canterbury to elect Becket as Archbishop, terminating his Chancellorship. In that capacity Becket proceeded to flout the King's orders and the King's men, until in 1164 he had to flee for his life to the Continent, by night and in disguise. The King was there already, but Becket was safe because Henry feared the power of the Pope.

The play begins with a recital by the Chorus of Women of Canterbury. They stand close inside the wall of the cathedral, where they may hear whatever is going on. There are no males in the Chorus; perhaps because the women of that time were the more religious, and stood for the Archbishop, whereas their husbands were likely to be the King's men. They will make seven long recitals, using up some thirteen of the forty-seven pages of the entire text. We will see a little later how they perform. After this Chorus, enter Three Priests in the ascending order of their rank and intelligence. The First Priest complains, and has no sense of policy; the Second is possessed by a policy which everybody knows is useless; and the Third is a wise person having much of the nobility of the Archbishop himself; at any rate he approves what Becket is going to do. Presently, enters the bouncy Herald, who tells them that the Archbishop has landed at Dover and now is very near Canterbury; he talks with the priests, and says finally,

> It is common knowledge that when the Archbishop
> Parted from the King, he said to the King,
> My Lord, he said, I leave you as a man
> Whom in this life I shall not see again.

So Becket, after his sorry seven years' absence from his post, is returning to die.

Then appears Becket himself, very quietly, and has not much to say but needs to retire and have a little rest. The next entry is that of the Four Tempters, one at a time, and in the ascending order of their station and intelligence. The first temptation to Becket is to do whatever the King requires of him, and that will bring peace to the turmoil. The second is to ask the King to restore him to his Chancellorship, where he will be in high favor as he used to be. The third is to fight the King, aligning with the King's Angevin and French enemies to bring about the King's fall. It is the Fourth Tempter only who surprises Becket, by advising the very martyrdom which Becket already intends; but he dismisses this Tempter too, not relishing the motive of his own everlasting glory which has been suggested.

When the Tempters have finished without any success, Eliot makes a cunning play by having the three groups of Chorus, Priests, and Tempters to speak successively and characteristically in four tercets. I quote the first two:

> C. Is it the owl that calls, or a signal between the trees?
> P. Is the window-bar made fast, is the door under lock and bolt?
> T. Is it rain that taps at the window, is it wind that pokes at the door?
> C. Does the torch flame in the hall, the candle in the room?
> P. Does the watchman walk by the wall?
> T. Does the mastiff prowl by the gate?

It is the foiled Tempters who speak most ominously.

At this point we quote a part of the third recital of the Chorus:

> We know of oppression and torture,
> We know of extortion and violence,
> Destitution, disease,
> The old without fire in winter,

> The child without milk in summer,
> Our labor taken away from us,
> Our sins made heavier upon us.
> We have seen the young man mutilated,
> The torn girl trembling by the mill-stream.
> And meanwhile we have gone on living,
> Living and partly living,
> Picking together the pieces,
> Gathering faggots at nightfall,
> Building a partial shelter,
> For sleeping, and eating and drinking and laughter.

The lamentation is touching in its homeliness. The prosody is not a free verse, but nicely rhythmed, and the lines finish without rhymes but with feminine endings instead. To break whatever monotony Eliot feels in these lines—and in all his modern rhythms he is very fearful of that—we have the little insert at the beginning of the last line; a rhythm without a partner. The Chorus of Women is responsible for the best verse in the play, and Eliot intended it to be so.

The Archbishop concludes this part with a soliloquy which begins as follows:

> Now is my way clear, now is the meaning plain:
> Temptation shall not come in this kind again.
> The last temptation is the greatest treason:
> To do the right deed for the wrong reason.

He has had a strenuous day, but there are three weeks before Christmas, and he will be fortifying his spirit and waiting.

The Interlude carries the Archbishop's Christmas sermon, announcing his approaching martyrdom. It is a firm but modulated sermon, preaching the gospel and speaking of martyrs with even temper. I wish I knew whether Eliot, who had a taste for sermons, composed it for the Archbishop; or whether it belongs historically to the Archbishop. If Eliot found it in J. C. Robertson's seven volumes entitled *Materials for the History of Thomas Becket,* published in 1885, he must at least have modernized the text.

In Part II the same characters appear, except for the Herald and the Four Tempters. In place of the Tempters, enter the Four Knights who have come to make their killing. They appear in the descending order of rank, and are well disciplined in their parts. They attempt to take the Archbishop, but are prevented by the Priests and Attendants; and when invited to dinner in the Archbishop's chambers, they propose to find their own dinner, and the sequel will be that they will be a little tipsy when they return. But in the meantime the Chorus is greatly excited, and the Women disclose much more imagination and command of language than we have supposed:

> I have smelt them, the death-bringers, senses are
> quickened
> By subtile forebodings; I have heard
> Fluting in the night-time, fluting and owls, have seen
> at noon
> Scaly wings slanting over, huge and ridiculous. I have
> tasted

> The savor of putrid flesh in the spoon. I have felt
> The heaving of earth at nightfall, restless, absurd.
> I have heard
> Laughter in the noises of breasts that make strange
> noises; jackal, jackass, jackdaw; the scurrying
> noise of mouse and jerboa; the laugh of the loon,
> the lunatic bird. I have seen
> Gray necks twisting, rat tails twining, in the thick
> light of dawn. I have eaten
> Smooth creatures still living, with the strong salt
> taste of living things under sea; I have tasted
> The living lobster, the crab, the oyster, the whelk
> and the prawn; and they live and spawn in my
> bowels, and my bowels dissolve in the light of
> dawn. I have smelt
> Death in the rose, death in the hollyhock, sweet pea,
> hyacinth, primrose and cowslip. I have seen
> Trunk and horn, tusk and hoof, in odd places; . . .

The semicolon is only a stop for taking a fresh breath; the Women will go on and on, as if they were accomplished in natural history. The lines have many rhythms and rhymes as their speech gets faster. But they will finish after a little, with apology to the Archbishop:

> O Lord Archbishop, O Thomas Archbishop, forgive us,
> forgive us, pray for us that we may pray for you,
> out of our shame.

The Four Knights return with Attendants of their own, and first they have a little sport at the Archbishop's expense. They too know Scripture, and they have made up a silly set of little stanzas so much alike that any one of them will do for a sample of the Knights' wit. Each Knight is responsible for one line:

> Are you washed in the blood of the Lamb?
> Are you marked with the mark of the beast?
> Come down Daniel to the lions' den,
> Come down Daniel and join in the feast.

They drag away the unresisting Becket into the cathedral and kill him. Next follows the ghastly anticlimax in which the Knights advance to the front of the stage and hold a sort of court to determine the cause of the Archbishop's death. The First Knight presides; but the Second Knight, surprisingly, is charming and winning though his argument is of no consequence. I would like to fancy that Eliot thought of the Second Knight as a boy fresh from Oxford, which Eliot knew well; and as having joined that mock Parliament, the Oxford Union, where the political aspirants, if they like, may practice the art of ingratiation; the only trouble being that Eliot knew that the University was not quite yet in being. The Third Knight rehearses all the treasons of Becket, and the Fourth pronounces the verdict: Suicide while of Unsound Mind!

But we are not quite finished. The intensity of the final action is not yet exhausted for Eliot. As the Knights and the people leave the cathedral there is speech among the Priests. But the First Priest talks so foolishly that the Third Priest does not wait for a speech from the Second, who will be little better than the First; but dismisses both from their holy office with a long and terrible curse; then prays thankfully to God for having given another Saint to Canterbury.

As the Women of Canterbury had started the play off, so they must finish it. They are calm and happy now; they pride themselves a little by reciting some of the metaphysics which they have received from the Archbishop and the Third Priest, as for example:

> Those who deny Thee could not deny, if Thou didst
> not exist; and their denial is never complete;
> if it were so, they would not exist.

They conclude:

> Lord, have mercy upon us.
> Blessed Thomas, pray for us.

Here ends my late but sincere commendation of Eliot's verse. Yet even now I find myself sensible of an uneasy tic in my conscience, over whether I ought not to sound a certain dissenting note as to his faith; or, if I am mistaken, a note which at the stage of his *Quartets* he might have approved.

I have reread the *Selected Essays* which he prefaced over the date of 1950, though the latest of the essays is dated 1935, when he wrote "Religion and Literature." I am afraid that he defines the Tradition principally in Roman Catholic terms. I had imagined that I would find him catholic with a little *c*, which would indicate a rather rare but very desirable virtue. But to be Roman Catholic in the Capital sense is to be a Roman and a Romantic; Romantic in almost the same sense as Shelley and Keats in their longer poems. Dante himself was a Romantic in his awesome yet beautiful *Divine Comedy*, giving us one part Historicity (with respect to the real persons who had lived on earth) and three parts Inferno, Purgatorio, and Paradiso, which are extravagantly unearthly. The Roman faith is, or has been, at once the strictest and the most metaphorical faith that a Christian can imagine.

I have never imposed my own faith on anybody particularly, but for this occasion I do not mind calling it Unitarian. I had backslid from my father's faith to that position even before I came upon Kant the Transcendentalist, who did not dare to make images of the Unknown God. And that is exactly the position which nowadays even the clergy of most churches, including the Roman Catholic, have found themselves desperately studying and frequently accepting. Wherever Christ is mentioned, not as the great Saint or Prophet but as a junior member of the Godhead, it is because he promised to his followers that immortality which Kant had named as the third of the three aspirations of the Pure Reason—the soul itself—even though it is the least capable of logical demonstration. And I think that most of the communicants, and many of the clergy itself, have little interest in that article of faith; but do not go about advertising their dissidence because they know that every now and then they will have to attend a service for the dead, where there will be a bereaved family who may find a vicarious comfort in the Promise read by the officiating clergy.

Once I took my family with me to Devonshire in England, of course with the assistance of the Guggenheim Foundation, and promptly called upon my great friend and former Oxford tutor, John Murray, who had become the Principal of Exeter College. Within ten minutes he made me engage myself to tutor, three mornings of each week, several exemplary young gentlemen from Egypt who had come to improve their English, both spoken and written. We had a pleasant time of it. But one of them had been trained for the priesthood, and came to me several times alone to read the English version of the Koran aloud, and tell me with a twinkle in his eye that the Mohammedans had but one God, but called their faith Mohammedan in honor of their greatest Prophet. I said little, but I had a smiling sense, thinking how perfect would be the analogy if the churches of the West called themselves Christian for a like reason.

But on the other hand: I have made two observations which suggest that Eliot might have agreed with my sentiments. First, even in *The Waste Land,* Eliot chose not to express an "orthodox" faith directly (even though he aspired to it) but to be content with making methodical and obscure references which his text did not expound. And furthermore, there is his important discovery of the Still Moment, and his preoccupation with it in the *Quartets,* where I count some sixty occasions; if I may count his mention of possible occasions, which his readers may follow up for themselves, along with the full and actual occasions which he describes. It was those occasions which gave a momentary sense of the Presence of the Creator who had contrived them.

But I suppose I must wait to ask some of Eliot's closest friends, when I see them, about the justice of referring these evidences to his conscious intention. In any event I have the greatest admiration for the power of his verse.

And now to my ill report of Shakespeare as compared with Donne. At least I take comfort from seeing that I had not done so badly by Shakespeare as by Eliot. I am pleased to notice that I took many of his sonnets to be metaphysical, like the sonnets of Donne; in respect to their terse and sometimes opaque style, and their careful arguments. (It is dangerous to deny any kind of merit to Shakespeare.) And I have restudied the sonnets. More of them than I had thought are innocent of my charge of anticlimax in their descending quatrains; and the final couplets are pithier and more adequate to their arguments. Here are two sonnets which turn out better than the opening lines would suggest. Shakespeare has to work for his living, and at the moment is on tour with his fellow actors a long way from London, and the blissful company of his patron, the Earl of Southampton.

XXVII. Weary with toil, I haste me to my bed,
The dear repose for limbs with travel tired;
But then begins a journey in my head
To work my head when body's work's expired;
For then my thoughts, from far where I abide,
Intend a zealous pilgrimage to thee,
And keep my drooping eyelids open wide,
Looking on darkness which the blind do see;
Save that my soul's imaginary sight
Presents thy shadow to my sightless view,
Which, like a jewel hung in ghastly night,
Makes black night beauteous and her old face new.
Lo! thus, by day my limbs, by night my mind,
For thee and for myself no quiet find.

XXVIII. How can I then return in happy plight,
That am debarr'd the benefit of rest?
When day's depression is not eas'd by night,
But day by night, and night by day, oppress'd?
And each, though enemies to either's reign,
Do in consent shake hands to torture me;
The one by toil, the other to complain
How far I toil, still farther off from thee.
I tell the day, to please him thou art bright
And dost him grace when clouds do blot the heaven;
So flatter I the swart-complexion'd night,
When sparkling stars twire not, thou gild'st the even:
But day doth daily draw my sorrows longer,
And night doth nightly make grief's strength seem stronger.

Surely this is excellent, vocabulary-wise; and apparently, in the honesty of its complaint, truth-wise. But no verse of Shakespeare's is really in his own "first person," except the sonnets; they are not made up to fit characters in the plays. But we shall wait a little before we wonder whether we should take the arguments as fact or fiction. That will be our most important problem.

And here is a "magnificent" sonnet which I disparaged; it is able to make a sort of dramatic claim to being close to his best; though there is pain in the conclusion, because the much-loved patron is strained with an offense.

XXXIII. Full many a glorious morning have I seen
Flatter the mountain tops with sovereign eye,
Kissing with golden face the meadows green,
Gilding pale streams with heavenly alchemy;
Anon permit the basest clouds to ride
With ugly rack on his celestial face,
And from the forlorn world his visage hide,
Stealing unseen to west with this disgrace:
Even so my sun one early morn did shine
With all-triumphant splendour on my brow;
But out, alack! he was but one hour mine;
The region-cloud hath mask'd him from me now.
Yet him from this my love no whit disdaineth;
Suns of the world my stain when heaven's sun staineth.

I had not done justice to this sonnet. It opens flamboyantly, but its early figuration is needed for the point of its ending. The greedy Earl with the "celestial" face must have been thankful for this beforehand apology by his slave, relieving him of having to make his own excuses for his fault.

I need not have brought Donne into my essay, especially on the strength of a mere bit of lyrical verse. Donne was junior to Shakespeare by eight years. But his thirst for knowledge and original speech was well fulfilled in his education, and in the early 1590's he was producing his peculiar lyrics while Shakespeare was getting into sonnetry. The "Holy Sonnets" were not written till about 1617. Shakespeare could not have known them. They number XIX, a small packet, but luxuriant verbally and steeped in theology. In spite of his authentic doubt as to his faith, they do not lack his accustomed wit and humors. I should imagine that if we weighed them against the usual anthologist's score or so of Shakespeare's sonnets, they would hold their own. One of Donne's advantages would be that he used the Italian sonnet form. There as everywhere, Donne is "metaphysical," the term which Doctor Johnson gave him a century or so later. But Donne twice at great length had referred to his own prose style (which was as choice as that of his verse), once as "metaphorical," and again as "paradoxical," and proved it by showing that he was only following the style of Christ's teachings. The three terms cited have about the same meaning.

It is easy to say emphatically that Shakespeare's production was vast as compared with Donne's. The two were perhaps about equal at sonnets, but these patterns can claim only a limited territory of letters. We know the sheer bulk of Shakespeare's plays, numbering some thirty-six or so. And I have just now reread the tragedies of *Macbeth*, *Hamlet*, *King Lear*, *Othello*, and *Antony and Cleopatra*. At the moment I must think of drama as the finest form of literature, and of *King Lear* as the masterpiece of plays; of Shakespeare *in toto* as the First Poet in the Western world. I cannot imagine many objections from my readers.

But having once introduced Donne into competition with Shakespeare, I should have chosen better examples than I did. In all his verse there is a preference for nicety and particularity which forbids the intrusion of commonplace words and phrases to fill up the lines. I should have commended and illustrated the virtue of the twenty-eight pentameter couplets of Elegy XVI, "On His Mistris," where he forbids the wife of his secret marriage to attend him on his Continental tour in the guise of a Page. For example, he warns her that

> Men of France, changeable Camelions,
> Spittles of diseases, shops of fashions,
> Loves fuellers, and the rightest company
> Of Players, which upon the worlds stage be,
> Will quickly know thee . . .

and commands her in conclusion,

> Nor praise nor dispraise me, nor bless nor curse
> Openly loves force, nor in bed fright thy Nurse

With midnights' startings, crying out, oh, oh
Nurse, O my love is slain, I saw him goe
Oer the white Alps alone; I saw him, I,
Assail'd, fight, taken, stabb'd, bleed, fall and die.
Augur me better chance, except dread Jove
Thinke it enough for me t'have had thy love.

And I should have quoted from "The Extasie," of nineteen lyric quatrains. The poem has the strictest logic, though its terms are metaphysical; which is to say that the items of which it is composed are largely fictions of the imagination.

Such is Donne's style; perhaps it is too singular to be compared with Shakespeare's profusion.

But it happens that one of the "Holy Sonnets" of Donne might be apt at this point. It is peculiarly suited for introducing the question of the bond between Shakespeare and Southampton. It is Sonnet XVIII, the next-to-last in the series, written just after the death of Donne's faithful wife, who in the preceding sonnet had been "ravished" into heaven, whereupon Donne though he mourned her knew that now he must attend to theological matters. But his use of scriptural terms proves a little embarrassing:

Show me dear Christ, thy Spouse, so bright and clear.
What! is it She, which on the other shore
Goes richly painted? or which rob'd and tore
Laments and mourns in Germany and here?
Sleepes she a thousand, then peepes up one year?
Is she self truth and errs? Now new, now outwore?
Doth she, and did she, and shall she evermore
On one, or seven or on no hill appear?

> Dwells she within us, or like adventuring knights
> First travaile we to seeke and then make Love?
> Betray kind husband thy spouse to our sights,
> And let my amorous soule court thy mild Dove,
> Who is most trew, and pleasing to thee then
> When she's embrac'd and open to most men.

We know that the Spouse or Bride of Christ is the Church; here is the text of Matthew 9. 14, 15:

> Then came to him the disciples of John, saying, Why do we and the Pharisees fast oft, but thy disciples fast not?
>
> And Jesus said unto them, can the children of the bride-chamber mourn, as long as the bridegroom is with them? but the days will come, when the bridegroom shall be taken from them, and then they shall fast.

The children of the bridechamber are the offspring of her womb, the members of the Church. The "She" to whom Donne refers is the Church of Rome, on seven hills, who had been robbed and torn in Germany and England by Luther and his Reformation. Donne had lost his Roman faith early, and now had attached himself to the Angelican Church and was a priest. The bridegroom has returned to his heaven, and instead of coming down himself (in the old Greek style) to take the Bride, delegates her to be the Church-on-earth, and to welcome the males who come to her, and the more the better. The Godhead is unexpectedly bisexual. And what is the gender of the women members of the Church?

The problem of Shakespeare and the Earl is secular rather than theological. But there is a confusion of sexes. The autobiography to which Shakespeare subscribes is brilliant, humble, long, and difficult, yet mostly sustained. At least he serves his patron by assigning to him the beauty of a woman's face, and lavishing a hundred endearments. The proud Earl is pleased, but without return of sexual feeling; the poet slyly attributes this to his own increasing age and homeliness. But the Earl is quite capable of resorting to women, including Shakespeare's own mistress; and of bringing into his court another poet, probably Chapman, to whom Shakespeare as a matter of policy imputes a greater talent than his own. Does it not seem very likely that patron and poet are playing at a game whose terms have been agreed upon in advance?

The anthologists in their omnibus selections have usually been discreet in picking their fifteen or twenty sonnets by Shakespeare. Yet I have known students who have suddenly discovered that the face which Shakespeare adored was that of a man! It frightened them. Other teachers have told me of their students' like revulsion.

Let us go back to the beginning of Shakespeare's luck in being enrolled among Southampton's protégés. He wrote, and dedicated to the patron briefly and formally, the composition called *Venus and Adonis.* Its argument concerns pederasty, but that was committed by the Queen of Love herself. It was fortunate that Shakespeare had decided to write consistently in abbreviated sonnets having each a single quatrain followed by a couplet ending; a wise apprenticeship. The work was inordinately long, but when did Shakespeare stint his invention? I count a hundred and six sestets. But evidently the work suited precisely the patron's taste and leisure. For Shakespeare's next offering was *The Rape of Lucrece*, containing two hundred fifty-four sestets. The theme is common rape, but the deed is consummated historically, by Tarquin the Proud, last of the kings of Rome; he would be promptly exiled by the citizens, who would declare for a Republic. But for our purposes it is significant that the Earl must have come into the highest regard for his subject on the score of the *Venus and Adonis*. Otherwise Shakespeare could hardly have dared to preface the new poem with a dedication professing his abject love; it runs in part at follows:

> The love I dedicate to your lordship is without end; whereof this pamphlet, without beginning, is but a superfluous moiety. . . . What I have done is yours; what I have to do is yours; being part in all I have, devoted yours.

We may feel confident that the pleas of Venus to Adonis, and those of Tarquin to Lucrece, are not different from those of Shakespeare to Southampton; except that his may have only a literary office designed for the occasion. And now Shakespeare is ready for the forthcoming sonnets.

I am greatly indebted to Peter Quennel's very good book, *Shakespeare: a Biography,* 1963; and especially to Chapter V, "His Sugared Sonnets." In 1598, Southampton's mother married Sir William Hervey; but he been acquainted with her and her household earlier, and her complaints over her son's refusal to marry. Mr. Quennel thinks that Sir William, who knew Southampton as given to the dissolute habits of other nobles of the period, may have asked Shakespeare to counsel him. Therefore Sonnets I to XVII contain the poet's advice that he marry and breed sons as lovely as himself. But presently, in Sonnet XX, Shakespeare seems to profess that there can be no possibility of a homosexual union with the patron, however he may have wished it:

> A woman's face with Nature's own hand painted
> Hast thou, the master mistress of my passion;
> A woman's gentle heart, but not acquainted
> With shifting change, as is false women's fashion;
> An eye more bright than theirs, less false in rolling,
> Gilding the object whereupon it gazeth;
> A man in hue, all hues in his controlling,
> Which steals men's eyes and women's souls amazeth.
> And for a woman wert thou first created;
> Till Nature, as she wrought thee, felt a-doting,
> And by addition thee of me defeated
> By adding one thing to my purpose nothing.
> But since she prick'd thee out for women's pleasure,
> Mine be thy love, and thy love's use their treasure.

Mr. Quennel says: "*The Sonnets,* in fact, may be described as a monument to homosexual love raised by an otherwise heterosexual poet"; and that "intellectual dishonesty seldom makes for true poetry"; though this assertion could hardly apply to the fictions of drama and sonnets. A little later he observes: "Southampton, as we have seen, was once accused of homosexual tendencies; and the elder man may have fallen a victim to the rakish and experienced youth." As for Southampton's homosexual affair once reported to Robert Cecil, Mr. Quennel has the fairness to suggest that "Cecil's self-righteous informer is, of course, a highly suspect witness"; but for the poet's victimization by the young patron there is no reported witness at all. Furthermore, Mr. Quennel has written sufficiently, like other good scholars, of the extravagant professions of love and endearment which the merry poets in the last Elizabethan decade tendered to the patrons who supported them. It must have been accepted generally that they were overdramatizing their actual feelings.

Now, so far as I can recall, there is not a single case of homosexuality in all the plays of Shakespeare. He was a strict moralist, aside from the venial sins; and he must have regarded the Commandment which forbade adultery as including the pederasty, the rape, and the possible homosexuality, of the three texts with which he furnished the patron. Nevertheless, there did come into the sonnets one stinging repudiation of the infamy which some person or persons chose to attribute to them. But it is a late sonnet, numbered CXXI, and incidentally one of the finest:

'Tis better to be vile than vile esteemed
When not to be receives reproach of being,
And the just pleasure lost which is so deemed
Not by our feelings but by others' seeing.
For why should others' false adulterate eyes
Give salutation to my sportive blood?
Or on my frailties why are frailer spies,
Which in their wills count bad what I think good?
No, I am that I am, and they that level
At my abuses reckon up their own;
I may be straight, though they themselves be bevel;
By their rank thoughts my deeds must not be shown,
   Unless this general evil they maintain,
   All men are bad, and in their badness reign.

Often I imagine what consultation beforehand was held by the poet and his lord, when new sonnets were to be written; which of them proposed the argument, or which was out-argued by the other. For the Earl had an honor to defend, and likewise the poet. But here there must have been agreement. Shakespeare must answer the false spies; but he would do it in his own person, as the Earl would prefer, though they would have been involved equally.

It remains only to tell of how the sonnets found their readers. *Venus and Adonis* was printed and registered by the Stationers in 1593; *The Rape of Lucrece* in 1594; but the *Sonnets?* Evidently neither of the partners intended publication, but would distribute handwritten copies among the other patrons and protégés, and in that way reach their proper readers. No printed edition was made until 1609;

for one Thomas Thorp had found copies, and his book was registered by the Stationers. His sales, however, were small, because the Sonnet Period was over; and the sonnets did not come into general notice till nearly a century afterward, whereupon its readers began to exclaim over its treasures and have done so ever since. And now nearly everybody is acquainted with them, and the moralist readers ponder sadly over the unsavory "problem" which they present. I have sufficiently indicated my own solution, though it is not especially original. I do know that after Shakespeare's death in 1616, there were plenty of panegyrists, and Ben Jonson, that knowing and forthright critic, found no fault in the man.